Frugal
Living
FOR
DUMMIES®

# Frugal Living

## FOR

# DUMMIES®

## by Deborah Taylor-Hough

WILEY

John Wiley & Sons, Inc.

**Frugal Living For Dummies**®

Published by
John Wiley & Sons, Inc.
111 River Street
Hoboken, NJ 07030
www.wiley.com

Copyright © 2003 by John Wiley & Sons, Inc., Hoboken, New Jersey

Published by John Wiley & Sons, Inc., Hoboken, New Jersey

Published simultaneously in Canada

For general information on our other products and services or to obtain technical support, please contact our Customer Care Department within the U.S. at 877-762-2974, outside the U.S. at 317-572-3993, or fax 317-572-4002.

Wiley publishes in a variety of print and electronic formats and by print-on-demand. Some material included with standard print versions of this book may not be included in e-books or in print-on-demand. If this book refers to media such as a CD or DVD that is not included in the version you purchased, you may download this material at http://booksupport.wiley.com. For more information about Wiley products, visit www.wiley.com.

Library of Congress Control Number: 2002114818

ISBN 978-0-7645-5403-2 (pbk); ISBN 978-1-118-07137-3 (ebk); ISBN 978-1-118-06969-1 (ebk)

1B/RV/QR/QT/IN

10 9 8 7

WILEY

# About the Author

**Deborah Taylor-Hough** has been living the frugal lifestyle most of her life. Whether she was shopping at every garage sale in town with her mother during high school or finding the best deals on groceries in order to feed her growing family on a limited budget, Deborah has learned the frugal ropes through personal experience, hard work, reading more books than she can count, and graduating with honors from the ever-popular School of Hard Knocks.

Deborah is the editor/publisher of the *Simple Times Newsletter*, an e-mail publication reaching tens of thousands of subscribers since 1998. She has authored several books on frugal living topics, including: *A Simple Choice: A practical guide for saving your time, money and sanity*, *Frozen Assets: How to cook for a day and eat for a month*, and *Mix and Match Recipes: Creative ideas for busy kitchens* (among other titles). She's been featured extensively in television, radio, and print media throughout the United States and Canada, and frequently conducts workshops on frugal living, voluntary simplicity, and assorted homemaking topics for conferences, retreats, women's groups, and church functions.

Deborah and her family live in the Puget Sound region of Washington State with four spoiled cats, a lizard, and far too many fish.

# Dedication

This book is dedicated to my three wonderful children — Kelsey, Ian, and Shannon — who waited patiently this summer for trips to the beach and help with broken toys while Mommy said, "Yes, just a minute . . . I'll be right there," probably a few too many times. I love the three of you more than words can say.

# Author's Acknowledgments

I'd like to thank my editors, Alissa Schwipps, Tracy Boggier, and Cheryl Gochnauer, and my agent, Jacky Sachs, for all your help bringing *Frugal Living For Dummies* to fruition. It wouldn't even exist without your encouragement, practical ideas, and steadfast belief in me and the project.

I'd also like to thank my husband, Stuart, for the long periods of time he gave me to concentrate and work on this book.

And a special personal "thank you" to Danita Bay, Stacy Andrus (and Bug), Catherine Levison, Gina Dalquest, Lisa Morales, Leanne Ely, Sean Hollen, Autumn Pickett, Karen Bierdeman, Gary Foreman, Larry Wilson, Christine Saunders, and the members of the Bell's home group for your friendship, prayers, and heartfelt support all along the way.

# Publisher's Acknowledgments

We're proud of this book; please send us your comments through our Dummies online registration form located at www.dummies.com/register/.

Some of the people who helped bring this book to market include the following:

*Acquisitions, Editorial, and Media Development*

**Project Editor:** Alissa D. Schwipps

**Acquisitions Editor:** Tracy Boggier

**Copy Editors:** Laura B. Peterson, Tina Sims

**Acquisitions Assistant:** Holly Grimes

**Technical Editor:** Cheryl Gochnauer

**Editorial Manager:** Jennifer Ehrlich

**Editorial Assistant:** Elizabeth Rea

**Cartoons:** Rich Tennant,
www.the5thwave.com

*Composition Services*

**Project Coordinator:** Maridee Ennis

**Layout and Graphics:** Carrie Foster, Joyce Haughey, Jackie Nicholas, Barry Offringa, Jacque Schneider, Scott Tullis

**Proofreaders:** John Tyler Connoley, John Greenough, Aptara

**Indexer:** Aptara

*Special Help:* Chad Sievers

*Publishing and Editorial for Consumer Dummies*

**Kathleen Nebenhaus,** Vice President and Executive Publisher

**David Palmer,** Associate Publisher

**Kristin Ferguson-Wagstaffe,** Product Development Director

*Publishing for Technology Dummies*

**Andy Cummings,** Vice President and Publisher

*Composition Services*

**Debbie Stailey,** Director of Composition Services

# Contents at a Glance

# Table of Contents

# Introduction

*H*ow many of these expensive — and often stressful — situations can you relate to?

- ✔ Indiscriminate corporate lay-offs
- ✔ Stagnant wages
- ✔ Increased cost of living
- ✔ New car loans
- ✔ Skyrocketing housing costs
- ✔ Daycare expenses
- ✔ Back-to-school shopping
- ✔ Doctor bills and insurance deductibles
- ✔ Exorbitant utility bills
- ✔ Excessive credit card debt

Do you ever feel like screaming, "Help! Somebody stop this merry-go-round . . . I want to get off!" Most people today feel the financial crunch of modern life in at least a few of these categories, and many face all of these dilemmas every day from the moment they roll out of bed until they rest their oh-so-weary heads on the pillow each night.

If you're feeling a financial crunch in your life, cutting back on your expenditures through frugal living provides a remedy. Frugal living is no longer a concept reserved for the newly married or for starving college students trying to stretch the macaroni and cheese for another meal. People of all ages and places in life need to cut back and discover how to live within their means. What previously passed for financial common sense in your grandmother's day is almost unknown to modern family members. Old-fashioned common sense just isn't so common anymore. People live their lives at break-neck speed . . . with their financial choices governed by the high cost of living often requiring both parents in a family to work full time, plus all the time pressures resulting from dual-career homes. Busyness keeps families spending more and more money just for the sake of "fast, easy, and convenient."

I wrote this book because I know there are other people just like me. Folks who want to attain specific goals in their lives, but feel money pressures are standing in their way. When my second child came along, I recognized my heart's desire was to be home full time while my kids were small. Even though my husband and I had consumer debt and outstanding medical bills, we paid off all our debts and happily realized our dream of having a stay-at-home parent for the past twelve years by reducing spending in nearly every area of our lives. Shopping at secondhand stores, cooking and buying food in bulk, and learning to live within a pre-set spending plan were not just wise financial decisions for our family, but life-changing ones as well. No matter what your personal or financial goals, frugal living can help you reach your dreams.

# About This Book

This book is designed to help steer you through the high cost of modern living. Whether you're looking for help saving money on groceries, or you need a few inexpensive ideas for school clothes, or perhaps holidays and birthdays are taking too big a bite out of your budget, this book provides easy-to-access information on a wide range of money- and family-related topics.

*Frugal Living For Dummies* is a ready reference for people seeking a less expensive lifestyle. You can read it from cover to cover, or you can skip to any point in the book as you look for the ideas and tips you need right now. For example, if the thought of back-to-school shopping — and what it's going to do to your budget — is making you feel a little faint, feel free to turn to the appropriate sections right away. *Frugal Living For Dummies* is set up so that you can get the tips and ideas you need as quickly as possible.

# Conventions Used in This Book

To help you pick out information from a page, we use the following conventions throughout the text to make elements consistent and easy to understand:

- Any Web addresses appear in `mono font`.
- New terms appear in *italics* and are closely followed by an easy-to-understand definition.
- **Bold** highlights the action parts of numbered steps or keywords in bulleted lists.

✔ Sidebars, which look like text enclosed in a shaded gray box, consist of information that's interesting to know but not necessarily critical to your understanding of the chapter or section's topic.

# Foolish Assumptions

As this book was coming together, I made a few assumptions about you, the reader, and what your needs may be. Here's what I assumed about you:

✔ You're facing a sticky financial situation in your life that makes keeping more money in your pocket attractive to you. You may be contemplating a job change, going back to school, feeling overwhelmed with consumer debt, considering staying home with a new baby, finding more month left at the end of the money, or all of the above.

✔ You're either brand new to frugal living concepts or you're looking for a quick refresher.

✔ You're looking for an easy-to-understand book that focuses on simple and effective ways to save money on basic family-related expenses right away.

✔ You're not looking for a stuffy book that contains in-depth budgeting and financial planning advice, or numerous pie charts and bar graphs of detailed information about investments, stock options, blah, blah, blah.

If you fit any of these criteria, *Frugal Living For Dummies* is just the book you've been looking for!

# How This Book Is Organized

This book is divided into five parts covering the necessary basics for any frugal person's life. Each of these parts is broken down further into individual chapters with smaller sub-headings, allowing you to find your way directly to any sub-topic you may want to browse (for example, you don't have to wade through information about frugal baby care if you're currently interested in battling costly teenage peer pressure). The following sections give you a brief summary of each part of *Frugal Living For Dummies*.

# Part 1: Getting Down to Basics

This section introduces you to frugal living and gives you the basics of personal financial planning. You find a quick guide to setting up a personal budget, tips for dealing with un-frugal family members, and ideas for identifying personal priorities to help you live true to your own frugal vision and lifestyle choices. These topics — especially budgeting toward a financial goal — can help you save lots of money by helping you keep your family's overall financial picture in mind. And after all, saving money is why you're reading this book, isn't it?

# Part II: Eating Like a King with a Peasant's Purse

Next to housing, food is often the single most expensive budget item for most families and also one of the few flexible items. This section takes you step-by-step through the maze of food-related expenses. You figure out how to frugally navigate around the physical layout of a grocery store and resist the allure of retail marketing strategies, and you also discover numerous budget-saving cooking techniques and meal ideas.

# Part III: Funding the Frugal Family

This section provides the tips and tricks you need to save big bucks on family-related expenses, from diapers to diplomas and every birthday in between. I also include a chapter with great cost-cutting personal hygiene and exercise ideas. You also find fun and frugal ways to celebrate the holidays as well as activities sure to please everyone — Mom, Dad, Billy, and sister Sue, too.

# Part IV: Enjoying a Frugal Home and Hearth

This section takes you on a tour of frugal living possibilities throughout your home, yard, and driveway. You find ideas for saving money on cars, home maintenance, large purchases, household cleaning, secondhand shopping, pet care, and general household upkeep.

## *Part V: Part of Tens*

This section contains a list of inexpensive gift ideas for family and friends and a list of cheap — not chintzy — ways to show your sweetheart how much you care.

# *Icons Used in This Book*

Keep an eye out for the following icons, which highlight important information throughout the book:

If you want a money-saving idea for something fun or super simple, keep your eye out for the Great Idea icon throughout the book.

If an idea or important point needs to be remembered clearly when you're done with a section of the book, a Remember icon highlights it for you.

If you're looking for big savings that give you the most return for your investment of time and effort, watch for the Super Saver icon.

You find time- and money-saving advice for applying frugal living basics to your daily life whenever you see the Tip icon.

The Warning icon signifies a major threat to your financial and budgeting health. Occasionally a Warning icon also represents an actual threat of bodily harm.

# *Where to Go from Here*

This book isn't structured in a linear fashion, so you can open to any chapter or section and not necessarily need to have read the chapters or sections that went before. If your dinner budget is a bit overextended, turn to Part II for a jump-start on food-related savings. If December gift-giving is giving your budget a black eye, skip ahead to Chapter 11.

And remember, contrary to popular opinion, frugal living doesn't have to mean deprivation, as you discover in the pages of *Frugal Living For Dummies*. So keep your chin up, a smile on your face . . . and go save some money!

# Part I
# Getting Down to Basics

The 5th Wave          By Rich Tennant

"I bought a software program that should help us monitor and control our spending habits, and while I was there, I picked up a few new games, a couple of screen savers, 4 new mousepads, this nifty pullout keyboard cradle..."

## In this part . . .

*I*f your idea of a savings account is a full change jar in the kitchen, or if you find money slips through your fingers and you never know where it all goes, you should read the chapters in this part. Part I includes practical ideas on the basics of frugal living, including setting financial goals, living on a budget, and dealing with spendthrift loved ones. You find some easy ideas for getting started on a new, less expensive lifestyle.

# Chapter 1

# Living Frugally in a Spendthrift World

Spending more money than you make each month is so easy in a consumer-driven society. Just pull out the ol' credit card and buy that new sweater, or golf club, or that $5 cup of ice cream. But eventually the bills come due, and, like it or not, the bills have to be repaid at some point — unless you're thinking personal bankruptcy would be a nice little addition to your résumé or credit report. But trust me on this one — you *don't* want to go there if you can help it! And you can help it by abandoning your spendthrift ways and adopting a frugal attitude. Does that sound like a novel idea to you? Then read on!

## Defining Frugal Living

Frugal living is making the necessary choices to live within your means. By living within your means, you keep yourself and your family from the bondage of consumer debt. Living frugally isn't the same as living a miserably unadorned, Spartan lifestyle. And being frugal isn't the same thing as being cheap or chintzy. Frugal living is simply being economical in the use of your resources. For example:

> ✔ **My house is filled almost to overflowing with my favorite Victoriana décor** — purchased at garage sales, thrift stores, and retrieved from Grandma's attic.

✔ **Our family of five dines in fancy restaurants on special occasions** — often with coupons or during special offers.

✔ **We see nearly every current movie we want to** — by waiting for it to hit the cheap theaters, by allocating some of our entertainment budget for a movie splurge in a first-run theater (eating before we go, of course, so we aren't tempted by $3.50 sodas and $4.50 bags of popcorn, and going early in the day to a discount matinee showing), or by waiting for the video release.

✔ **My three kids are dressed in fashionable, brand-name clothing** — usually purchased secondhand or from the clearance racks at their favorite stores.

✔ **We eat high-quality, delicious foods at home** — lovingly prepared from sale items at the grocery store.

Don't slip into the extremes of saving or spending money, but find a balance that works for you and your family members. Sometimes money's so tight that you have no choice but to be a miser. Other times you need the comfort — and the therapy — of a nice restaurant dinner with your spouse, far away from the kids and the pressing responsibilities of life.

# To Be or Not to Be: Reasons for Living a Frugal Lifestyle

"To be or not to be." Hmm. Well, Hamlet may have been dealing with bigger issues than whether or not to spend his money on gourmet coffees, but deciding to live a more frugal lifestyle in the midst of commercialism run amok isn't necessarily an easy decision. I mean, after all, what will the neighbors think if your family is still driving the same old car five years from now?

Keep in mind the reasons you live a frugal lifestyle: getting out of debt and then staying out of debt, living within your means, saving for college or a down payment on a house, affording nice vacations, or living through a financial crisis (such as a job loss) without losing your shorts. If you're satisfied with the choices you're making in your life, don't worry about what other people think about your frugal lifestyle.

For many families today, frugal living isn't so much a matter of choosing not to join the consumer spending spree as it is a matter of necessity. The rising cost of living, stagnant wages, unexpected corporate layoffs, compounding personal debt, and high medical bills all contribute to the modern family's financial difficulties.

Whether you need or choose to adopt a frugal lifestyle, living frugally can help you achieve your financial goals and live through financially tough times.

## Saving money and meeting financial goals

Whatever your personal or family goals may be, cutting back on regular expenses can help free up money for other, more highly valued, purposes. For example, if your family wants to take an exceptionally nice vacation next year, but you don't want to work an extra part-time job to pay for it, what can you do? Well, an easy solution is to cut back on your regular expenses throughout the year, and then save the difference for your dream vacation. Europe, here we come! (See Chapter 2 for goal-setting advice and Chapter 3 for budgeting advice.)

## Dealing with stagnant wages or low income

It'd be great if every job provided regular raises, adequate medical coverage, and cost-of-living increases, but unfortunately, not all employers are able to provide these benefits for their workers. But by cutting back on personal and family-related expenses, a family may be able to continue living within its means, even if the cost of living creeps higher than wage increases. For example, if you're spending $700 per month on groceries to feed your family and then you cut that amount in half, your family just received a $350 per month raise. (Don't think cutting your monthly grocery bill by a few hundred dollars is possible? Check out Chapter 4.)

Some families value having a parent stay at home while the kids are young. In today's economy, however, two full-time incomes are almost a financial necessity just to afford the rent or mortgage and other basic needs of life. But by tightening your money belt and keeping true to your personal priorities, affording a stay-at-home parent can become a reality for your family.

## Living through a job loss

A major job loss can be devastating for any family. To make matters worse, many families are living so close to the edge financially that even a brief period of unemployment can be just enough to send their house into foreclosure and make their utilities unaffordable. If you're unemployed right now, a drastically reduced spending plan for your family can mean the difference between drowning under a load of debt and staying afloat until the current crisis passes.

Even if you haven't lost your job, discovering how to live frugally can help you build up a financial cushion that will carry your family through any unexpected downturns in your family's financial state or in the overall economy.

## *Reducing consumer debt*

Are you living a lifestyle that's beyond your means? Do you have all those new clothes, furniture, cars, and restaurant meals only because your credit is maxed out? Financing an expensive lifestyle on credit may be possible, but it's not the wisest course of action. Eventually you reach the end of your credit limits and a time of reckoning comes.

Reducing your consumer debt load is a good idea no matter how well you may be balancing your payments. I highly recommend you set a reasonably frugal budget, evaluate your spending habits by tracking your expenses for at least two to three weeks (better yet, for three months so you don't miss quarterly expenses such as insurance premiums or tuition payments), and make a plan to get out of debt as quickly as possible (I explain budgeting tactics in Chapter 3). A budget or spending plan isn't financial prison. If you take the time to think carefully through your regular expenses and plan ahead accordingly, you'll find that staying on track financially is not nearly as difficult as it seems at first glance.

# *Look on the Bright Side: Adjusting Bad Attitudes*

You can list off a number of excellent reasons for living frugally, but in order to not feel deprived or discouraged, you may need to make a few attitude adjustments. If you feel sad and depressed every time you forego a designer ice cream bar at the supermarket or an expensive pair of shoes at the mall, contentment is going to be a difficult goal to achieve. By focusing on the benefits of frugality and living within your means instead of focusing on the little things you may have to give up to save money, you'll find a lifestyle of financial responsibility is more satisfying than excessive personal debt or financial disaster.

## Clearing out the contentment thieves

Discontentment is an illness that infects many people everyday. Look around your life and see where germs of discontent are breeding. Do the glossy photos of perfect houses on magazine covers make you dissatisfied with your cheery but humble home? If so, drop those magazines off at the doctor's office waiting room. Are catalogs telling you that you *have* to have that new whirlygig for your backyard? Just toss the catalogs in the recycling bin before you even glance at them.

Get rid of whatever makes you discontent. Throw it away. Recycle it. Cancel its subscription. Stop going to the mall or the auto store or the ice cream smorgasbord if you end up buying things you don't need, or if you find yourself regretting your life choices after seeing the latest and greatest consumer gadgets paraded before your eyes. Getting rid of the contentment thieves enables you to live happily within your means and saves you untold dollars in the process.

## *Canceling your reservation for the pity party*

If your friends show off their new bedroom set to you — and you're still sleeping on the same old mismatched hand-me-downs you received from your in-laws ten years ago — just say, "That's nice!" and leave it at that. Don't go home and have a pity party, whining and moaning about all the sacrifices you're making to live within your means.

 Always keep a positive goal in mind. Instead of seeing frugal living as something you have to do ("Poor pitiful me, I'm so broke!"), remind yourself continually that frugality is something you've chosen to do to meet future goals or to live the lifestyle you want.

A sure-fire cure for the discontented blues is to start keeping track of the things in your life that you are thankful for. Do this by making an ongoing list in a blank book or journal of things that bring you joy in your life or that you're grateful for. When life is difficult, focusing on the good things in life can really improve your attitude.

## *Accepting that your money supply has a limit*

A friend of mine says that whenever he gets paid, he gets to be a "Two Day Rich Man." A couple thousand dollars in the bank makes him feel temporarily wealthy — until he writes out the mortgage payment and pays his credit card bills. So much for riches.

The money coming into your home has a limit. Spending all your paycheck on fun and games during the first half of your pay period doesn't leave much for bills and groceries and emergencies later on. Everyone's finances have a limit, even wealthy folk's. Don't act like the money supply is never-ending. Instead, keep to a written budget (described in Chapter 3), remember your long-term financial goals, and realize that all things fun and worthwhile aren't equally important. Identify your priorities in life and spend money on the things you deem most important. Say "no" or "wait" to lesser priorities so they don't eat up your current budget.

## *Reveling in the fact that you're free from credit card debt*

Even if you have thousands of dollars available on your credit cards, paying with credit to enjoy things now just puts you in hock to your creditors later. Take it from someone who knows the pain and frustration of excessive consumer debt firsthand — debt can take a while to catch up with you, but when it does, it's a mean task master. Debt eats up your future and limits your life choices. (And the prison of excessive debt doesn't give you time off for good behavior!)

Instead of falling further in debt, live frugally, pay off your credit card debt, and live within your means. Think of all the things you can do with the money you save when you don't have to pay on credit card accounts! For more information on getting out from under consumer debt, see Chapter 3.

## *Finding freedom and financial strength with a budget*

For some people, the word budget brings to mind images of ledger pages with columns of cold facts and figures — very confining and overwhelming. But I've discovered that the discipline and seeming confinement of a budget actually frees me from the bondage of consumer debt and bills that can't be paid on time.

A budget isn't just for the financially irresponsible — it's a valuable tool that enables you to live within your means and to make intelligent choices about your money. And a wise budget always includes some discretionary cash that you can spend on anything you want. (Remember, your budget isn't your prison; debt is.) Read Chapter 3 for more information about setting and keeping to a reasonable budget.

## Adopting wise spending habits: Saying no to impulse purchases

Do you ever make a quick trip to the grocery store just to pick up a $3 gallon of milk, and then come home $20 poorer because you saw so many things you suddenly thought you needed? Well, welcome to the not-so-wonderful world of impulse spending. Whatever your particular spending impulses are, you can resist the marketing and sales tactics designed to separate you from your hard earned cash by making a few simple changes:

- ✔ Go to a "cash only" basis for budgeting. For example, when I go grocery shopping, I shop with cash because it limits the amount I can spend and forces me to keep on track with my budget. I don't bring my entire monthly grocery budget to the store with me at one time, though, or I may be tempted to spend the money impulsively. Instead I decide in advance how much to spend and limit myself to only that amount. If I'm overspending, I put things back or reshop for less expensive items.

- ✔ Cut down on buying expensive snacks and gourmet coffees at work by bringing your own homemade or less expensive varieties. (See the "Resisting impulse purchases on the job" sidebar in this chapter.)

- ✔ Shop from a list for everything from food to clothing to holiday gifts. Keep to the list and don't give in to the temptation to buy enticing items not on the list.

- ✔ Consolidate your little trips to the grocery store into one weekly trip. That way you save money by using less gas running all over town, and you also keep yourself away from impulse purchase temptations that loom every time you enter retail stores.

✔ Stop before every purchase and ask yourself, "Is this something I want or is this something I truly need?" If it's not a true need, and money is extremely tight, don't make the purchase this time. If you discover that you really do need it, find out if this is the best deal or if you should wait to find the item on sale or at a discount store. Make yourself wait 24 hours before deciding to purchase any item over $15.

Chapter 4 discusses additional suggestions for how to stand firm against the onslaught of impulsive temptations in the stores around you.

## Resisting impulse purchases on the job

A common budget problem that often goes unnoticed is buying snacks and drinks at work rather than bringing them from home. Let's do the math by adding up the amounts spent on a few common items:

✔ Espresso bar on the way to work = **$3**

✔ Mid-morning doughnut and coffee = **$2**

✔ Lunch with the gang at the sandwich shop = **$6**

✔ Afternoon snack or coffee = **$2**

✔ A bottle of soda and a bag of chips for the commute home = **$2**

Oops! That's **$15** down the drain in one day, and that's assuming a relatively low-cost lunch. If you spend $15 a day, five days a week for a month, that's $300 out of the monthly budget just for snacks and lunches for only one person — or $3,600 per year! Multiply that by two family members out in the workplace and you've got enough money going out of your budget for snacks to almost make a part-time job necessary.

Now let's compare the cost of bringing the same items from home:

✔ A thermos of coffee (enough to replace both coffee breaks during the day) = **50 cents**

✔ A boxed lunch from home = **$2**

✔ A small snack or two (pretzels, an apple) = **50 cents**

✔ A can of soda for the drive home (purchased in bulk and on sale, of course) = **25 cents**

Bringing your own treats and lunch from home costs just over **$3** per day, or about $75 per month (double this for a two-adult household), which is one-fourth of what you pay when you buy the same things at work or during your commute.

# Establishing Goals, Budgets, and Good Financial Habits

Not knowing what your financial goals are is almost like setting out on a long car trip for parts unknown without a road map. If you drive long enough, you'll definitely end up somewhere — but probably not where you were hoping to go. All destinations are not created equal, whether you're talking about current vacation plans or your long-term life goals (I discuss setting financial goals in Chapter 2).

After you establish your financial goals and your family's financial goals, you need to set a budget. I know, I know — budgeting sounds like a pain, but living within a budget doesn't have to be the equivalent of a financial straightjacket. I provide basic budgeting information in Chapter 3, which will help you evaluate your current financial situation and set a reasonable budget so you can free yourself from debt and live happily within your means.

Once you've put a budget in place and have your goals in mind, work to control your spending by adopting good, frugal spending habits. Here's a list of some simple habits you may want to instill into your financial life:

- ✔ Keep your check register balanced and up to date. That way, you know exactly how much money is left in the bank at all times. Occasionally I was too busy to subtract checks from the balance as I wrote them out, and before too long I found myself without funds. Seeing a running total keeps you from thinking you have more to spend than you do.

- ✔ Keep a written record of all the money you spend throughout the day, no matter how insignificant it seems at the time (coffee, newspaper, sodas, cigarettes, gum, and so on). The process of writing each purchase down helps you see clearly where the money's dripping out of your life. If you find your money's going out to incidentals and impulse purchases, writing them down can actually help you say "No!" to overspending.

- ✔ Don't pull out your credit card for every purchase. Better yet, leave your credit cards, debit cards, and checkbooks at home unless you're traveling.

- ✔ Avoid carrying a lot of cash unless you need it. The more cash I have on hand, the more tempted I am to spend it. Unless I'm grocery shopping with cash (to limit the amount I spend),

I hardly ever carry more than $10 of the actual paper stuff with me at any given time. A friend of mine puts her cash into a sealed envelope labeled, "Emergency Only!" inside her wallet. This forces her to think twice before forking over $2 at the office vending machine for a spur-of-the-moment snack.

✔ Set up a small fund of discretionary money that you can spend on whatever strikes your fancy. Essentially you're giving yourself an allowance. If you have access to a free checking account at your bank, you can set up a special account just for discretionary spending and deposit a small portion of each paycheck into the account. Or if you're using a cash-only budgeting system, have a special envelope for your "allowance."

✔ Deposit a portion of each paycheck directly into your savings account and leave it there. Many banks can put money directly from your paycheck into a savings account. By putting money into savings right off the top, you're less likely to spend it on something else.

By changing one habit at a time, you can turn your entire financial picture around in a relatively short timeframe. But remember, new habits take a while to become ingrained — about a month, if you listen to the experts. Many people don't realize this and make developing new habits more difficult than it needs to be by not allowing themselves enough time or by trying to change too many habits at once. Try to work on only one new habit a month. In a year's time, you can establish twelve new habits with relatively little stress and strain.

## Eliminating budget-killing personal habits

Not only is quitting smoking good for your health, but it's also a godsend to your budget. Easier said than done, I know, but you may want to seriously consider kicking the habit if money is tight and you're finding it difficult to survive financially from month to month. Cigarettes vary in price from one location to another, but if you estimate the average cost is about $3 per pack, that's $90 each month going up in smoke.

Regular drinking, gambling, purchasing collectibles, and recreational shopping can also cause untold damage to your family's budget if you do these things excessively and impulsively. By finding less expensive hobbies and recreational activities (or by limiting these to a specific budgeted amount each month), you'll be better able to live within your means.

# Bringing the Family Aboard

If you're the only person in the family who is making sure the pennies don't slip needlessly out of the family coffers, you may think keeping a budget seems impossible. But with careful communication and a commitment to living true to your family's financial vision for the future, you can even bring that spendthrift spouse or peer-pressured teen in line and within budget. Chapter 2 has information on working with your non-frugal family members.

Introduce your family to the joys — and dramatic savings! — available through shopping at secondhand stores, garage sales, and other reduced-price locations where they can find top-quality furniture, games, and clothing (to name just a few items) for a fraction of the new prices. See Chapter 16 for more information on secondhand shopping.

# Finding Ways to be Frugal in Every Area of Your Life

Although some areas of everyday spending are easier to cut back on than others, if you make a concentrated effort to cut back a little bit everywhere, you'll see faster results and a healthier checkbook, too! Here's a quick overview of some frugal living basics for life in general (I discuss these topics in detail later in this book):

- ✔ **Cut costs on food-related expenses.** Frequent trips to the drive-through and panicked calls for pizza delivery all add up to disaster for the average person's budget. But when life's too busy and you're running fifteen different directions at once, you need some quick and easy ways to save money and get dinner on the table without breaking the bank. You find helpful ideas for avoiding the retail marketing traps of the grocery store in Chapter 4, and Chapter 5 helps you plan easy, cheap meals that go beyond plain boiled potatoes or macaroni and cheese every night.

- ✔ **Keep a rein on kid-related expenses.** When a young couple first gets married, they often think two can live as cheaply as one, which can be true. But when the two of you become the three or four of you, watch out! Frugal living becomes not only more difficult but also a lot more necessary for the financial survival of your family when kids are added to the picture. From diapers and formula to designer clothes and school dances, the costs of raising kids are a continual challenge to the frugal plans of their parents. Check out Chapters 7 and 8 for money-saving tips on basic kid-related expenses.

✔ **Cut back on gift expenses.** Gift-giving opportunities abound, and with them, expectations. If your extended family gives elaborate gifts to the entire clan at the holidays every year, perhaps you can explain in a tactful way that you or your immediate family have chosen to simplify your lives and are cutting back on gift giving this year. Suggest just buying gifts for the children, or drawing names out of a hat, or just exchanging "family" gifts that everyone in the household can use together rather than giving separate gifts to each individual. You may find that the others want to ease their gift-giving burden as well, but are hesitant to rock the boat first. See Chapter 18 for further frugal gift ideas.

✔ **Keep general upkeep expenses under control.** Whether you're keeping your home, car, or yourself in tip-top shape, do it within budget. Chapters 9, 13, and 14 tell you how.

✔ **Be wise and frugal when investing in big-ticket items.** Even the most frugal family needs to occasionally spend money on something expensive (house, car, plane tickets, college education, appliances, vacations). The most well-thought-out frugal plans can be significantly set off course by making a single mistake with one of these high-ticket purchases or expenses. Chapter 15 gives practical help for finding frugal options for many of these items. One of the most frugal options is to buy secondhand. See Chapter 16 for tips on getting the most out of the previously used market around town.

# Chapter 2

# All in the Family: Establishing a Frugal Front

*In This Chapter*
▶ Working with your spouse to set financial goals
▶ Teaching children monetary responsibilities

*F*inding financial common ground can be difficult when one spouse is a spendthrift and the other's a full-fledged miser. Frugal living is a choice that's easiest to live with if both partners share the same general financial goals, even if their money styles are a bit different. If you both want to save money, get out of debt, live within your means, and attain mutual long-term goals, it's important to discuss your different approaches to money management and find some common ground. Otherwise your frugal efforts may be voided by your partner's poor spending habits.

Children can also be difficult to win over to frugal living. If you listen carefully, you can probably still hear the echoes from the latest whine-fest: "But Mommy, I want it NOW!"

This chapter helps you work with money management differences and also investigates a few ideas for instilling healthy money habits in your kids.

## Working with Your Partner to Achieve Financial Goals

Wouldn't it be nice if everyone were exactly the same? Well, of course not. I know I sure don't want to live in a boring world of identical clones that look, think, and act exactly alike. Variety is the spice of life, and it's also the spice of relationships, even in the area of finances. Just like the ingredients in your favorite meal, the right amount of spice can make the mix of flavors absolutely perfect — but too much spice is almost unbearable. You don't need to do away with each and every difference; you just need to blend the flavors together.

Resolving (or at least discussing openly) any financial differences between you and your partner is important if frugal living is a goal for you both. In order to fully adopt many of the frugal practices in this book, everyone involved needs to understand the benefits of a frugal lifestyle and how important it is to control any impulsive spending habits.

## Recognizing your financial strengths and weaknesses

If you're currently involved with someone and considering a serious commitment, or if you've never discussed your spending habits with your spouse or significant other, take some time to talk about your financial mindsets. Identify your differences and spend some time planning how you want to handle them in your relationship. By dealing with your financial differences, you'll not only cut down on many arguments later in life, but you and your partner will become a united frugal front working toward common financial goals together.

 Sit down together and share details about the practical aspects of your personal money style. (If you're already married, use this opportunity to reevaluate your current financial situation.) Ask yourselves, individually, the following questions and then compare answers:

- ✔ Do I carry credit cards? How many? What kind: gas cards, department store cards, general credit cards? Do I pay the cards in full each month, or just the minimum payments?

- ✔ Do I carry cash with me? How much? What do I use it for? How do I keep records of cash spent?

- ✔ What does my credit history look like? Any debt problems, overdue bills, repossessions, bankruptcy filings, or late payments?

- ✔ What sort of insurance coverage and financial contingency plans do I have for medical expenses and other emergencies?

- ✔ Do I have a system for paying bills? What is it?

- ✔ How do I keep track of receipts and any tax-related paperwork?

- ✔ Do I buy lunch at work every day or bring it from home?

✔ Is recreational shopping a favorite pastime? What sort of limits, if any, do I set for my personal shopping sprees?

✔ How do I decide to make a major purchase such as a car, new furniture, large appliances, or a home?

✔ How much of my income do I save each month, and what sort of system do I use for saving money?

✔ What is my philosophy about financially assisting elderly, disabled, or cash-strapped relatives?

✔ Do I want (or want my spouse) to stay home after we have children?

✔ Is tithing or regular philanthropic giving important to me?

✔ How far in debt can I go and still feel comfortable?

You may find that your significant other is a spendthrift and you're a miser or vice versa — opposites tend to attract each other. I believe one reason opposites attract is that on some unconscious level, people are aware of their own weaknesses and short-comings and know almost instinctively what they need to complete themselves. If you have trouble keeping to a written budget, you may choose a life partner whose greatest joy is keeping detailed written records of every flower growing in the yard or every penny spent on bubble gum by the kids — and you balance each other out in the process. Having differences is healthy, but I also know from experience that these differences can test your limits of grace and reason.

If you are the spend-a-holic in the relationship and are already convinced of the need for financial change in your life, the road ahead is much easier. Unfortunately, reforming a loved one from their spendthrift ways can be difficult and requires much tact. Don't allow yourself to become adversarial with the spend-a-holic in your life. Instead, be reasonable and show how adopting frugal living habits can reduce outstanding consumer debt, free up money for fun activities such as vacations, and help to finance large future expenses such as buying a house or paying for your children's college tuition.

## Identifying long-term goals

You've probably heard the old cliché, "If you don't know where you're going, how will you know when you get there?" Well, it holds true in the area of family finances, too. Establishing long-term goals for yourself and your family helps to keep your current financial picture in perspective. For example, if one of your goals as a couple is to have a full-time parent at home when the new baby arrives, you can start cutting back on spending now in order to get out of debt and establish some savings before the big day. Keeping your long-term goals in mind will help keep you on track whenever you're tempted to spend money on extras.

A necessary step toward working together as a financial team is to establish your life goals and review them with your significant other. Ask yourself the following questions to help you determine your long-term financial goals:

- What hobbies do I want to pursue to add recreation and fun to my life?
- What place does education hold in my future or that of others in my immediate family?
- How important is home ownership in my future?
- What are my career goals? What further training, if any, do I need to reach those goals?
- How much time, money, and effort do I want to give in the near future to charity or church-related activities?
- What character traits do I value most and want to develop in my own life and the life of my children? Are my financial goals and decisions in line with those character traits?
- What are my retirement goals?
- How will I take care of future healthcare concerns?
- How soon do I want to pay off any outstanding consumer debt?
- At the end of my life, what things may I regret if I choose to spend my money on less important pursuits?

Writing out your goals and the values that are important to your family can go a long way toward keeping your life and finances on track. But even if you don't write down your goals, thinking through your priorities and keeping them in mind as you make decisions (financial and otherwise) is a good habit to develop.

## Establishing savings goals

After you've discussed your financial desires and goals for life, set some savings goals. If you and your partner are not accustomed to working together toward a financial goal, start with something relatively small like saving for a new couch or your next short vacation. You can usually reach these goals within six months to a year, and so you get a fairly quick return on your savings investment — and an opportunity to reinforce the value of working together toward a savings goal. After you've seen that you can work together toward small goals, start working on long-term goals like retirement and the kids' education.

One way to set up a savings plan is to set aside a small amount of money in a special account from each paycheck until you've reached your short-term goal. Or keep a big jar on the dresser in the bedroom where you can empty your pockets and purse of any loose change. One summer, we financed a long weekend at the ocean for our family with just the change my husband and I threw into a jar every day. Seeing a successful example of how easy it can be to reach a savings goal can be just the impetus many spend-thrifts need to give second thought to their impulsive spending habits. See Chapter 3 for more advice on budgeting.

## *Finding peaceful solutions to financial differences*

Above all else, it's important to discover the art of diplomacy when you identify significant financial differences between you and your spouse. Money problems are the root of all sorts of marital discord and strife. But even when you're in the middle of a major disagreement about finances or your savings goals, the relationship doesn't have to break down if you continue to treat each other with kindness and respect. You can never convince people to change their minds by yelling at them, calling them names, manipulating their emotions, or giving them the silent treatment.

---

### The three checking account system

One way for partners who each have their own income to deal with differing money habits is to open three checking accounts: one joint account (for paying bills) and an individual account for each person. (*Note:* It's important to first establish a workable budget before implementing the three account system so each partner knows how much to deposit each pay period to cover the basics. See Chapter 3 for budgeting basics.) When you receive your paychecks, you each deposit a predetermined amount into the joint account. The joint account is then used for paying bills and for short-term savings for future expenses. The individual accounts are for the money left after you both pay for the basic essentials. If one partner wants to fritter his money away on designer coffees and video rentals, fine. The other person can be happily saving for that nice vacation she's been dreaming of for years — whether she chooses to take the spendthrift spouse with her on vacation may be another story, though.

TIP

If you are beyond the talking stage and are in the yelling, crying, door-slamming stage, consider seeking help from a trained financial counselor with a local debt-counseling agency. You can contact the National Foundation for Credit Counseling (a nationwide nonprofit network of Consumer Credit Counseling Service offices) at 1-800-388-CCCS. The NFCC can put you in touch with a counseling office near you. Find more information online at www.nfcc.org. Even if you're not dealing specifically with debt issues, a financial counselor can help you work through financial planning decisions in a calm, reasonable fashion. Many religious communities and churches offer free counseling of this sort, too. Just having an uninvolved third party helping you think calmly through your financial choices can be tremendously helpful.

# Taming Childhood and Teenage Spending

The phrase "frugal children" is an oxymoron (a contradicting combination of words) if I've ever heard one. Children and money are easily parted, or at least that's what happens in my house. But children can be raised to understand the value of money, budgets, and frugal living. This section explains how parents can set their kids up for frugal living successes throughout their childhood and beyond.

## Explaining that money doesn't grow on trees

Help your children learn the value of the money they spend at an early age. Talk to your kids about how many hours you need to work in order to buy that expensive charm bracelet or video game. If your children are older and have part-time jobs of their own, remind them how many hours they slave away over that hot grill flipping greasy burgers to pay for that prom dress or CD player.

Include your kids occasionally in discussions about the family financial situation, so that everyone takes part in setting goals and watching spending. If you're having serious financial difficulties, go easy on the details so that your kids don't worry. They need to be able to trust that Mom and Dad are in control of the situation and that they'll all be taken care of. But don't be afraid to be honest with your kids and tell them you can't afford something they ask for if it's not in your budget. "I'm sorry, Honey, but we can't afford a plane trip to Dino-Land Adventure this year, but we're going to go camping up the coast for a week instead. We'll have a great time!"

## Instilling good spending habits

To instill sound decision-making and shopping skills in your children, talk to them regularly about the decision-making processes you use when making various purchases. For example, regularly including your children with you on grocery shopping trips is an easy way to introduce them to comparative shopping, using coupons, watching for sales and loss leaders, and learning to read labels.

If you like to shop at garage sales and thrift stores, take your kids with you and let them see firsthand how far their money goes for secondhand clothing, toys, and sporting goods. My 15-year-old daughter takes great pride in her ability to buy a whole new wardrobe of fashionable, high-quality clothing at the thrift store for the same amount of money most of her friends spend for only one pair of designer jeans or a couple of blouses.

A casual discussion around the dinner table about the pros and cons of the new washing machine you're considering buying can go a long way to help kids see what's involved in making well-informed spending decisions.

Be sure to set a good frugal example for your children. Do you use shopping and spending as a personal reward for yourself? Do you shop when you're bored? Do you buy a new dress when you're depressed? Do you carry high credit card debt? Just as in other areas of life, your kids are watching and following your lead on how to handle finances and material goods.

## Budgeting 101 for kids — from preschoolers to college students

Teaching kids that the money coming into their lives isn't just for spending willy-nilly is an ongoing challenge for parents. This section outlines ways you can help tots and teens manage money.

### Setting up a system of four banks

We've discovered a technique that works incredibly well in our family and in other families we know who've tried it. It helps kids understand that not all money they earn or receive through gifts or allowances can go immediately into their pockets to spend. In a short period of time, they recognize that only a portion of the money is theirs to play with — the rest goes to help others, save for future expenses, and use to reach long-term life goals.

Here's what we do as a family to help our children manage their money in a simple, yet meaningful, way. Our kids divide up any money they receive from allowances, gifts, babysitting, and other jobs into four banks. The banks can be store-bought piggybanks from the dollar store, or just something as simple as clean milk cartoons with hand-drawn labels. The four banks are labeled as follows:

- ✔ **Giving** (10 percent). This amount goes to church, a needy family, or a favorite charity.

- ✔ **Spending** (30 percent). This is discretionary, spend-it-where-they-want, money. If children want to stock up on gum balls or plastic eggs from the talking duck machine at the grocery store, so be it. They eventually learn that by frittering their money away on small items, they don't have money available for bigger, more expensive purchases.

- ✔ **Short-term savings** (30 percent). Savings is for something fairly expensive and special, perhaps a new bicycle or a CD player.

- ✔ **Long-term savings** (30 percent). This is for things later in life such as a first car and important learning experiences (foreign travel, occupational education, or college expenses). My oldest daughter used her long-term savings accumulated over the course of three years for a two week service project to Mexico with her youth group at church.

Long-term and short-term savings goals should be approved by the parents, but allow the children to have total say-so over their spending money. Even if they make mistakes (and they will!), they'll learn important firsthand lessons through the process of dealing with the direct consequences of overspending or spending on lesser priorities.

### Role playing the family budget with younger kids

If you have young kids (12 and under), role playing about the family budget can help them grasp family money management concepts such as the value of money and how to cover the basics of life and still have money left over to save for the future and use for fun stuff. This isn't a long-term money-management plan for kids but is a great way to teach them about household money management over a relatively short period of time (perhaps in one or two months).

Give the kids a set amount of play money from one of your board games, and then say, "This month you have to pay your own way. Here's the cash from your monthly paycheck, so now let's figure out your share of the rent, utility bills, food costs, and gas." Have the children write out their budget with you so you can make sure they've allowed enough in each category to cover the basic living expenses plus savings and fun stuff. Then have the kids pay you with the play money for their expenses. If they spend any of their real money during the month, have them take it out of the play money, too, so that they can see how spending money on trinkets at the dollar store affects their ability to pay for necessities, like rent and food, down the road. Sit down with them once a week, review their budget, and determine how much money they have left. Weekly reviews keep things current and fresh in their minds, so the lessons learned hit home sooner and in a meaningful way.

Or rather than using play money, set up a blank checkbook register and some "checks." Teach them how to write checks, balance their checkbook, and plan their expenses. Give them "bills" throughout the month for their share of the family expenses.

### Asking teens to manage real money

You probably spend a certain amount of money on your teens each month for necessities and more frivolous incidentals like clothing, movie tickets, club dues, school yearbooks, CDs, craft materials, make-up, and hair accessories. One way to instill good money management habits is to average how much you spend each month on these items and turn over that amount to your teens and allow them to budget for these items. This isn't really an allowance. It's money you were spending anyway, but now you're giving your teens the opportunity to budget their expenses for themselves. Sit down with your teen and explain everything that you expect him or her to be able to pay for out of this money. They need to understand that if they don't budget the money properly — and don't have money to go to the movie with friends because they spent too much on CD's — they have to live with the consequences of overspending. Don't bail them out or you defeat the purpose of this technique.

Set your children up with a ledger or a home budgeting book to record their budget, anticipate expenses, and write out actual expenditures. Sure, they may have a class on consumer math in high school, but learning to budget first hand with their own money is going to sink in a lot more than if they're only pretending to budget for a made-up family in a textbook.

A second way to help your teens manage money is to require that they pay for all their own entertainment expenses with money they've earned through odd jobs, babysitting, or part-time employment. You pay for the basics, and your teen pays for the extras. That way, not only do they have some control over their finances, but they also see that their money only goes so far and then it's gone. It's much easier to do it this way than having little Suzy come to you with her hand out every other day asking for money to eat lunch at the mall or a couple bucks to take in the bargain movie with her friends.

If your children want to go to camp or on a special trip, have them pay for half or the entire fee themselves. By working to pay their own way, they appreciate the trip more or maybe decide that it's not really something they want that badly. If Mom and Dad pay for everything, kids can easily say "Yes! I wanna go!" to activities that don't really mean much to them.

Some families don't believe in giving their children a specific allowance every week because they believe that most allowances are just free money that's not tied directly to work and consequently pays kids for just being alive and breathing. But their kids are always asking them for $10 for this or $5 for that activity. I think this not only teaches children to whine, but it probably costs the parents more in the long run. Just as parents don't have an unlimited supply of money (I can't run to my publisher and say, "Hey, I need an extra $100 for our family trip"), kids need to learn that their parents can't bail them out every time they overspend their budget on clothes or entertainment.

## Helping your kids deal with peer pressure

Unless your children live in a tree house completely removed from the outside world, peer pressure affects them to some degree or another. "But, Mom, *everyone's* got a tattoo. I need one too!" Saying "no" to a tattoo is probably fairly easy for most parents, but saying "no" to the latest clothing fashions can be considerably harder, especially for parents of teens. We don't want our kids to be laughed at by their peers, but we also don't want to end up in bankruptcy court after paying for too many school clothes or top-of-the-line bicycles on credit cards year after year.

The best method for conquering peer pressure is to encourage altruistic tendencies in your children. As a family, sponsor a child through a relief agency like World Vision (www.wvi.org) or Compassion International (www.compassion.com). Having your children contribute a portion of their allowance or job earnings to help the sponsored child or having them take a trip with a youth group to an impoverished nation can have a life-changing effect on even the most materialistic teen.

# Chapter 3

# Eliminating Debt and Setting Up a Budget

*In This Chapter*
▶ Undoing the damages of severe debt
▶ Trying out budgeting tactics for beginners

*P*eople choose to limit their spending and live a frugal lifestyle for a lot of reasons: Saving for long-term goals, living within your means, having a stay-at-home parent, or surviving a sudden financial downturn. Making a simple, workable budget is an important step toward meeting those goals. This chapter contains a few budgeting basics combined with ideas for digging your way out of debt.

## Digging Out of Debt

Excessive consumer debt can be a prison, holding you captive to past financial decisions and overspending. You need to pay off your debts to free up money for your current lifestyle and future plans and dreams. In addition to living an all-around frugal lifestyle, the following steps help you get debt-free.

### Step 1: Acknowledge the problem

The most important step toward digging your way out of debt is acknowledging the problem and realizing you need to actively do something about it.

If any of the following statements are true in your life, consumer debt is a problem for you. Make paying off your debt a high priority or you may face a major debt-related problem such as utility shut-off notices or even a personal bankruptcy in the not-so-distant future.

✔ You have little or no savings and are at your limit on most of your credit cards.

✔ You juggle bills each month, deciding which ones to pay and which need to wait until the next payday, even if it means paying after the bill's due date and incurring subsequent late fees.

✔ You've taken at least one cash advance from a credit card account or other line of credit to make payments on other debts.

✔ Your debt load (including car payments but not including your mortgage) exceeds 20 percent of your income. Most budgets can reasonably handle a 10-15 percent debt load, but more than that is excessive.

If you use credit cards to finance your lifestyle, you're living beyond your means. It's time to remedy the situation.

## Step 2: Cut the cards

Identifying the problem is the first step to digging out of debt. The second step is often difficult for hard-core credit card junkies: cut up your credit cards. Yep, pull out the scissors and start snipping.

Some credit providers can't officially close the account until you've paid in full, but consider it closed to your usage. Do not, under any circumstances, use a credit card until your debts are paid in full. If you're deeply in debt, this can take several years. But after you're out from under the burden of excessive debt, the relief you experience more than makes up for the inconvenience of going without credit for a long stretch of time.

Sometimes you need a credit card of some sort for making airline reservations, buying online, or renting a car. If so, get a check card from your bank. You are essentially paying cash because the money immediately comes out of your checking account. But this way you can take care of any personal business that requires a credit card without deepening your credit debt.

## Step 3: Set a frugal budget and live within it

When planning your budget, be realistic about what you need to spend in each category, but don't be overly generous with yourself either. (I discuss constructing a budget that's right for you later in this chapter.) You need to cinch in your money belt if you're serious about repaying your debts so that you have the money to budget for your debt-repayment plan. The frugal tips throughout this book can help you get in shape to pay off those debts as quickly as possible.

## Step 4: Contact your creditors

Communicate directly with your creditors and explain to them that you're having problems meeting your payments. Tell them about your frugal budget and ask whether they'd be willing to accept slightly lower payments for a period of time. Many creditors are more than happy to lower monthly payments if that prevents a customer from filing bankruptcy — a smaller payment is better than no payment at all.

Some creditors, though, would rather play hardball and force you into bankruptcy before accepting a lower payment each month. If you have difficult creditors, contact a credit counseling agency. These agencies have experience communicating directly with creditors and working out solutions to debt repayment problems. If you search online, you find a large number of credit counseling agencies, but I strongly recommend beginning your search with the National Foundation for Credit Counseling at 1-800-388-2227 or www.nfcc.org for help locating a counseling agency near you. This network of credit counseling agencies is nonprofit and doesn't have a vested interest in making money off the debt-ridden consumer.

## Budgeting for the Future

Does the word "budget" send chills up your spine? I know it did for me for many years, but I've since had a change of heart. Now I realize that budgets allow you to be organized and have some control over what you spend. They help you to decide how to spend your money, plan for your future, pay off existing debt, and save a few pennies each month by reducing wasteful and impulsive purchases.

### Step 1: Categorize your expenses

When you begin setting up a monthly budget, start with big categories before breaking your budget down into smaller expense categories. A good list of basic budget categories to begin with includes

✔ **Housing:** mortgage/rent, repairs, property taxes, cleaning supplies, homeowner's/renter's insurance, utilities, furnishings, décor

✔ **Food:** groceries, meals out, pizza delivery, snacks and beverages at work

✔ **Transportation:** car payments, insurance, gas, oil, parking, repairs/maintenance, public transportation fees

✔ **Medical:** insurance, out-of-pocket expenses such as deductibles and non-insurance covered medical services, pharmacy, eye care, dental

✔ **Clothing:** new purchases, dry cleaning, repair

✔ **Personal:** cosmetics, haircuts, cleansers

✔ **Insurance:** life insurance and any other insurance not covered under home, transportation, or medical expenses

✔ **Education:** tuition, dues/fees, school pictures, yearbooks, school supplies, books

✔ **Credit accounts:** major credit cards, department store cards, lines of credit through your bank or other lender, any other outstanding debt

✔ **Gifts:** holidays, birthdays, graduations, weddings, showers

✔ **Recreation:** vacations, movies, books, magazines, newspapers, cable TV, restaurants, sporting events, sports equipment

✔ **Savings:** long-term and short-term goals, as well as retirement

✔ **Donations:** charities, churches

## Keeping family relationships as a priority

Most people at the end of their life don't wish they'd spent more time at the office, but they do often regret not spending more time with their family, especially when their children were young. Unfortunately, people who find themselves with debt payments that exceed what they can reasonably afford usually cast about for ways to increase their income. But instead of taking a part-time job, working overtime every week, or getting involved in a get-rich-quick scheme, look at your budget for ways to cut back your spending. Decreasing spending is usually a lot easier than increasing your income. Plus, you won't sacrifice time with your family in exchange for a paid-off credit card. By cutting back and tightening your money belt, you can pay off your bills *and* watch little Johnny's championship T-ball game on Saturday afternoon.

You need to set aside money each month for those yearly and quarterly payments that often sneak up on you when you least expect them. If you spend $1,200 on your yearly property taxes, divide that number by 12 and set aside $100 per month so that you aren't caught off guard by your property taxes, insurance payments, or any other periodic bills.

Within each general budget category, some items are essential (the mortgage or rent payment, the electric bill, and groceries), but other items are extra (new furniture, gifts, and pizza delivery). From your first list of general budget items, develop two separate budget lists, one for essentials and the other for extras. (I can't dictate what's essential and what's extra for other people, so I haven't divided up the lists for you. Some people may have to eat out regularly because of work-related issues and so dining out is an essential item in their life rather than an extra. Others may consider charitable giving an extra while their friends down the street consider it non-negotiable because of religious convictions.)

After you divide your expenses into two lists, look through both your essential and extra lists to find flexible budget items such as clothing, groceries, and other food-related expenses where you can cut back using the tips and advice throughout this book. Make a star next to flexible items in each of your lists so that you can identify them easily.

Extra and flexible budget items are the main places to focus your frugal living tactics. You're always going to have to pay your water bill, but cable television may be an extra utility that can be done away with for awhile if money's needed in a more essential budget category. Turn to the different sections in this book dealing with each budget category to find ways to cut back on the extras, and save a bit on the essentials, as well.

## *Step 2: Estimate what you spend*

Go through your checkbook and any other receipts or records you've kept over the past few months so that you can track how much you actually spend on essentials. Then for one month, keep a detailed diary of all your extra purchases, even for cheap things like newspapers or coffee from the vending machine at work. Little expenses quickly add up to big money when they're made on a daily basis, and these smaller out-of-pocket purchases that are frequently made with cash usually won't show up in your check register, so writing them all down helps make you aware of where the cash is dribbling out of your life.

After you've discovered exactly where your money goes throughout the month, you may need to reevaluate your written budget lists if you find your actual spending differed from your anticipated spending.

## Step 3: Calculate and adjust

Now that you've made two lists of budget items (essentials and extras), use the two lists to see if your spending habits are keeping you in the red.

Add up the essentials list and the extras list separately. Subtract the essentials total from your monthly income. If you have money left over, subtract the extras total from that amount. If you still have money left over, great! Look into a savings or investing plan (talk to your bank or a certified financial planner for help setting up a plan). But if your extras list takes you into negative numbers, start looking for places to cut back (for example, cancel your newspaper delivery or eat out once a month instead of once a week). You can also trim from the extras list in order to put more money toward debt repayment if that's a high priority in your financial picture. The rest of this book is dedicated to helping you save money on various expenses, so don't give up hope if you find you need to drastically cut your spending in order to stick to your budget and live within your means.

## The envelope system

The simplest budgeting plan is frequently referred to as the envelope system. My husband and I revolutionized our financial situation by simply setting aside cash in envelopes labeled with the various expense categories that we could pay for in cash: bus fare, gas and oil for the car, groceries, lunch money, toiletries, office supplies, and so on. (For things like utility bills that need to be paid with checks, we didn't technically use the envelopes.)

The envelope system made all the difference in the world for us because we could visualize how taking a few dollars from the grocery envelope to pay for a movie is actually stealing money from a budget category. When your money is just a lump of abstract figures in your bank statement, taking a little bit here and there for non-budgeted items is easier to do. But taking only cash to the grocery store made me shop more carefully, plan my meals more frugally, and put things back on the shelves if I went over the budgeted amount.

For keeping track of your budget, take a look at office supply stores for an easy-to-use, inexpensive family budgeting book. If you want something small that you can carry with you at all times, the Budget Map (http://budgetmap.com/) is a specially designed ledger that fits in your personal checkbook and takes the fuss out of making and sticking to a budget. I've found it to be easy, effective, and relatively inexpensive

A simple tip for taking care of your budgeting woes for regular bills is to pay for a part of each budget item each time you get paid. Our utility bill is due every two months, but my husband gets paid twice a month. So we figure out what our average two-month utility bill is and then divide that number by four. That amount then comes out of each and every pay period for utilities. Sometimes you can plan for a small payment every two weeks easier than for one large payment once every other month. If you have a monthly mortgage payment and get paid twice a month, write a check for half the mortgage payment each pay period. If you have an insurance payment that's due every six months, write out twelve small checks, one on each pay period.

# Part II
# Eating Like a King with a Peasant's Purse

The 5th Wave          By Rich Tennant

"We're trying to save money by buying in bulk, Caviar?"

## In this part . . .

The grocery bill is one of the few flexible items in the average family's budget, and one of the largest too. By using a few easy guidelines and simple tricks, anyone can shave a considerable sum of money off this budget category. Part II deals with shopping frugally for food items and preparing inexpensive meals — and no, you won't be eating macaroni and cheese every night 'til you pay off your kids' college loans.

# Chapter 4

# Going to the Grocery without Being Taken to the Cleaners

*In This Chapter*

▶ Escaping the lures of impulse buying

▶ Discovering simple money-saving tricks

▶ Keeping tabs on prices with a price diary

According to a 1995 paper published by the North Dakota State University Extension Program, the average American family spends about 15 percent of its monthly income on groceries and food-related expenses. To spend all that money, a family member's probably in the local grocery store more often than once or twice a month. And the more often you're at the store, the more opportunities the store's marketers have to entice you with the latest and greatest items. Supermarkets are in business to make money, and their marketers are savvy about the buying tendencies, weaknesses, and temptations of the average shopper, so the single greatest money-saving tip for grocery shopping I can share with you is to beware of *impulse purchases* (or buying more than you intended when you just go in for one or two things). Impulse buys can easily drive up that quick trip to the store for milk and eggs into a $30 experience complete with designer coffee and frozen éclairs.

In this chapter, I explain how you can avoid falling prey to impulse purchases and how you can combat common budget-breaking snares and pitfalls at the grocery store.

## Avoiding Common Gimmicks and Tricks of the Grocery Trade

Grocery stores spend money specifically to learn how to fool you into parting with your hard-earned money in their store. Whether it's enticing you into the store in the first place with sale items sold below what the store paid for the items, or convincing you to buy more expensive items, it's helpful to be aware of some of these tactics.

## Seeing through the aisle switcheroo

When you walk into the local grocery store and realize all the aisles have been reorganized and everything you usually purchase isn't where it usually is, you're experiencing a common grocery store *gimmick* (or a scheme for tricking you into spending money you wouldn't have spent otherwise). Yes, your grocery store actually moves items around just to make you, its loyal customer, feel confused and unable to find anything.

So, do you want to know the method behind the madness? If you shop at a particular store regularly, you know where everything you buy is located in each aisle, right? Without realizing it, you've developed a form of tunnel vision and don't really see anything except for what you need. But what happens when the store rearranges the aisles or moves items from one position on a shelf to another? You have to look around and actually focus on each aisle and every shelf. By losing your tunnel vision for a time, the possibility of something new catching your eye increases dramatically, and consequently your impulse purchases increase, too.

 Avoid making impulse purchases and sending your grocery bill through the roof by being extra vigilant about sticking to your shopping list. If you notice your store is going through a major overhaul and rearranging everything on the shelves, know that impulse buys are lurking around each corner and on every aisle. Turn on your tunnel vision and beware!

## Understanding the store's layout

If you've ever run into the grocery store after work to buy a gallon of milk and a dozen eggs for breakfast the next day, you've probably questioned why you have to walk all the way to the back of the store just to find those two items. Here's the answer: Most grocery stores have the same general floor plan — they keep produce, bread, dairy, and meat products along the edges of the store or up against the walls. Oftentimes the stores put commonly purchased items against the farthest wall or way off in a back corner. Store marketers know that if a customer has to walk to the back of the store for one little item, they pass numerous displays and shelves full of goodies.

Customers constantly walking past attractive displays in the local grocery store encourages every store manager's favorite customer activity: impulse buying!

One way to stop most of your impulse buys is to curtail aimless wandering through the store. Plan your menu and shopping list around the items against the store walls, and then plan for a single quick trip down each of the following aisles:

- ✔ The freezer aisle for frozen juices

- ✔ The pasta aisle for spaghetti noodles or other pasta needs

- ✔ The baking supplies aisle for flour, baking soda, cooking oil, and other home baking items

- ✔ The cereal aisle for breakfast cereal and oatmeal (but be careful about impulsively buying expensive boxed cereals, especially if your children are shopping with you!)

Plan your shopping around the aisle arrangement in the store and you won't be nearly as apt to wander past those tempting donuts that weren't on the shopping list — even though sometimes I can hear those donuts as they sit there, ever so softly calling my name.

When you shop the edges of the store, you find yourself saving considerably on your grocery bill. Plus, the perimeter carries the healthiest items in the store. Your waistline — and your budget — will be healthier on a diet consisting of fresh fruits, vegetables, and lean meats, rather than potato chips, boxed dinners, and processed luncheon meats.

## Escaping the store with only the loss leaders you went in for

When you see a price on something in a store flier that seems too good to be true, chances are you're looking at what's called a *loss leader*, those items the stores sell at (or below), the wholesale price paid for the merchandise. Stores advertise products for essentially zero profit to entice new customers into the store for the drastically reduced item, and then hopefully to keep the customer browsing around, giving in to a couple of impulse purchases. Many customers even plan to do all their shopping in whichever store has the most loss leaders, thus bringing their entire grocery budget that week into the store with the highest discounts. The stores are willing to take a loss on selected items because they plan to recoup their loss through higher sales in general due to the increased traffic.

Supermarkets usually offer more loss leaders at deeper discounts than convenience stores because the larger stores carry a broader line of products and usually sell higher volumes of goods. You can usually find loss leaders advertised on the front and back pages of the ads and circular sections. You can also find the loss leaders splashed across the reader boards or signs on the store.

Occasionally, stores will match a competitor's price if the customer brings in the ad or flier with the competitor's price displayed. So even a loss leader offered at another store could still reap benefits for you at your regular store if your store has price matching policies. If you find an excellent deal, and then don't have to drive around to different stores to get the better prices, you'll save even more.

The key to taking advantage of loss leaders without letting loss leaders take advantage of you is to not give in to temptation. Stop at several different stores to take advantage of their loss leaders, but be careful about those impulse buys. Stopping in for a couple cans of tuna fish, but then buying $20 worth of holiday decorations that aren't on sale, is hardly a good way to save your family's hard-earned money.

Here are a few tips to help you take advantage of loss-leader savings:

- ✔ Loss leaders frequently have a limit on the number of items you can buy at the discounted or coupon price, so you have an opportunity to take the troops (your spouse and kids) to the store with you. Send little Bobby and Suzy into their own checkout lines with their own supply of loss leaders. They feel grown up and you save additional dollars. But if the special specifies "one per household," this send-in-the-troops technique won't be an honest way to save a few pennies.

- ✔ You can also plan on making multiple trips to the store to stock up on the loss leaders. If you walk or jog by the store, duck into the store each day as you pass. You don't want to make too many extra trips to the store in the car because you use up your savings in gasoline, but if you have to go past there anyway, stock up!

- ✔ When you're sitting down to plan your weekly menu, look for loss leaders in the grocery ads. Scanning the ads can help your budget considerably if you plan your meals around the items that are deeply discounted each week.

- ✔ When you go shopping, do your loss leader shopping first, and then finish the remainder of your grocery shopping at whichever store you've discovered has the best prices in general.

Don't consider loss leaders an excuse for splurging. Stock up on those items you can reasonably store and use. Having a six-year supply of toothpaste is probably overkill. And be sure to check the expiration date on any loss leader purchases. Oftentimes these items are getting near their expiration date and the store is trying to clear off their shelves before the "sell-by" date arrives. Even toothpaste and cans of soda pop have expiration dates, so check the labels carefully before buying items with too-good-to-be-true price tags.

## Looking high and low: Finding the best bargains on the shelves

If you're like most people, you first notice the items at eye level. Because marketing experts are also experts in human behavior, they've noticed the eye-level tendency we all have — and they plan store displays accordingly.

If you want to find the best values on the grocery store shelves, look high on the top shelves or bend down and look at the bottom shelf. The brand-name and higher-priced products are located at eye level, while the generic, store brand, and lower-priced items are in the more awkward places to see.

# Using Coupons and Rebates

The world today is full of coupons and rebates. People either love these money-saving techniques or find them to be more work than they're worth. (You've probably seen those Coupon Kings on TV talk shows who spend only 63 cents for a month's worth of groceries — all from the wonders of coupon magic. More power to 'em!) Even though I'm probably not going to spend my spare time involved with a super-colossal coupon or rebate system, I'm always out there looking for a good bargain, and I find coupons and rebates to be a valuable addition to a well-rounded approach to saving money.

## Boning up on coupon basics

Most people use coupons occasionally at the grocery store, but lightly scanning the ads in Sunday's newspaper and clipping one coupon good for 25 cents off five cans of tomato paste isn't going to result in tremendous savings on your grocery bill. But if you make a habit of looking carefully through the Sunday and Wednesday ads, and other assorted coupon circulars, for considerable savings on items and brands you regularly buy, the pennies and dimes add up to substantial savings over time — maybe even hundreds of dollars over the course of a year.

One of the most important tips for effective coupon use is to be organized about the process. Every coupon you need but can't easily locate is cash slipping through your fingers. You've probably seen those little wallet-shaped coupon organizers you can slip into your purse or pocket to keep your coupons organized by category. If you ever find one of those coupon caddies at a garage sale for a dollar or two, snap it up! The caddie more than pays for itself in a short time. Go through your coupon organizer about once a month to check for expired coupons. If you keep the coupons in their appropriate sections in the order of their expiration dates, you can easily cull the outdated ones.

### Knowing when to coupon

Some areas of the United States have stores that double and triple coupons, even coupons from competitors. If you find a $1 off coupon for a $3 item and take it to a store on triple coupon day, you just purchased the item for free. Free is a difficult price to beat, anywhere! Stores with double and triple coupon deals usually have a limit. For example, they may only triple coupons up to 50 cents, so be aware of any limitations. Also, be aware that stores that double and triple coupons usually make up for the savings by having slightly higher prices overall than other stores. Buy the deeply discounted coupon items, and then take the rest of your shopping to the store you know has the lowest prices.

Coupons are great, but they're not always the best deal at the grocery store. For example, sale prices without a coupon are oftentimes less than brand-name items with a coupon. Also, some store brands and generic items are often less expensive than similar brand-name items with a coupon. But if you find you really don't like your store's house brand of spaghetti sauce, and your family only eats a particular brand name, then using coupons for the more expensive version is definitely going to be a money saver for you in the checkout line.

Look for coupons for items that are already on sale. You'll save twice with this tactic, unless the coupon specifies that it can't be combined with other offers. Be sure to read coupons carefully and check for limitations.

### Knowing when not to coupon

Don't buy items just because you have a coupon. If you find a coupon for $1.50 off of a type of cereal you never use and nobody in your household enjoys, you're not going to be saving money by purchasing something that may just sit on your shelf. Keep in mind that manufacturers provide coupons to entice you to buy their product; they don't care about saving you money.

Along the same lines, don't plan your shopping list around the manufacturer's coupons you've collected. Make up your regular shopping list first, and then go to your coupon wallet and see if you have current coupons for the items you're buying.

Also, if you have a coupon for a convenience item you can easily make yourself (for example: taco seasoning packets, tuna skillet meal boxes, instant oatmeal single-servings), skip it — you probably save more money with the homemade variety rather than the pre-packaged item at the store, even with a coupon. Plus, you have a healthier product because you can choose the ingredients yourself. See Chapter 5 for information on finding homemade alternatives to store-bought goods.

## Rebating for fun and profit

Most rebate aficionados consider rebating to be a hobby, not just a money-saving technique. The thrill of hunting for those elusive rebate opportunities, the process of filling out and filing the forms, and the ecstasy of receiving the refund checks in the mail all add up to fun for many people. And rebates can really be a dream come true on large ticket items, such as washers and dryers, kitchen appliances, or even vehicles. Personally, I find rebating requires more organizational talents than I was born with ("Now, which pile did I file that rebate offer in?"). To participate in rebates in large quantities, you need a purposeful system for organizing your rebate forms, proof of purchase materials, and cash register receipts. But the folks who love playing the rebate game, really love it! And who knows? You may turn out to be one of those people, too.

"How does rebating work?" you ask. Well, you're probably familiar with the in-store displays enticing buyers to purchase a new-and-improved water filter system (what was wrong with the old one, anyway?). If you buy the new advertised system, the manufacturer will send you $15 back from your original purchase price. Wow! What a deal!

In order to receive the rebate, you must fill out a rebate form and mail it along with proof-of-purchase materials (usually your original cash register receipt and the Universal Product Code [UPC] or barcode) to the manufacturer.

Occasionally, a store will offer rebates in the form of store credit rather than money back from the manufacturer. If you shop in a store regularly, credit for shopping there again can be helpful to the budget. But be careful you don't use the store credit as an excuse to buy things you normally wouldn't purchase. Remember, the store isn't really trying to save you money — they're trying to entice you into spending more money.

If you're interested in more information about rebating, you can find current rebate offers through several different sources. Probably the best resources are the Refundle Bundle newsletter (you can subscribe at www.refundlebundle.com) and the popular Web site www.couponsandrefunds.com.

# Saving Even More Money, Let Me Count the Ways

There are countless ways to quickly and easily save money on your grocery bill. The following sections contain many of the best ideas grouped together for easy reference. Sometimes minor changes in how you think about your grocery shopping can bring major benefits at the checkout stand.

## Locating in-store specials

You can discover current specials at your local supermarket in the latest flier sent out by the store. In addition to the copy you receive in the mail or in the Sunday supplements of your newspaper, you usually can find a copy of the flier displayed near the store's entrance or on the store's bulletin board. Bulletin boards are often located near the entrances and in the hallway by the restrooms. Many stores also post in-store specials throughout the store on signs attached to the shelves directly below the product.

While the cashier rings up your order in the checkout line, watch the prices coming through on the cash register's computer carefully. Sometimes the store has the wrong price entered into the computer system, or the cashier may press the wrong key. Be gracious about it if you see a mistake. More often than not, it's not the cashier's fault but an error in the system. Stores sometimes provide incorrectly scanned items for free.

Some grocery stores offer discount cards to their regular customers. Cardholders then have access to discounts and sale prices non-cardholders won't be able to use. Usually there isn't a charge for these cards, so if your favorite store offers a discount card, it's definitely worth taking advantage of the added savings.

Some stores also offer additional discounts for senior citizens, and military personnel and their families. Occasionally, a store may have a special day of the week for senior citizen discounts. Be sure to check with your local grocery store to see if you qualify for any of these special offers

After you're in the store, at the end of each aisle, the grocery store marketing gurus place eye-catching displays of on-sale products called *end caps.* But beware! That current special on lasagna noodles may be an excellent price, but the cheese and pasta sauce displayed with the sale item may not be on sale at all. The store's marketers are attempting to entice you into impulse buys by putting high-priced, but related goods next to their deeply discounted items.

## *Taking advantage of seasonal sales*

You're probably aware of the annual January White Sales held by many stores, where you can find great bargains on linens to use throughout the new year. Did you know many food items go on sale at regular times from year to year, too? For example, March is National Frozen Food Month in the United States. (Unless you work in the grocery trade, I bet you didn't know that.) To celebrate this prestigious event, most grocery stores offer significant discounts on frozen foods during the month of March. Throughout the rest of the year, other food items are seasonally offered at discounts. The lower prices usually reflect what's currently growing at local farms. Fruits and vegetables that aren't in season can still be found in the produce department, but the price is higher because the stores need to pay higher shipping costs for importing the food from other regions.

The following list includes food items you can find on sale or at the lowest prices each month of the year:

- ✔ **January:** Turkey, apples, grapefruit, oranges, and pears
- ✔ **February:** Post-Valentine's Day candy and chocolates

✔ **March:** Frozen vegetables, meats, breakfast items, and TV dinners

✔ **April:** Eggs, broccoli, and cauliflower

✔ **May:** Sodas, hot dogs, hamburgers, buns, asparagas, and pineapple

✔ **June:** Dairy products and tomatoes

✔ **July:** Strawberries, corn, berries, cherries, squash, watermelons, cantaloupes, tomatoes, plums, peaches, and nectarines

✔ **August:** Squash, green peppers, salad fixings, berries, apples, melon, peaches, apricots, and fresh fish

✔ **September:** Apples, broccoli, cauliflower, and canned goods

✔ **October:** Pumpkins, cranberries, grapes, oranges, sweet potatoes, and yams

✔ **November:** Turkey, sweet potatoes, yams, and post-Halloween bags of candy

✔ **December:** Oranges, apples, and grapefruit

## Buying in bulk

Purchasing frequently used items in bulk can save substantial amounts on your budget. You probably don't need a year's supply of bananas — and I know you don't need the year's supply of fruit flies that come with them! But what about having enough toilet paper on hand so you never run out unexpectedly?

## Packing away bulk purchases

Do you think you don't have room for bulk purchases because you don't have a pantry? Well, take a look at the back of your linen closet shelves behind the folded towels. If you're like many people (including me), you may have some empty space just waiting to be filled with a stack of cans, boxes, or packages. What about that empty corner in the garage? Or take a look underneath your beds, and what do you see? Empty space and dust bunnies? Any of these places can be potential storage spots for a case or two of extra stewed tomatoes or refried beans. You can also split bulk orders with a friend or relative if you really don't have the room but want to experience the savings to be found in bulk purchases.

### Calculating the "per-unit" price

It pays to bring along a calculator on your trips to the supermarket or warehouse store so you can figure out the per-unit price of different items, especially if you're planning on doing any bulk buying.

To figure out the unit price of an item, decide which unit you want to use — do you want to figure out how much per ounce or how much per pound something costs? Canned goods should be figured out per ounce, while items like fresh produce and meats should be figured on a per pound basis.

For example, if you're looking at a 15-ounce can of tomato sauce and trying to figure out if it's a better deal than the 32-ounce can next to it, take the total price of the first can and then divide that number by the number of ounces in the can. This gives you the per-unit price of the first can. Do the same thing for the second can. Whichever can comes up with the smaller per-unit price gives you the highest savings.

### Avoiding impulse purchases

At warehouse stores, you can often find great prices on vast quantities of items, such as baking soda, salad oil, and paper plates. If you have the storage space, go for it! (See the "Packing away bulk purchases" sidebar in this chapter for helpful hints on where to store the items you buy in bulk.)

The biggest drawback I see to warehouse stores is impulse buying. Maybe you need to purchase a couple cases of soda for a party, but you walk out of the store with the soda, a 12-pack of tube socks, six ten-pound packages of frozen chicken breasts, three books, and four snow tires. Impulse buying is often stronger and more devastating at warehouse stores — after all, people can find it tough to pass up a 100-piece bath towel set on sale from a top designer.

Along with being careful about impulse buying at warehouse stores, you also need to diligently check the per-unit pricing of everything you want to buy. Maybe the 15-pound can of tomato sauce looks like a great bargain, but if you check the pricing per ounce and compare it with the sale price per ounce at the regular grocery store (as I explain in the previous section), you may find you're not getting quite as good a deal as you thought. Keeping a price diary, which I discuss later in this chapter, can really be beneficial. Remember, just because the can is big doesn't mean the savings are equally huge.

## Opting for generic products or store brands

Many stores carry *store brands,* items with the store's name on the label. Or they may carry *generic products,* those items labeled without a brand name of any sort. If you're willing to be a bit adventurous, keeping your eye out for inexpensive store brands and generic products can shave a substantial amount from your grocery budget. People often tell me they don't care for the taste or quality of store brands or generic items, but you may be surprised to discover that many products carrying generic or store brand labels are actually top quality, name brand items packaged under a different label.

If you're uncertain whether your local store carries generic grocery items that meet your family's expectations or taste requirements, you can give the items in question a try. Don't stock up on ten jars of the generic spaghetti sauce until you've purchased a single jar as a trial. If your family approves its taste, you've found an excellent way to save some money on your grocery budget.

I've personally had the best luck with generic versions of:

- ✔ Tomato sauce and paste
- ✔ Canned and frozen vegetables
- ✔ Margarine
- ✔ Canned soups
- ✔ Cookies and crackers
- ✔ Dairy products (milk, butter, and cheese)
- ✔ Coffee and tea
- ✔ Bread, rolls, and buns

## Building relationships with shopkeepers and store employees

Do you know the Muffin Man? No, I'm not talking about the one who "lives on Drury Lane" in the old children's rhyme, but do you know the bakery worker at your local supermarket? If you don't, you should. Grocery store employees can be the gatekeepers to great savings.

If you're a regular shopper, take a few minutes to chat with the various employees in the store. They may remember you if you come in regularly, and they're usually more than happy to answer questions. Don't hesitate to ask the meat counter employee what time each day ground beef is reduced in price, or feel free to check with the produce manager to see what time she pulls the past-its-prime fruit and vegetables from the produce department displays.

Many grocery stores throw away day old bread and less-than-perfect produce. Ask the store manager what their policies are. You may even be able to get these items for free! I've known several people who stop by their local grocery store several times a week to cart away the bread, produce, and dented cans that the store would've tossed in its dumpster. They often cart away so many extra food items, they can't use them all — so they share the food generously throughout their neighborhood, their church, and their circle of friends.

# Experiencing the Wonders of a Price Diary

Ever question if you should stock up on your favorite salsa at the current sale price, or if you should just purchase the amount needed for tonight's nachos? Maybe you're out of toilet paper and can't recall offhand if the brand-name, two-for-one sale is worth filling the empty space in the linen closet with rolls of toilet paper. Well, imagine having a magic genie in your purse or pocket that can instantly answer those questions for you. Wouldn't it be great? Well, I don't have an actual genie for you, but I do have an idea that's almost as effective: the price diary!

"Dear Diary, I'm so proud of myself! Today I only spent 25 cents each for cans of cooked kidney beans!" (Just kidding, that's not an actual price diary entry.) A price diary isn't a place for recording the emotional thrills of saving your dimes and dollars. A price diary is a handy checklist to refer to whenever you question if an item on sale is worth stocking up on or not. By purchasing items when they're on sale at ultra-low prices, you can avoid paying full retail. Otherwise, if you wait until you need to add items to your shopping list because the pantry's empty, you have to pay whatever the current price for those items happens to be.

Setting up the price diary can be a bit of work, but the diary is well worth every minute if used properly. If the price diary just sits on your desk gathering dust, then you aren't investing your time, effort, or money well.

Here's how to set up your own price diary:

1. **Find a small lined, spiral-bound notebook or mini three-ring binder.**

   Choose a diary that easily fits in your pocket or purse when you head out the door to the supermarket; you need to carry the diary with you when you shop in order for it to be effective.

2. **Go through your cupboards, pantry shelves, refrigerator drawers, and freezer space and make a list of every item you buy regularly (or use at least once every other week).**

   These items are what you should stock up on when they go on sale.

3. **Organize the items.**

   You can organize alphabetically, or separate the frequently used items according to subtopics, such as meat, dairy, bread, pasta, vegetables, canned/boxed items, spices, frozen foods, paper products, cleaning products, and so on. Or you can arrange the list by aisles in your grocery store. The goal is to find the item entry you're looking for quickly while you're in the store. See Figure 4-1 for a possible page layout. Use a layout that makes sense to you.

**Beef**

| Item | Store | Best Price |
|------|-------|-----------|
| Ground Beef | Oscar's | $0.88 per pound |
| Roast | Shop-Fast | $1.39 per pound |
| Steak | Oscar's | $1.49 per pound |

**Figure 4-1:** An example price diary page layout.

4. **Transfer the list to your price diary.**

   Only put one or two items on each page.

**5. Write down (in pencil!) the lowest prices that you find for each item.**

You can take the list with you to the store or jot down prices as you browse through your local grocery stores' ads. You can start by listing prices on old grocery receipts. When you find a lower sale price than previously listed, erase the earlier number and write in the new lowest price.

Don't forget to list the store name where you found the lowest prices. Use abbreviations that make sense to you for the store names and food items in the price diary. (If you do all your shopping at only two stores in town, feel free to only record the prices from those stores in your price diary.) Be sure to list unit pricing too. For example, don't just say, "Beans — 25¢ per can." You'll find it more effective to write something more detailed like, "Beans, kidney, 15-oz. can — 25¢ per can." And keep a small calculator with your price diary. Figuring all those cost-per-serving or cost-per-ounce numbers can be challenging to do in your head. (See "Calculating the 'per-unit' price" section earlier in this chapter for more information on unit pricing.)

You want to record the lowest sale prices so you'll know when the advertising fliers come out on Wednesday if ground beef is priced so low, it's a "stock up the freezer" sort of sale, or if it's just an average "buy this week's ground beef" sale. While you don't want to run all over town to every grocery store within driving range, if the store across town is having a stock-up sale on chicken, it's worth a trip out of your way if you're going to be buying enough to stock your freezer for several months' worth of chicken meals.

So the next time you see an item advertised on sale or a banner splashed across the store's ad circular screaming at you about deeply discounted items, consult your price diary. Compare the supposed sale price to the lowest price listed in your diary and see if the item is really on sale. You may find spaghetti sauce on sale for $2.50, but then discover, through the wonders of your handy-dandy price diary, that the store is selling the sauce for the same price as always. Sometimes stores advertise something as being on sale so they can later raise the price, and then customers won't blink.

For a sample of the types of items you may want to include in your price diary, see the following list:

✔ **Baking supplies:** Baking chocolate, cooking oil, dry and evaporated milk, honey, raisins, and yeast

✔ **Bread:** Dinner rolls, hamburger and hot dog buns, and sandwich bread

✓ **Canned goods:** Applesauce, broth (canned: beef, chicken, vegetable), mushrooms (whole and sliced), soups, spaghetti sauce, tomato paste, tomato sauce, and tuna

✓ **Cleaning supplies:** Bleach, dishwashing detergents, fabric softener (liquid, sheets), laundry detergent (liquid, powdered), and laundry stain remover

✓ **Condiments:** Ketchup, lemon juice, lime juice, mayonnaise, mustard (Dijon, honey, regular), pickles (sliced, sweet, whole), relish, soy sauce, and Worcestershire sauce

✓ **Dairy:** 2 percent, 4 percent, and whole milk, butter, flavored coffee creamers, light cream, margarine (cubes, tub), and whipping cream

✓ **Frozen:** Beans (green), corn, french fries, mixed vegetables, peas, and spinach

✓ **Meats:** Beef (ground, roasts, steaks, stew meat), chicken (breasts w/bone, boneless breasts, ground, drumsticks, thighs, whole fryer, wings), ham (sliced, whole, turkey ham), deli meats (ham, chicken, roast beef, turkey), pork (chops, ground, roast, sausage), and turkey (ground, whole, hindquarter)

✓ **Paper products:** Facial tissue, paper plates, paper towels, toilet paper, and feminine hygiene

✓ **Pasta:** Egg noodles, elbow macaroni, fettuccine, linguini, manicotti shells, penne, rigatoni, seashells (large, small), and spaghetti

✓ **Pre-packaged items:** Bouillon cubes (beef, chicken, vegetable), gravy mix packets, hot chocolate mix, jams and jellies, peanut butter, rice (brown, instant, long grain, white, wild), sunflower seeds, and vinegar (balsamic, cider, red wine, white, white wine)

✓ **Produce:** Apples, bell pepper (green, red), carrots, lettuce (green leaf, head lettuce, red leaf, romaine), onions, potatoes (baking, bagged, red, sweet), and tofu

✓ **Refrigerator/freezer supplies:** Cheese (cheddar, Monterey Jack, mozzarella, Parmesan, ricotta, Romano, Swiss), cottage cheese, eggs or egg substitute, juice (lemonade, orange, mixed), lemon juice, sour cream, tortillas (corn, flour), and yogurt (flavored, plain)

✓ **Spices:** Allspice, basil, chili powder, dill, nutmeg (ground and whole), onion powder, onion salt, oregano, paprika, pepper (black and white), rosemary, sage, salt, thyme, and vanilla extract

If you buy toiletries (face soap, shampoo, shaving cream, make-up) at the grocery store, you'll also want to include a section in your price diary for these items.

Over time, you may find you've saved so much money you can actually write in your regular journal about a vacation or new computer you paid for with the money saved with the price diary's help. Your new entry may read: "Dear Diary — I went to the ocean this weekend and had such a wonderful time! I'm so glad I took the time to keep track of my grocery expenses this year so I can enjoy another carefree weekend with my friends."

# Chapter 5

# No More Macaroni and Cheese, Please! Creating Frugal Meals

. . . . . . . . . . . . . . . . . . . . . . . . . . . . . . . . . . . . . . . . .

### In This Chapter

▶ Deciding on a frugal family meal plan

▶ Saving money on each meal of the day

▶ Using leftovers to reduce grocery bills

▶ Growing your own vegetables

▶ Saving on homemade mixes

. . . . . . . . . . . . . . . . . . . . . . . . . . . . . . . . . . . . . . . . .

*E*ven if you know how to shop frugally and are already saving money hand over fist in the grocery store's checkout line with coupons and store sales, your efforts really won't do much good if the meals you prepare at home are expensive to begin with. Eating homemade meatloaf is obviously more frugal than eating New York steak.

But if you think frugal eating is equal to eating nothing but generic macaroni and cheese for the rest of your life, think again! In this chapter, I provide easy ways to make your mealtimes nutritious, adventurous, tasty, and cheap — all at the same time!

## Creating a Meal Plan to Avoid the Fast-Food Trap

Do you remember the old cliché, "When we fail to plan, we plan to fail"? Well, not only is it true in work life and personal goal setting, but it also applies to family meal planning. By not planning meals ahead of time, you can easily fall into the drive-through or pizza delivery trap. (When I first started investigating frugal eating habits, I discovered that about half of my family's food dollars were going to fast food, convenience items, and pizza delivery — about $120 each month, which translates into $1,440 a year! I'd rather spend that same money on family activities, education for my children, or sock it away in long-term savings.)

Don't get me wrong — going out to eat can take its rightful place as an occasional treat. But instead of making a meal of fast food a daily occurrence, I plan ahead and save big bucks on my family's food bill each month. Not only does a menu plan help you avoid the fast-food trap, but it also helps you prepare your grocery list each week and provides variety in your diet.

Here are two easy steps you can follow to create a family-pleasing meal plan and save money, too:

1. **Make a list of your family's favorite meals.**

   Ask your family to participate in the meal planning by brainstorming all the different recipes and foods they enjoy eating regularly for breakfast, lunch, and dinner.

2. **Write out a menu at the beginning of each week or month.**

   Refer to your family's list of favorites and plan a particular type of dish for each meal of the day. For example, dinner — Monday's dinner can be pasta, Tuesday can be chicken, Wednesday can be vegetarian, Thursday can be hearty soup, Friday can be seafood, Saturday can be pork, and Sunday can be a family barbeque night (depending on the weather). Now do the same for breakfast and lunch. What meals you choose for each day of the week doesn't matter. Just make the menu work for you and your family's tastes.

 Tape the menu inside a kitchen cabinet or on the refrigerator door. That way, your family sees an official weekly menu of breakfasts, lunches, and dinners. Having the menu out on display cuts down on those never-ending "What's for dinner?" questions.

# Breaking Your Fast, Not Your Budget!

Articles in magazines and ads on TV remind me constantly of the importance of eating a good breakfast, especially for children facing a long day at school trying to get their brain cells to function at a high level for hours on end. So I know feeding the kids well each morning is important. But feed them a healthy meal *and* keep it frugal at the same time? Hmmm . . . that seems like a whole 'nother kettle of fish. Lucky for you I have some frugal breakfast ideas to share. Read on!

## Enjoying generic breakfast favorites

If you're like me and you live with several big eaters who can polish off a single $5 box of cereal in one meal, breakfast can be one of the most expensive meals of the day. If your kids have to pour milk on a bowl of cereal or it's not really "breakfast" in their eyes, give the generic versions of your favorite cereals a try. Or if your family members enjoy brand-name breakfast pastries and juices, try the generic or store brand of those, too — your family may never taste the difference, but your pocketbook will surely take note.

All your favorite lunch and dinner foods come in less-expensive generic versions as well. Generic versions of spaghetti sauce and canned fruits and vegetables are easy to find in grocery stores.

If the kids complain that the generic items just don't taste as good, keep your eyes open for sale prices on brand-name breakfast items. For example, I try to never spend more than $2 per box on brand-name cereals, and even then, I usually buy them only for a special celebration like a birthday or for an occasional treat. I can buy brand-name cereal at less than $2 per box by combining a store's sale price with a good coupon. (Boxed cereals are one of the best items for using coupons.) Finding a favorite brand of cereal on sale for $2 per box and then handing in a $1-off coupon that's doubled buys a box of cereal for the best price of all: Free! (See Chapter 4 for more on coupon basics.)

Making homemade versions of frequently purchased breakfast items, such as frozen waffles or instant oatmeal, can save substantially compared to the cost of purchasing the premade varieties at the store. By looking at the ingredient list on the package, you can often get a good idea of what to use instead. For example, make instant oatmeal at home by briefly whirling oats in the blender or food processor. Then just stir in boiling water as you normally would for instant oats. Adding a bit of powdered milk and spices like cinnamon and nutmeg to the oats before adding the water makes it tasty, too. (See the "Making your own mixes and convenience items" section, later in this chapter, for more information.)

## More fast and cheap breakfast ideas

Sometimes I wake up feeling uncreative. Uh, oh! Breakfast boredom means I've entered dangerous territory — can you hear the fast-food drive-through calling my name? To keep temptation at bay, I make a list of favorite breakfast ideas and hang it on the inside of my cupboard door. Here are a few items on my breakfast list in case you need a little inspiration on some bleary-eyed, creativity-deprived morning:

✔ **Breakfast shakes or smoothies:** Blend a few ice cubes with your choice of fresh or generic canned fruits and juice.

✔ **Fresh or canned fruit:** Whole, sliced, or stewed.

✔ **Rice, oats, or other cooked grains:** Serve hot with milk, sweetener, raisins or finely diced apples, and a dash of cinnamon or nutmeg. Many grains can be purchased inexpensively in bulk and stored in air-tight containers in your kitchen cupboard for several months without getting stale.

✔ **Omelets:** Use up leftover pieces of meat, vegetables, and cheese to keep omelets inexpensive.

✔ **Crepes:** Fill with leftover meats, inexpensive homemade cheese sauces, or fruit and whipped cream you've purchased on sale.

✔ **Yogurt:** Homemade is easy and cheap. Most natural foods cookbooks have a recipe or two. Add bits of leftover fruit or stir in some jam or vanilla for flavoring.

✔ **Bagels:** Serve toasted and spread with butter; or spread with generic cream cheese. Sliced strawberries, when they're in season, and generic cream cheese on bagels is an almost decadent breakfast treat. Look for sales on bagels and stock up. They keep for weeks in the freezer.

✔ **Mule Food:** Stir together uncooked rolled oats, raisins, and nuts (if available). Serve cold with milk and your choice of sweetener (honey, sugar, brown sugar, maple syrup, vanilla, fruit juice, almond extract) and milk; or just stir the "Mule Food" into your favorite flavored yogurt. Make this treat in bulk and store in an air-tight container for a great substitute for brand-name boxed granola.

## *Pulling breakfast out of a hat . . . or the freezer*

One of my favorite appliances for fixing frugal breakfast meals is my freezer. Yep, you read that right. The freezer. And I'm not talking about just stocking it with boxes of store-bought frozen waffles from the warehouse store down the road (although that's not a bad idea, either, if I can find a great price). A breakfast made from store-bought frozen waffles can cost a family several dollars, but the same meal made with homemade frozen waffles usually costs less than one dollar for the entire family. Saving about $2 on breakfast every day can equal $730 each year.

I frequently make breakfast items ahead of time to store in my freezer. When it comes time to eat, I can just throw something in the toaster or microwave rather than whip up a big breakfast meal from scratch each morning. (See Chapter 6 for more money-saving tips on preparing and freezing large quantities of food to serve later.) Breakfast sandwiches and burritos can be made from left-over meats and cheeses, and eggs purchased on sale. By making French toast and waffles in large quantities, you can buy the ingredients in bulk and save substantially. The following breakfast items freeze and reheat well:

- ✔ **Homemade waffles, pancakes, and French toast:** When reheating waffles, pancakes, or French toast, just pop them (still frozen!) into the toaster on the lowest setting. They thaw and reheat easily this way; plus, the toaster method helps them keep their shape. Microwaving these items makes them soggy and limp, and not particularly appetizing. Just reheat your home-frozen breakfast items the same way you'd toast frozen waffles from the store. Add fruit, nuts, or raisins to spice things up a bit.

  Heat the syrup before serving. The syrup not only tastes better, but it also goes farther because warm syrup is a bit thinner than cold syrup. Be sure to give generic syrups a try — they're considerably less expensive than brand names and are similar in taste and quality.

- ✔ **Breakfast burritos:** One of my family's favorite breakfast meals is simply a soft flour tortilla rolled with pre-cooked breakfast items inside. I don't really use an official recipe, but just mix together whatever I have on hand (scrambled eggs, sausage, onion, cheese), and then roll it all up together in tortillas burrito-style. Place the burritos in a single layer on a cookie sheet in the freezer until frozen solid. After they're frozen, put them in zip-top freezer bags. Breakfast burritos reheat beautifully in the microwave. Yum!

- ✔ **Breakfast casseroles and quiches:** I put these together in a mix-and-match fashion just like with the breakfast burritos. I've found a large selection of breakfast casserole recipes on the Internet and in assorted cookbooks lying around my house, so just use any recipe that sounds appealing to you. For making a breakfast quiche, I prepare my favorite pie shell recipe (or a store-bought frozen shell if I've found a good sale), and a handy quiche recipe I keep around. Rather than follow the recipe exactly, I substitute the recipe's filling with breakfast ingredients like bacon, sausage, and onions. For freezing, prepare the quiche or casserole completely, cool, and then cover in foil or plastic wrap to freeze. If you freeze the casserole or quiche in a microwave-safe dish, you can reheat it in the microwave.

✔ **Muffins and breads:** Zucchini bread, banana bread, or any dessert bread or muffin makes a delicious, simple, and cheap change of pace for breakfast. Prepare them according to your favorite recipes, then wrap in heavy-duty plastic wrap, and freeze until ready to use. You can warm the bread in the microwave or serve it cold. *Tip:* Spreading butter or peanut butter on the bread while it's still frozen makes the spreading easier.

✔ **Breakfast sandwiches:** To build your own breakfast sandwiches, use slices of English muffins or halved biscuits and top with whatever breakfast items you have in the fridge — scrambled or fried eggs, a slice of breakfast meat, and a bit of cheese. Simply wrap in heavy-duty plastic wrap, freeze together in large zip-top freezer bags, and reheat in the microwave. Much less expensive — and healthier — than making a trip to the local drive-through for a breakfast sandwich, let me tell you!

# Stretching Your Lunch-Time Dollar

A friend of mine signs all her e-mail with the sentence, "If you are what you eat, then I'm fast, easy, and cheap!" Boy, if that's not my motto when it comes to mealtimes — especially lunch — I don't know what is!

If you pack your lunch to take to work, don't think of preparing the meal as just another chore, a bit of drudgery to be overcome. Instead, see it as an opportunity to picnic outside each day. If weather permits, find a sunny spot to eat with co-workers, or maybe alone with a good book in the shade of your favorite tree with a view of the water, or in the local park by the fountain.

## Counting the savings

If the adults in your house are spending $5 per day at the lunch counter or vending machine at work, that means $100 per month, or $1,200 per year, are going out of your food budget for sandwiches, fries, coffee, and sodas. And daily lunch prices are often closer to $10 per day — which takes that daily lunch expense up to a whopping $3,000 per year for one person! Yikes! By making lunches at home for roughly $1 per day, you can easily shave about $900 per year per person off your family's food budget (and that's on the low end!).

Many schools offer hot lunch programs at such a bargain price that it doesn't really pay to make lunch at home. But if your hot lunch program is taking a bite out of your food budget, you may want to think about packing your kids' lunches instead. Packing your child's lunch can stretch the budget or break the bank, depending on the choices you make about what to include in it.

## Packaging your lunch

The idea of "brown-bagging" it to work or school is almost old-fashioned now. With the advent of reusable drink bottles and lunch packaging, anyone can pack a lunch fit for a king — and save money in the process by not having to buy sandwich and lunch bags continually. Many inexpensive plastic containers are available at the supermarket, but to really save money, look for them at thrift stores and garage sales.

The following list gives some ideas for quick and frugal lunch bag tricks you can use for everyone — from Dad's lunch pail to the kids' field trip days:

- ✔ **Have official lunchboxes for each person.** You save a few pennies by not buying brown paper bags. The lunchboxes for adults today are more stylish than they were years ago, plus they're well insulated and frequently come with their own drink bottles. Shop around a bit. You don't need to resort to a big metal can or a plastic box with cartoon characters anymore.

- ✔ **Pack lunch items in reusable storage containers.** Because the lunchbox comes back home each day, you don't have to worry about not seeing your little sandwich boxes or plastic drink bottles again. (Fill the plastic drink bottles with reconstituted frozen juice instead of buying the individual juice boxes with the little straws.)

- ✔ **Invest in a wide-mouthed, insulated container.** It's great for keeping foods hot or cold and also allows you to take single servings of warm leftovers such as chili, homemade soup, and pasta.

- ✔ **Repackage large bags of snacks.** Buying individual portions of chips and snack items is expensive. Instead, put handfuls of pretzels, snack crackers, or chips into smaller lunch-sized zip-top reusable bags. Place the smaller bags into a large storage bag until ready to toss into the lunch boxes.

Save time while you save money by preparing lunches in an assembly-line fashion, especially if you're making food for several people. Make all the sandwiches at once, slice and add the dessert (if you're giving them any) to each bag, pour juice into all the juice bottles, and so on.

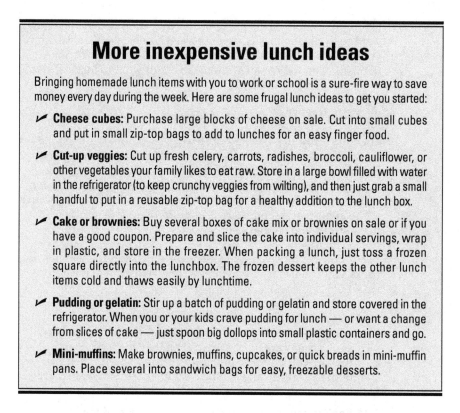

## More inexpensive lunch ideas

Bringing homemade lunch items with you to work or school is a sure-fire way to save money every day during the week. Here are some frugal lunch ideas to get you started:

- **Cheese cubes:** Purchase large blocks of cheese on sale. Cut into small cubes and put in small zip-top bags to add to lunches for an easy finger food.

- **Cut-up veggies:** Cut up fresh celery, carrots, radishes, broccoli, cauliflower, or other vegetables your family likes to eat raw. Store in a large bowl filled with water in the refrigerator (to keep crunchy veggies from wilting), and then just grab a small handful to put in a reusable zip-top bag for a healthy addition to the lunch box.

- **Cake or brownies:** Buy several boxes of cake mix or brownies on sale or if you have a good coupon. Prepare and slice the cake into individual servings, wrap in plastic, and store in the freezer. When packing a lunch, just toss a frozen square directly into the lunchbox. The frozen dessert keeps the other lunch items cold and thaws easily by lunchtime.

- **Pudding or gelatin:** Stir up a batch of pudding or gelatin and store covered in the refrigerator. When you or your kids crave pudding for lunch — or want a change from slices of cake — just spoon big dollops into small plastic containers and go.

- **Mini-muffins:** Make brownies, muffins, cupcakes, or quick breads in mini-muffin pans. Place several into sandwich bags for easy, freezable desserts.

## *To sandwich or not to sandwich*

When I think of bringing lunch from home, sandwiches are the first thought that enters my mind. Homemade sandwiches are definitely a frugal alternative to the wares at the deli in your office building, but lunches brought from home can also include creative fare that goes a step beyond the bread-meat-and-cheese routine.

### *Thinking inside the breadbox*

Sandwiches don't always need to come served between two pieces of white bread . . . or even whole wheat bread. For a change of pace, make sandwiches with bagels, English muffins, raisin bread, or pita pockets. Look for sales on day-old bread items and stock up your freezer with a variety of sandwich fixings.

Some simple, frugal, and always family-friendly sandwich filling ideas to consider are

- Tuna or egg salad
- Peanut butter and jelly (yes, kids still love the old standby)

✔ Cream cheese with sliced cucumber, avocado, or alfalfa sprouts

✔ Assorted leftover meats and cheeses

✔ Leftover salads or rice stuffed into pocket bread

✔ Bean spreads with assorted sliced veggies

### Thinking outside the breadbox

Sandwiches are always easy and provide filling lunchtime fare, but don't be afraid to think outside the breadbox. Leftovers, such as cold slices of quiche and frittatas, pizza, and various salads (green salad, potato salad, cole slaw, pasta salads) all make great lunchtime meals, too.

For a different — and delicious — hot weather meal, stuff a whole tomato (cored) with tuna fish or egg salad. You can use almost any leftover salad, cooked vegetable, or rice mixture. Be sure to pack a knife and fork to cut the stuffed tomato.

Those prepackaged lunchtime meals in the plastic trays are really popular, and equally as expensive. Why not make your own? Save the tray from a TV dinner and fill the compartments with assorted cheese, crackers, and veggies. Wrap in foil or plastic wrap to keep fresh.

# Deciding "What's for Dinner?"

I used to spend about $700-$800 each month on food-related items for my family of five. I found that the largest portion of our family food budget was all going toward one meal: dinner. Not only is it usually the largest meal of the day, but it's also the one in the midst of the five o'clock family rush hour — Dad and Mom are just getting home from work, kids are tired after school and ready to eat *now,* and last minute errands need to be run. All these add up to making dinner one of the most difficult meals to plan and prepare, and you become tempted to fall back on expensive alternatives to eating frugal, home-cooked meals.

I try to limit the cost of dinner to no more than $4 for the entire meal (that feeds five of us). For example, if I buy a package of chicken drumsticks that feeds the whole family on sale for $2, I still have $2 to spend on salad fixings, veggies, side dishes, or desserts for that meal. Or instead of spending that extra $2, I can serve a fresh salad prepared with lettuce and fixings from my garden, use a little homemade Italian dressing, and save that extra $2 for another meal. By cutting costs slightly on each meal throughout the week, I can use the savings to splurge occasionally on more expensive cuts of meat, or maybe even take the family out for dessert for a fun family evening.

## Serving breakfast for dinner

Who says breakfast foods are only for breakfast? Bacon and eggs may be a fairly expensive breakfast to serve the family, but it's a very cheap meal compared to most dinner menus. Making an occasional breakfast for dinner can be a real treat, especially with everyone running out the door in the morning to work and school. Who really has much time to fix a typical breakfast meal during the morning crunch? And speaking of breakfast items at dinner, omelets are delicious for any meal — just vary the side dishes. Instead of hash browns, serve steamed vegetables or rice at dinnertime.

Many of the ideas shared in the lunch and leftover categories in this chapter can easily be adapted to your frugal family's dinner menus as well.

## Focusing on the sides

If you're not a vegetarian, think of meat as a side dish rather than the main course. A small serving of chicken with a large tossed salad and a generous serving of steamed vegetables or rice can save tremendously compared to having the meat be the largest item on your dinner plate.

Buying large bags of rice in the Asian food aisle of the grocery store is another economical side dish choice. I've known quite a few people who thought they didn't even like rice until they tried one of the delicious Asian brands.

Be sure to check out Chapter 6 for more tips on buying more time between visits to the grocery store by making foods go farther. (Honey, we've got company! Add a little water to the soup.)

# S.O.S. = Saving on Snacks

The front door bursts open, a backpack's flung on a chair, and a child bellows, "I'm home! What can I eat?" Ever hear that from your returning troops? Do you find yourself wondering if they *ever* think of anything else besides food? I know I sure do. For some frugal snack ideas, try

 ✔ **Crackers with toppings:** Spread peanut butter or cream cheese on a cracker, or top with sliced meats and cheeses.

- **Assorted cheeses:** Serve cubed or sliced cheeses alone or with slices of apple, crackers, celery sticks, or meats. Try spreading cream cheese onto these items, too.

- **Popcorn:** This has to be my favorite frugal snack for our family. For very few of our hard earned pennies, I can make a huge bowl of popcorn and feed all my kids and their friends after school. Sprinkling popcorn with flavored salt or a bit of Parmesan cheese makes for a nice change of pace.

- **Fresh fruit in season:** Apples, pears, oranges, plums, nectarines, peaches, apricots, and so on make a healthy and economical addition to the family menu. Just be sure to limit afternoon snacks to one piece of fruit per person or the cost can quickly become prohibitive.

  Serve sliced apples with toppings. I personally like apples with sliced cheese or cream cheese, but my kids prefer their apples smothered in peanut butter.

- **Cut-up veggies:** Keeping cut-up celery, carrots, cauliflower, broccoli, or other veggies on hand and easily accessible in the fridge makes healthy snacking a piece of cake, or in this case, a piece of vegetable. (See the "Growing your own produce" section later in this chapter for information about growing these healthy eats in your own garden.)

- **Cinnamon toast:** Just toast the bread, spread the butter, sprinkle on a bit of sugar and cinnamon, and you're good to go. Buy an inexpensive salt shaker from the thrift store, and keep your own homemade sugar and cinnamon mixture on hand — much cheaper than the store-bought mix.

- **Fruit shakes or smoothies:** Just blend your favorite fruit (canned or fresh) with some milk and ice cubes.

Anything that keeps you from grabbing bags of expensive snack items at the grocery store or local mini-mart will save substantially on your food expenses. The following items can be made ahead and frozen for fast and easy snacks:

- **Grapes, blueberries, and strawberries:** Yep, just freeze them whole. You can even eat them still frozen if you want a delicious and nutritious hot weather snack.

- **Homemade granola bars:** Recipes for these abound in healthy foods cookbooks and on the Internet.

- **Cookies, cakes, muffins, cupcakes, and quick breads:** Prepare according to your favorite recipes and then just wrap as individual servings for freezing.

✔ **Homemade freezer pops:** Various juices, powdered drink mixes, flavored yogurt, milk mixed with the jelly left at the bottom of jars, prepared pudding mix, and even boxes of flavored gelatin make great-tasting freezer treats. Just prepare and freeze. And believe it or not, frozen gelatin actually makes drip-proof freezer pops.

# Having Your Cake without Busting the Bank: Dessert Ideas

Because I only serve desserts as a treat on special occasions, my children don't expect dessert every night. When they do find sweets and desserts at the end of the meal, the kids really appreciate the special treat. But buying premade dessert items at the store or bakery can wipe out a frugal meal in an instant, so go with homemade versions whenever possible. Here are a few simple — yet frugal — dessert ideas:

✔ **Cookies:** Make up a bunch of cookies in advance, and rather than store them in the cookie jar, put them into large zip-top bags and store them in the freezer. Only thaw out the cookies you plan to serve immediately. This helps cut down on those late-night cookie monsters making their way into the kitchen for an evening munch.

✔ **Cakes:** Make cakes from scratch for maximum savings or purchase cake mixes when they reach a stock-up price. Be sure to check out the section in Chapter 4 on creating a price diary so you know a good price when you see it.

✔ **Fresh fruit:** If you want to eat something a little sweet (but healthy, too), fruit makes a wonderful dessert. We often serve it with sliced cheese.

# Using Leftovers Creatively

Tossing a glob of warmed-up old noodles onto a plate doesn't entice many appetites. But if you use a little creativity, leftovers can be fun and tasty meal starters — and still dirt-cheap. (I talk more about cooking with leftovers in Chapter 6.)

## Making a buffet

I try to plan one meal each week that uses up the assorted leftovers accumulating on the refrigerator shelves. It's like getting a free meal every week.

My family calls a meal of leftovers the Party Tray. After accumulating about half a dozen containers of leftovers, I reheat them (usually in the microwave) and portion out a little bit of everything onto each person's plate. Nobody usually ends up with more than a spoonful or two of any one item, but the variety of items gives it the look of a full plate after you've gone through a buffet line at a party: a dab of lasagna, a bit of chili, a couple of spoonfuls of gelatin, a meatball or two in sauce, a forkful of several types of salad. Toss some crackers, sliced cheese, and fresh cut-up veggies into the mix, and you've got an easy dinner that's enjoyed by the whole family.

I find it helpful to camouflage the leftovers from meal to meal. Even your pickiest eaters may have trouble recognizing the roasted chicken from dinner two nights ago in today's pasta salad luncheon.

| *Bread (loaf ends, dry slices)* | *Eggs (hard-cooked)* |
|---|---|
| Bread pudding | Casseroles |
| Casserole topping | Egg salad |
| Croutons | Salad topping |
| French toast | Sandwiches |

| *Meat, poultry, or fish (cooked)* | *Vegetables (cooked)* |
|---|---|
| Casseroles | Baked potato topping |
| Enchiladas | Casseroles |
| Fried rice | Soup |
| Pot-pies | Pot-pies |

# Put it all in the pot and what have you got? Dinner!

A fairy lives in my freezer. Really. You don't believe me? Well, come on over and look sometime. She's a covered, plastic bucket and she does wonderful magic with leftovers and food scraps. Her specialty is soup. Mmmm, boy can she make soup! Every night when clearing off the table or picking up the scraps from food preparation, I throw everything that's edible, but not big enough to save for another meal, into the plastic bucket in the freezer — bits of meat, vegetables, potatoes, rice, beans, pasta, and so on. When the bucket is full, I make a big pot of either tomato, chicken, or vegetable broth and throw the entire hodge-podge of contents from the freezer bucket right into the soup pot. Add a few spices, cook until hot, serve with some fresh bread or a green salad, and you've got a meal fit for a king. It always reminds me a bit of that old children's story, *Stone Soup*.

A friend of mine found out the hard way the Freezer Fairy's magic doesn't work with fish. Adding pieces of fish to the bucket really doesn't make an appetizing meal because the fishy smell and flavor overpowers everything else. But if you save your fish scraps in a separate bucket, they can make a delicious fish chowder. Just prepare a cream soup base, add some simple vegetables like carrots and potatoes, toss in your spices and seafood scraps, heat, and serve.

## Sandwiching leftovers into savings

One of my favorite uses for leftovers is making sandwiches for lunch or dinner. Whether it's leftover roast beef made into French dips, or sliced meatloaf with mayo and ketchup, or an open-faced turkey sandwich smothered in gravy, I love the options two simple little slices of bread give to my menus.

Rolling leftover meats and veggies into a cold, flour tortilla with a bit of cream cheese is also a delicious way to add some variety to the typical sandwich presentation.

## Safety is as safety does . . .

Remember to keep those budget-stretching leftovers safe for you and your family. It's not helpful to your overall financial well-being if those frugal meals send everyone to the doctor with food poisoning! Here are some general guidelines for keeping your leftover foods safe:

- Cover and place leftovers in the refrigerator within two hours of the meal (preferably within an hour).
- If you keep leftovers around in your fridge longer than three days before eating them, store them in the freezer.
- Thaw any frozen leftovers in the refrigerator rather than on the kitchen countertop so that harmful bacteria doesn't have an opportunity to breed as quickly.

# Finding Alternatives to Store-Bought Items

Store-bought isn't always a necessity, and homemade ideas are often healthier and better tasting than their more expensive store-bought counterparts. Whether you're looking for alternatives to store-bought mixes, or you just want to add a little fresh produce to your backyard garden, you can find several money-saving ideas worth considering in this section.

## Growing your own produce

Whether you have a large or small yard (or no yard at all), you can grow a garden that drastically cuts down your produce bill five months out of the year. Here's how:

- ✔ **Pick a prime location.** The garden should get 6-8 hours of sun a day and be in close proximity to both your house and the water supply.

  If you don't have a big sunny spot in your yard for a full garden, just scatter vegetable plants throughout the yard. Or try container gardening, which works wonders on small decks and patios.

- ✔ **Decide what veggies to grow.** Start with about four or five easy-to-grow varieties of vegetables (such as tomatoes, bush beans, lettuce, cucumbers, and zucchini) — whatever your family eats regularly and works well with your soil and climate conditions. For specifics about regional growing recommendations for your area, consult a local home and garden center or ask your friendly gardening neighbors what they suggest.

- ✔ **Weed and enjoy!**

Be sure to check out *Gardening For Dummies* by Mike MacCaskey and the editors of the National Gardening Association and *Container Gardening For Dummies* by Bill Marken and the editors of the National Gardening Association (both books published by Wiley) for more gardening tips and tricks.

## Making your own mixes and convenience items

For the sake of convenience — and sometimes just out of sheer laziness — I buy expensive premade and prepackaged products (such as salad dressing, taco seasoning, and cookie and cake mixes) to ease my time spent in the kitchen. But when money's tight, all the convenience in the world doesn't make up for spending too much on groceries and going over my budget. And it goes without saying that homemade is not only cheaper, but it's also considerably healthier. I can choose which ingredients to use, and I also know that no flavorings, colorings, or preservatives are added.

## Exploring backyard meat production

Growing livestock, poultry, and even fish at home isn't something just for farmers or folks living on 50 acres in the mountains. Backyard meat production is actually a very economical way to provide fresh, drug-free, cruelty-free, organically fed meat for a family. You can find helpful books at the library about raising your own backyard chicken flocks, rabbit farms, sheep and cattle "ranches," and even fish farms. Or check out the following resources:

✔ Chickens: You can find a helpful collection of information about raising poultry for eggs and meat at: "Management Guide for the Backyard Flock" www.ces. uga.edu/pubcd/L429-w.html.

✔ Rabbits: For a primer on backyard meat rabbit raising practices, go to www. qsl.net/ki0dz/rrr.htm.

✔ Pigs: For an introduction to raising pork, see the article, "Raising the Backyard Pig" online at: www.ume.maine.edu/CESPSQ/feedpig.htm.

✔ Cattle: The vast majority of information on the Internet about raising beef and milk cows involves large-scale commercial operations. For backyard production information in the United States, consult your local county cooperative extension office.

✔ Fish: Fish farming (aquaculture) is a worldwide activity. You can find recommended resources at: "Basic Information on Aquaculture" www.lib.noaa.gov/ docaqua/basicaqua.html.

Before you run out and buy a calf to raise in your backyard, check with your city to make sure you understand the rules about livestock in your locale. Some municipalities have rules against actual farm animals (cows, chickens, pigs, goats, sheep), but may not have laws against meat-producing animals that are frequently kept as household pets (rabbits, for example).

You can find recipes for convenience items by looking at the ingredient lists on the package and getting a good idea of what to use, browsing through all-purpose cookbooks and cooking-related books at the library, and logging on to www.recipesource.com/ misc/mixes/ or www.frugalitynetwork.com/frugalrecipes. mixes.html.

When you find a good recipe for something you use regularly, like taco seasoning, prepare the mix ahead of time to store in the refrigerator or on the pantry shelf. Pre-measure the mixes into individual plastic zip-top bags, and then place the individual bags into larger zip-top bags. When you need some taco seasoning, you can just reach in and grab out a small bag. You're ready to cook without worrying about running to the store for last-minute ingredients.

# Chapter 6

# Quick and Thrifty Cooking Tips

Sometimes in order to save money, you only need to make a slight adjustment in the way you prepare foods. In this chapter, I discuss making a few meals ahead of time to store in the freezer, putting together a couple of meals from planned leftovers, sharing cooking responsibilities with friends and neighbors, and keeping certain ingredients on hand to make fast, yet frugal meals that help you avoid the fast-food trap. These ideas are just the ticket to eating well while living within a modest food budget.

## Freezing Food = Freezing Food Bills

 Probably the single greatest money-saver I've discovered is cooking ahead for the freezer. When I first started cooking most of our dinner meals for the freezer, our $700 per month food bill dropped immediately to around $300. And that was before I'd even started doing anything else to make our meals and food budget more frugal and cost effective. Now, by having our dinner meals already prepared, we aren't as tempted to run to the fast-food restaurant, order pizza, or rely on convenience items from the supermarket. My family of five can sit down for a delicious home-cooked meal every night, and save money in the process.

## Easing into bulk cooking

The idea of cooking for the freezer puts off many people. They hear terms referring to *monthly* cooking or *30-day* cooking, and they roll their eyes. Because I only had a small fridge-top freezer for many years, I can understand their hesitations.

 If you don't have the freezer space, energy, or organizational gifting for a full month of cooking in one pop, try twice-a-month, or even once-a-week. Or just double and triple recipes as you prepare them. For example, make three meals of homemade chili at a time. Eat one tonight, and then package the extra in clearly labeled freezer bags. You now have two meals ready to go in just minutes for those nights when you're in a hurry. Just pop the freezer bag in the microwave or pour the thawed chili into a pan on the stovetop, toss together a green salad, and dinner is served.

To ensure your meals are thawed and ready to heat up at dinner time, plan your dinners two days in advance. Most frozen casseroles take about 48 hours to thaw completely, so thinking ahead really saves reheating time. While you can reheat many items directly from the frozen state, doing so adds significantly to the preparation time.

Another way to ease into bulk cooking is to use a method I call mini-sessions. By preparing meals for the freezer based on their main protein ingredient (chicken, ground beef, tofu, and so on), you plan your bulk-cooking sessions around the supermarket's cur-rent sales. For example, the grocery store recently had whole fryers on sale for 57 cents per pound — a stock-up price in my *price diary.* (See Chapter 4 for complete details on setting up your own price diary.) I bought the maximum number of fryers the store allowed per customer in one day (four), came home, and quickly did a chicken mini-session. After cutting up the four fryers, I pre-pared and froze a number of meals for my family. Some of the meals I prepared were:

- ✔ **Two or three meals worth of marinated thighs and drum-sticks in plastic freezer bags.** The chicken marinates while it's frozen and also while it thaws. In this case, I just used homemade Italian-style salad dressing for a marinade. To serve, thaw completely, pour off the marinade, and then throw the chicken pieces onto the barbecue or under the oven broiler until cooked through.

- ✔ **Two meals of chicken cacciatore.** The freeze-ahead version I usually make consists of sliced chicken breast, a jar of spaghetti sauce, stewed tomatoes, and some sautéed onions and green pepper strips. I usually thaw and serve the cacciatore over pasta, but it's good over rice, too.

✔ **Several meals worth of cooked chicken.** I cut the chicken into medium-sized chunks to use in skillet meals or casseroles. Having freezer bags with precooked and frozen chicken pieces makes later meal preparation a snap.

✔ **A large pot of homemade chicken noodle soup.** Soup is usually good for at least two meals, maybe more, depending on how hungry the troops are when they're ready to eat.

In case you're wondering, yes, I interspersed the chicken meals with other foods, so please don't think my poor family saw nothing but chicken for weeks on end. Be sure to mix your menus up a bit to keep the troops happy.

## Freezing tips for homemade meals

Freezing prepared meals and still maintaining the quality of each item requires a bit of know-how. Keep in mind that as long as food is frozen solid the entire time, it is safe to eat indefinitely. But the quality of the taste, texture, and color of frozen foods begins to suffer after about two months, so use frozen meals within six to eight weeks. But if you find a bag of frozen spaghetti sauce hiding in the back recesses of your freezer, don't be afraid to eat it if you know it's been frozen the entire time. Here are a few more food freezing tips:

✔ You don't have to run out and buy top-of-the-line plastic containers to store your frozen meals — inexpensive plastic food storage boxes from the grocery store work equally well. The most important thing to look for is an air-tight seal to prevent freezer burn and moisture loss. Plastic margarine tubs don't give an air-tight seal, so only use them for storing frozen foods for less than a week.

✔ To save the most money (and the most space in your freezer), freeze as many items as possible in high quality, heavy-duty, zip-top freezer bags, which can be washed and reused several times. (But don't reuse bags used to store meats.) You can freeze most sauces, marinated meats, and meals you reheat in a saucepan in freezer bags. Freeze layered casseroles like lasagna in inexpensive glass baking dishes that you can find at garage sales for about 25 cents each. You can also use the disposable foil pans.

✔ Label all your frozen meals carefully with the name of the meal and the date frozen. You don't want to stand at your freezer door trying to guess whether the frozen reddish blob in the bag is homemade chili or chicken cacciatore and whether it's been hiding in your freezer for ten months or only a week.

✔ Cool food in the refrigerator or by dipping the pan carefully into a shallow sink of ice water before putting it in the freezer. Never let food cool (or thaw) on the counter at room temperature because bacteria then has a chance to grow.

✔ To prevent freezer burn, remove as much air as possible from the package before freezing. If you're using freezer bags, close the top of the bag but leave a small corner open for a drinking straw. Use the drinking straw to suck out any extra air from the bag, and then quickly slip out the straw and close the bag the rest of the way. You don't need to invest in a vacuum sealing machine if you do the drinking straw trick. But if you already have one, it's handy for freezer cooking.

## Choosing what to freeze

Take a walk through the freezer section of your grocery store to get an idea of what types of meals and individual items freeze well. If you're wondering if your family's favorite dinner is a candidate for freezing ahead, take out a single serving next time you prepare it, wrap thoroughly, and freeze. Give it about a week, thaw it, reheat, and see if it meets your criteria.

More things freeze well than don't, but here's a small list of items to be careful about:

✔ Mayonnaise, sour cream, and cream cheese separate during the freezing and thawing process. They work much better if they're mixed into a recipe — as part of a sauce or casserole, for example.

✔ Potatoes and pasta get soft and mushy. They can be frozen succesfully, but you need to be extremely careful not to overcook them before freezing.

✔ Hard cheese crumbles and changes in texture, but can be successfully frozen if grated first.

✔ Salad greens do not freeze. That may seem like common sense, but I've had several people tell me they've unfortunately tried doing that when bags of salad were on sale at the grocery store.

# Planning Ahead for Leftovers

Most of the time I think of leftovers as those little bits and pieces remaining in the casserole dish or vegetable steamer after everyone's eaten — they're staring at me, daring me to find a creative use for them. I accept the challenge by planning meals and menus around the leftovers. I simply cook bigger meals on the weekend, and then plan the meals during the week around using up the leftovers. Planning ahead really cuts down on the food bills and keeps me from cruising the aisles in the supermarket every afternoon waiting for something appetizing to reach out, embrace me, and say, "Invite me to your house for dinner tonight!"

Planned leftovers are an especially good idea if you're only cooking for one or two people. You can take advantage of buying items in larger quantities (such as inexpensive cuts of meat, turkey, or anything that comes in big packages), but not have the excess go to waste. Making a turkey dinner for yourself and your teenager? You're probably thinking, "No way! We'll be eating cold turkey sandwiches for a month!" With a little planning, the leftover turkey can be used in casseroles, omelets, skillet meals, and assorted sauces.

## Stretching the bird

My good friend Leanne loves to fix rubber chicken for her family. Yep, you read that right. Rubber chicken. But Leanne's idea of rubber chicken isn't an honest-to-goodness rubber chicken served with a Ping-Pong ball in its mouth. Rubber chicken refers to those chicken meals that just keep stretching — and stretching — and stretching from one little fat fryer. For her family of four, Leanne can usually stretch at least three meals from each chicken purchase: a roast chicken dinner meal consisting of the drumsticks, thighs, and wings; a casserole, stir-fry, or skillet meal prepared with the cut breast meat roasted the night before; and a hearty, homemade chicken soup made from any leftover meat and bones. Each time she buys a chicken, she plans ahead for the three chicken meals she'll serve throughout the week.

Another friend of mine stocks up on frozen whole turkeys when they're on sale and in season, near the Thanksgiving holiday. She has almost made a new family tradition. She takes her kids, grabs two shopping carts, and then purchases 12 frozen turkeys, one for each month of the year (she has two freezers in the garage, by the way). Then, every month, she prepares a turkey dinner with all the trimmings and uses the leftovers in other meals throughout the month: casseroles, soups, sandwiches, and stir-fry. If you have the freezer space — and your family loves turkey — you can easily cut down on some of your monthly food costs throughout the year. I always seem to get at least five or six meals from every turkey we purchase, so it really does go a long way. According to the U.S. Department of Agriculture, frozen turkey can be kept indefinitely, so don't hesitate to stock up when you find a great price.

## Considering other creative concoctions

Here are a couple of planned leftover ideas easily incorporated into your meal planning:

- ✔ **Chicken**
  - First meal: Oven-roasted chicken dinner
  - Second meal: Sandwiches (chicken salad, cold sliced chicken), chicken soup, fried rice, casseroles, or chili
- ✔ **Roast beef**
  - First meal: Roast beef dinner
  - Second meal: Sandwiches (cold roast beef, French dip, sliced beef with barbeque sauce), stir-fry, or shepherd's pie
- ✔ **Turkey**
  - First meal: Roast turkey dinner
  - Second meal: Sandwiches (open-face hot turkey with gravy, cold turkey with cream cheese and cranberry sauce), quiche, potpie, curry and rice, or tetrazzini
- ✔ **Ham**
  - First meal: Sliced ham dinner
  - Second meal: Sandwiches (hot ham and cheese, cold ham and cheese, deviled ham), ham and Lima bean soup, split pea soup, omelet, fried rice, macaroni salad with ham, scalloped potatoes with ham, or Monte Cristo sandwiches
- ✔ **Corned beef**
  - First meal: Traditional corned beef dinner
  - Second meal: Rueben sandwiches, homemade soup, or corned beef hash

> ✔ **Meatloaf**
>
> - First meal: Meatloaf dinner
> - Second meal: Meatloaf sandwiches, crumbled into soup or spaghetti sauce

# Cooking Cooperatively

Another way to save money is to buy in bulk and prepare your meals with someone else. You split the work, split the cost, and have some fun and friendship time to boot.

 Be extra cautious about food safety when preparing food to exchange with your friends and neighbors!

## Making cooking fun — sharing with a friend

Working together with someone else makes your bulk-cooking day go much, much faster. You also have someone to laugh and sing with, and even to cry with while cutting onions.

Here's how it works: Get together in advance and do some creative menu planning. For a full month of frozen meals, you want to pick about ten meals that both families enjoy and then triple each recipe so you can serve the same meal three times throughout the month (triple it for each family). For example, if you decide to make lasagna, you need three lasagnas for each family, or six lasagnas total for the two of you. Then, the day before you get together for the cooking extravaganza, head out to the store together and split the grocery bill in half. You get all the money-saving benefits of cooking ahead (buying in bulk, avoiding the fast-food trap, reducing waste), but you also benefit from time spent working and laughing with a good friend.

 If cooking a month's worth of meals sounds too ambitious, you can prepare a week or two of meals at a time instead. Whether you cook for a week or a month, cook at the person's house with the most freezer space, or you may be stuck with a bunch of room temperature foods quickly going bad.

## Exchanging frozen meals

Several women at my church participate regularly in group-meal exchanges. They don't actually cook together in a group, but they do their meal planning together, and then designate a time when they all get together and exchange the premade frozen meals. The frozen meal exchange idea works best if you don't try to include side dishes or salads.

When I participated in one of the meal exchanges, I not only saved some grocery money, but I also had fun. At the preplanning meeting, everyone brought a list of three recipes they were willing to prepare for the group, and then each of us voted on which meals they wanted from each person's suggestions. We had to unanimously vote in favor of a recipe for it to be used. (Be sure to voice the "my-kids-won't-eat-anything-with-visible-onions" types of mealtime difficulties.) By choosing three family favorite "what-we-serve-to-company" types of recipes, you rarely come away with no one wanting you to make anything. If that does happen, though, you can use a recipe brought by someone else that the group thought sounded good.

The group had 17 women, so I had a regular assembly line going in my kitchen as I prepared 17 separate casseroles on my countertops. The trickiest part was fitting all the foil-wrapped casseroles into my freezer. For the actual exchange of meals, we met at the church parking lot. Everyone brought their fully frozen meals stored on ice in coolers or wrapped in heavy blankets. Each woman placed the meals she'd prepared in the back of her car or van, and we just went around to everyone's open car and helped ourselves to one of each meal from each vehicle. All I had to do was make 17 of one recipe, but I came home from the exchange meeting with 17 completely different meals. I had an easier time making 17 of one meal than preparing 17 completely different meals all by myself.

Keep the following ideas in mind if you and your friends decide to put together your own food exchange program:

- ✔ A meal exchange like this works best with families of similar size, but two families in our group had more than eight members while the other families all had five or fewer people. To figure out how many servings to make of each meal, plan to fix enough food to feed the largest family in the group. The smaller families will have more leftovers that they can save to serve for additional dinners, lunches, or snacks.

- ✔ Be sure to use disposable foil pans or heavy-duty plastic freezer bags rather than pans or dishes that need to be returned. You don't want 17 casserole pans making the rounds of all your friends.

✔ Don't forget to share food allergies and take other people's food allergies seriously. Eating something you're allergic to can be more than a little annoying; it can be deadly!

When I first mentioned the group-meal exchange idea to my husband, he looked at me a bit cross-eyed and said, "But I like your cooking. I don't know if I'll like Susie's cooking or not." So you know what I did? Bad little wife that I am, I just didn't tell him! After about four days of eating meals from the group-meal exchange he said, "You've been trying a lot of new recipes this week, and they've all been really, really good!" I 'fessed up at that point, but I discovered through the process that sometimes what they don't know won't hurt 'em.

## *Trading hot, home-cooked meals*

If you live in a neighborhood with similar sized families, consider exchanging hot meals with other families instead of exchanging the premade, frozen variety. I know of a hot-meal exchange group that had four families in it. The families were each assigned one day per week (Monday through Thursday), and then each family was on its own over the weekend because not everyone was home or even in town then.

The families had a monthly planning meeting where they made decisions about what each family would prepare throughout the month. During this meeting, they discussed food preferences and allergies.

Whoever was assigned to Monday dinner cooked for all four families and delivered the meal to the doorsteps at a predetermined hour, piping hot, and ready to eat. The other three weekdays, someone else showed up at the door with a main dish, vegetable, salad, and dessert. The group made the families feel like they were having a catered vacation away from fixing dinner three days a week!

You may want to have the families pick up their meals from the prep person's house so that the prep person doesn't spend all afternoon cooking and then arrive at an empty house when delivering the meals. The prep person can commit to being home during a certain time window (say, 4:30-6:00 p.m.). This gives the other families flexibility in their schedules (for instance, no need to worry if you're caught in traffic), and simplifies keeping the dinners warm because the prep person's oven is already fired up.

Keep your cooking partners appraised of your schedule or any sudden changes. If it's your night to cook on Tuesday and you suddenly get called out of town for an emergency, you need a back-up plan in place. You can either buy "you-bake" pizzas for everyone, or each family can plan on having a dinner stored in the freezer for unexpected problems like this.

You don't always need to have the meals hot and ready to serve at the actual delivery time. People can easily warm something up in the microwave or on the stovetop and the people making the deliveries don't have to fret trying to keep four meals hot in transit. Also, foods like spaghetti noodles can be prepared easily from scratch so they're not gummy or sticky when delivered. Let people in your group know in advance whether they need to prepare anything themselves or not, so they can plan their evening accordingly.

# Fixing Your Food Fast

Sometimes you're tempted to get an expensive fast-food dinner just because the ingredients you have at home take at least an hour to make into a full meal. By keeping ingredients on hand for some of these quick and simple meal prep ideas, you can have dinner on the table in a jiffy.

## Stir-frying

*Stir-frying* is a process where the meat and vegetables are cooked rapidly in a small amount of oil. (The process is very similar to sautéing, but you use less oil, hotter temperatures, and usually a wok instead of a skillet.) Even including preparation time and cutting vegetables, I can usually have a stir-fry meal on the table from start to finish in about 15-20 minutes. Stir-fry is usually served over inexpensive noodles or rice and can be made inexpensively using fresh vegetables from your garden, leftover meats and veggies from other meals, or whatever's currently on sale at the market.

If you do a lot of stir-frying, keep an eye out for the following staples when they go on sale. Then you can be ready to stir-fry at a moment's notice.

| | |
|---|---|
| garlic powder | Chinese spice blend |
| crushed red pepper | ground ginger |
| sesame seeds | soy sauce |
| red chili paste | teriyaki sauce |

| | |
|---|---|
| rice | rice vinegar |
| water chestnuts | beef broth |
| Asian noodles | sherry |
| chopped peanuts and cashews | cornstarch |
| sesame and peanut oil | canned bamboo shoots |

Any good general cookbook has basic stir-fry instructions. Or take a look when you're at the library for books on Asian cooking. The Internet's full of stir-fry recipes, too. Just do a general search at your favorite search engine such as www.yahoo.com.

## Grilling and broiling

One of my favorites parts of summertime is firing up the barbecue and grilling our meals. We cook on the grill anything from chicken, hamburgers, and hotdogs, to zucchini and corn on the cob fresh from our garden. For detailed instructions on grilling, add *Grilling For Dummies* by Marie Rama and John Mariani (published by Wiley) to your cookbook collection.

When the weather outside is frightful, the oven broiler is still delightful. I cook almost anything under the broiler that I'd normally cook on the outdoor grill. Food cooked on the broiler isn't quite as tasty, but it's good in a pinch.

My freezer's one of the greatest helps for grilling and broiling. Some of the useful, grill-ready foods I keep in my freezer are:

- Chicken and assorted cuts of beef frozen in zip-top freezer bags with tasty marinade
- Premade hamburger patties
- Hotdogs purchased on sale
- Hotdog and hamburger buns bought at the bakery outlet store (you can buy day-old bread and bakery items for a fraction of the supermarket's price)

## Dusting off the old slow cooker

If you like the experience of walking in the door and smelling dinner cooking without you slaving away in the kitchen to prepare the meal, you'll love the convenience of a *slow cooker*. Take a few minutes in the morning before work or school to throw some ingredients into the pot, set it, and forget it. When you come home at dinnertime, the heavenly aroma of an easy dinner greets you. What could be better than that? The slow cooker also allows you to cook larger meals, providing leftovers and possibly even a second meal from one cooking time. You can also use vegetables and stew meats bought on sale for easy and inexpensive meals.

Some of the benefits you find from dusting off that lovely retro-slow cooker in the back of Grandma's attic are:

- ✔ You can buy tougher (and less expensive) cuts of meat because the slow cooker acts as a tenderizer.

- ✔ Meat shrinks less when cooked in the slow cooker and doesn't dry out. Also, flavors have time to develop while your meal slowly cooks all day.

- ✔ A slow cooker doesn't heat up the kitchen nearly as much as the stovetop or oven, so it's a perfect hot weather cooking appliance.

- ✔ A slow cooker frees up space in the oven and on the stovetop when doing a large cooking session for the freezer.

- ✔ Tofu, an inexpensive meat substitute, tastes better cooked in a slow cooker because it has time to soak up the flavors of the broth, spices, and other ingredients.

For complete details and recipes for the slow cooker, read *Slow Cookers For Dummies* by Glenna Vance and Tom Lacalamita (published by Wiley). You can also find a large selection of slow cooker recipes at www.crockerykitchen.com.

 A pressure cooker has many benefits similar to the slow cooker. For example, you can make large batches of chili or stew (and freeze any leftovers) and cook tougher, less expensive cuts of meat until they're tender and juicy. A pressure cooker is also much faster than a slow cooker, so if you don't have all day for your meal to simmer on the counter, the pressure cooker is a great option.

## Making magic in the microwave

I can remember when my mom got her first microwave oven. I think we were the only family on the block with one, and all the neighbors came over to "ooh" and "ahh" over this wonderful new miracle appliance. Now, microwave ovens are as common as toasters, and probably used a lot more often.

Reheating leftovers, warming premade frozen dinners, or preparing a breakfast burrito for the kiddos in the morning is so easy these days with the magic of the microwave. By making cooking easier and faster, microwave cooking can really help cut down on those fast-food trips. And anything that keeps you out of the drive-through lane keeps your food bill down (and your waistline smaller), believe me!

# Additional Money-Saving Tips and Tricks from the Kitchen

Every little tip helps when you're trying to save money in the kitchen, so I compiled a list of easy ideas to share with you. I use these tips and tricks to help cut the cost of general food preparation, cooking, and family eating.

- ✔ Serve small portions to small children so that you have less food going to waste. If they eat everything on their plate, then give them a little more.

- ✔ Check to see if powdered milk is cheaper than fresh milk in your area (prices vary by region). If it's less expensive, try mixing fresh milk together 50/50 with reconstituted powdered milk. (**Note:** Powdered milk tastes best if you let it get icy cold before you drink it.) Also, use reconstituted powdered milk as a substitute for fresh milk in recipes.

- ✔ Keep lettuce fresh longer by first rinsing and drying it thoroughly. (Use a salad spinner, if available.) Then cut or tear the lettuce into salad-size pieces, place into an air-tight zip-top bag, suck out all the excess air with a straw, and then store your bag of lettuce in the refrigerator. Each time you use some of the lettuce, suck the air out again. Lettuce keeps for as long as a week this way if you make certain it's dry before placing it in the bag.

- ✔ Purchase resealable bottles of soda rather than cans. Pour a single serving of soda into a small glass with ice cubes. Reseal the bottle and save the rest for later.

- ✔ Save the bits and pieces of leftover pie crust in a zip-top bag in the freezer. When you have enough in the bag, you can make another pie crust or two from the thawed pieces.

- ✔ Cook up a large pot of your favorite dry beans (kidney, white, red). Look in a general cookbook for instructions. Scoop the cooked beans into zip-top freezer bags, two cups to a bag. When you're making soup, casseroles, chili, skillet meals, or burritos and need some cooked beans, thaw a frozen bag and throw it in the pot. This is much cheaper than buying cans of prepared beans, and much faster than cooking beans from scratch each time you need them.

- ✔ Use half the amount of meat called for in the recipe when making a casserole or skillet meal and then add inexpensive vegetables or pasta to fill in for the missing meat.

- ✔ Stretch ground beef in hamburgers, meatloaves, and meatballs by stirring in cut-up bread crusts, oatmeal, homemade breadcrumbs, cracker crumbs, or plain cereals. This is a great way to use up stale crackers.

- ✔ Use turkey hot dogs instead of beef or pork. Turkey is often half the price.

- ✔ Buy blocks of cheese when they're on sale, grate, and place in a large zip-top freezer bag. Use cheese as needed. If the cheese clumps together in the freezer, just bang the bag of cheese against the edge of the kitchen counter once or twice to loosen.

- ✔ Buy eggs when they're on sale and freeze for later use in baking, omelettes, and scrambled eggs. Don't freeze the eggs whole; crack each egg into a section of a clean plastic ice cube tray. When frozen, remove the egg cubes from the tray and package in a large zip-top freezer bag. Use as needed. The thawed out eggs should be used quickly — they're very perishable.

- ✔ Fill the entire oven with baking potatoes when you have to heat it up to bake a few potatoes for dinner. Eat tonight's potatoes, cool the leftover ones, and freeze in zip-top bags. For a quick and inexpensive meal or side dish, reheat the frozen potatoes in the microwave. (Microwaves use a lot less energy than the oven.)

# Part III
# Funding the Frugal Family

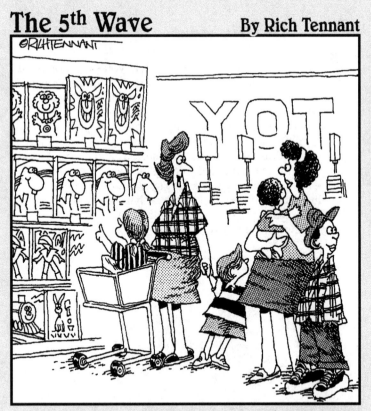

The 5th Wave    By Rich Tennant

"I FIND IT EASIER TO SAY 'NO', IF I IMAGINE THEM SAYING, 'MOMMY, CAN I HAVE THE LATEST OVER-HYPED, OVER-PRICED, COMMERCIAL EXPLOITATION OF AN OBNOXIOUSLY ADORABLE CARTOON CHARACTER."

# In this part . . .

Part III provides information to help you save money on the regular expenses of family life — from diapers and shampoo to school clothing and college tuition. You also find information on annual expenses like birthdays, as well as other seemingly never-ending — and never-paid-off — holiday gifts and celebrations throughout the year. And just so you don't think I'm always serious and cheap, I give you a few ideas for fun and frugal family activities. If yours is like most families, you want to spend time together, bonding with each other through activities you all enjoy. You'll be pleased to discover my idea of a fun family evening isn't sitting by the fireplace clipping coupons.

# Chapter 7

# Cutting Kid Costs: Providing the Basics on a Tight Budget

*In This Chapter*
- Bringing up baby without breaking the bank
- Clothing the kids without losing your shirt
- Encouraging the kids to pitch in on extras

*P*eople are often amazed that I've stayed home full time for most of the time I've raised my children. "But kids are so expensive! How do you do it?" Well, raising children is expensive, but sometimes people make many "unfrugal" choices that make it more expensive than it needs to be.

For example, furnishing the new baby's room can quickly dent your budget if the designer crib sirens sing their song in your direction. And the clothing needs for growing children are practically never-ending. In this chapter, I share simple tips for saving money on some of the basic necessities (like food and clothing!) involved with having kids. I also give some hints about how the kids can help out with those things "they just gotta have."

## Budgeting for Babies and Toddlers

Spend, spend, spend. Buy, buy, buy. Those words are all too familiar to today's parents, aren't they? Many of the everyday expenses for babies and toddlers are a lot more costly than they need to be, mainly because today's parents are busy and are looking for faster, more convenient alternatives. The prevailing attitude of parents seems to be, "Who wants to spend time washing diapers or grinding baby food?" But sometimes by making small sacrifices in convenience, families can save huge amounts of money.

## Affording furniture and other big-ticket baby items

One of the biggest expenses facing parents-to-be is baby furniture. An easy way to save money on these items is to borrow from friends or family members. If you know someone with older children, ask if you can borrow large, big-ticket baby items such as cribs, changing tables, playpens, highchairs, car seats, and cradles. Be sure to take good care of any borrowed items and return them in good repair to the owners when your child no longer needs the items.

Be careful to identify your *needs* versus your *wants*. Marketing specialists want to make you feel that you're not a good parent if you don't have top-of-the-line baby equipment with all the extras. In all our years of parenting, we never had a changing table. Those heart-warming ads for baby furniture stores tried to make me believe that all well-equipped parents need a changing table, but we just changed our babies on their crib mattress when they were tiny and on the carpet or bed when they got bigger. We never had a cradle, either. We did have a bassinet, but only because my mom saved my bassinet from when I was a baby. Otherwise, the only big-ticket baby furniture we had was a crib, a small dresser for clothing, and a highchair.

One item that you can't avoid owning is a car seat. Not only are they mandated by law in most places, but they're also a safety issue where you don't want to skimp too much. Many hospitals give away free car seats when the babies go home, so be sure to ask if your hospital has a car seat program. I don't recommend buying a used car seat from a garage sale or thrift store because you don't know the history of the car seat, and any car seat that's been through an accident should be discarded. But if you have a friend whose children have outgrown their car seat, ask if you can borrow it.

Even if you're borrowing from friends, always carefully inspect borrowed furniture (such as car seats and highchairs) for wear and tear, and be sure that the items meet current safety standards (for example, the railings on the crib aren't too far apart).

If someone throws a baby shower for you, hint that you'd really appreciate everyone pitching in together to buy a high-priced gift — like a playpen, a car seat, or a stroller — rather than a collection of cute outfits your baby may wear only once or twice. If you do end up receiving expensive designer outfits, but what you really wanted was a playpen, you may be able to return the clothes to the store and exchange them for the more expensive item you actually need. You can also return the adorable $30 infant dress bought as a gift at the mall and use the money to buy five outfits at a discount store — or head to the consignment store and buy ten slightly used items.

# Saving on diapering needs

 I used disposable diapers for my first child, and they were very convenient. But disposables also cost an incredible amount of money — and create a mountain of stinky trash in the landfill! After the birth of my second child, I decided to try cloth diapers, which I found to be just as easy to use and way more economical than disposables. Over the course of our diapering needs for our last two children (we have three children total), we saved hundreds of dollars by switching to cloth diapers washed at home. Cloth diapers also cause less diaper rash than disposables, and with the diaper covers available today with self-fastening tabs (no diaper pins!), cloth diapering is as easy as using disposables.

Another advantage to durable cloth diapers is that you can use them for child after child. After I bought the first round of diapers, I was all prepared for my next baby's diaper needs. And after I had my last child, I was able to pass the diapers and diaper covers on to a friend.

Although using a diapering service may not fit in your budget, contact a diaper service to ask about buying some of the "retired" diapers. I was hesitant to do this at first, but I quickly discovered that retired diapers were serviceable, cheaper than dirt, and able to stand up to at least another year or two of wear and tear. Even though we replaced the retired diapers twice during the course of our diapering needs, they were still an incredibly inexpensive option.

 Another easy way to save on diapering needs is to make your own baby wipes. Just buy a bunch of white cotton washcloths and keep a slightly damp one handy in a zip-top bag for quick little wipe-ups. To clean the washcloths, just toss them into the laundry with the diapers and diaper covers. You can also find instructions for making your own baby wipes from paper towels at www. thefrugalshopper.com/articles/babywipes.html.

# Feeding baby inexpensively

Frugal hardly seems like a word to use in the same sentence as "baby food." Those little jars of creamed vegetables, baby formula, and infant apple juice really take a bite out of the ol' budget. But buying the expensive prepackaged baby foods isn't the only way to feed baby. The new frugal parent has numerous less expensive options.

 The least expensive baby food available is the mother's milk: it's free. If you can breastfeed your little one, you save a bundle compared to buying formula. Even if you're working full time outside the home, breastfeeding is still an option. For breastfeeding tips, contact a local breastfeeding organization such as La Leche League (www.lalecheleague.org) or ask your local hospital or doctor's office to recommend a lactation consultant.

When your child is ready for solid foods, don't run out to Bob's ShopAway and buy expensive jars of premade baby food. Why pay dollars for something you can make just as easily at home for pennies? Serve your baby tiny servings — well-processed in the blender or food processor first — of most anything the family is eating: potatoes, carrots, peas, or even homemade chicken soup. Take care to leave out spices and any additives in baby's portion.

Prepare a large batch of baby food at one time so you don't need to do it at every meal. Cook and puree a big bunch of carrots, freeze the puree in ice cube trays, pop out the frozen food cubes, and place in labeled zip-top freezer bags. When your baby's ready to eat, just take out a frozen carrot cube, thaw it, warm slightly, and dinner is served. Mmm . . . mmm . . . good!

Be careful not to heat the food too hot. Microwaves can be efficient but often heat the center of the food to temperatures inappropriately hot for a baby. Be sure to stir the food thoroughly and double-check the temperature before feeding to your precious little food processor.

If you buy premade baby food, buy the largest jars available. The little bitty jars may be meal-sized for baby's tiny appetite, but they're expensive too. Be sure you don't feed the baby directly from the larger jars, though. Putting the spoon into baby's mouth and then into the jar again adds saliva to the jar, which actually begins breaking down the food (like in digestion) and spoils it for use later. If you open a large jar, spoon out a small portion onto a plate or bowl and then cover the jar and put it in the refrigerator. Your baby's large jar of food lasts for about two meals this way, rather than just one.

The special baby juice at the grocery store isn't really anything fancier than diluted regular juice. Just buy regular 100 percent juice in frozen concentrate form (with no additives or sweeteners), but then add twice the amount of water recommended when you're reconstituting the juice.

## Providing toddler toys and games

When my first child was born, money was tight and I actually wondered to myself, "How in the world are we going to afford toys for this baby as she grows?" Well, I shouldn't have worried. My daughter, and the two children who followed her, have had as many toys as any other child I've ever known. The majority of our family's toys and games come through hand-me-downs, yard sales, gifts, and thrift stores. We've hardly had to fork out money for toys at all. When the children outgrow toys or games, we share them with other families, sell the items at our next garage sale, or stop by the Goodwill donation station down the street.

A helpful way to cut back on the greedy "gimmies" of childhood is to not go to toy stores. Just imagine a great big "Quarantine" sign hanging over the front door of all toy stores and avoid them like the plague. Honestly, if your kids never set foot inside one of those giant toy stores, they'll never miss it.

# Clothing the Kids

During my regular rounds of thrift stores and garage sales, I always keep an eye out for clothing possibilities. Whether we need school clothes, play clothes, jammies, or church outfits, I find things all the time that work for my kids' clothing needs. Dressing your child well doesn't have to equal dressing them expensively. Even if your family's wardrobe consists of almost nothing but secondhand clothing, you can all still look great.

A wardrobe of basic colors and simple styles makes mix-and-match dressing practical, easy, and much less expensive than buying outfits made of pieces that can only be worn with each other.

## Making the most of hand-me-downs

Most clothes are still in reasonably good condition when children outgrow them, so making use of hand-me-downs is a wonderful way to save money and recycle still serviceable clothing items. When I was a child, I had a stylish cousin a year older than me and a size or two bigger. Every season, my mom received a big box from her sister filled with my cousin's outgrown clothing. It was like receiving a care package from the clothing fairy! Not all the clothes matched my taste or fit perfectly, but finding several fashionable "new" shirts and school dresses in the box was so much fun.

If you have friends and family with kids slightly older than yours, ask them to save Buffy and Skip's outgrown clothing for you. Most parents are more than happy to save clothes for a friend, but may not know offhand who is interested in receiving their hand-me-downs. Feel free to offer to pay your friend for hand-me-downs if it makes you feel more comfortable, but most people are pleased to find a new home for their castoffs and are more interested in helping a friend than making a few pennies.

For more information on shopping for quality secondhand clothing, be sure to read Chapter 16.

## Exchanging outgrown clothing with friends

Several women at my church arrange regular group clothing exchanges throughout the year. Everyone brings her family's outgrown or discarded clothing, displays it all on a table, and then sorts through everyone else's castoffs to find clothing for her own family. At the end of the exchange, the leftovers are boxed up and sent to a local charity-run thrift store. You can do this very informally with a group of friends in someone's home, too. To make the exchange work smoothly, plan on two days: the first day for dropping off clothes and setting up the exchange tables, and the second day for the actual exchange (and clean-up).

## Shopping seasonally and planning ahead

At the end of each season, you can find huge savings on seasonal clothing items. The best *selection* of clothes is usually at the beginning of the season, but the best *bargains* are found at the end.

Watch for big seasonal sales at local stores, where you can stock up on items you'll use throughout the year. A chain store in our area has a regular "half-off" sale on their red-white-and-blue clothing after the 4th of July. We use this opportunity to stock up on printed T-shirts and socks. Another store in our area has all its socks and hosiery items on sale for half off on the day after Thanksgiving. One of my friends buys all of her family's hosiery needs during that one-day sale each year.

If you buy clothes in bigger sizes, your kids can grow into them as time passes. When I see an excellent sale price on assorted clothing or find the perfect sweater at a yard sale, I stock up on larger sizes. I keep a box full of clothes in each kid's closet for them to grow into. Then when the seasons change and I'm putting away shorts or taking out winter mittens, I pull the box off the shelf and see if my kids have grown into any of the bigger sizes yet.

## Saving on school clothes

Anyone who tells you that dressing your children well for school doesn't matter probably hasn't been inside a classroom for at least a century or two. Kids aren't always sweet little angels to each other, and unfortunately, the oddly dressed child still receives more than his or her share of jeering and name-calling.

By waiting until the school year begins to buy the bulk of their school clothing, your kids have a chance to see what's "in" and what's "out" fashion-wise this year. Then they won't worry about buying something totally dorky and out of style. Waiting until after school starts is also the perfect time to take advantage of clearance sale prices at department stores, thrift stores, and second-hand shops.

## Removing stains from kids' clothes

Removing stains from children's garments helps prolong the life of the clothes. I have good luck generously using a solid stick-style stain remover for almost any stain. Here are some ideas to try for some common stubborn stains:

✔ **Baby formula: Apply stick stain remover as soon as possible.** Let sit overnight, and then launder as usual. If the stain persists, soak overnight in a solution of non-chlorine bleach mixed with warm water (use ¼ scoop bleach per gallon of water). Launder again.

✔ **Blood: Rinse immediately with cool water.** Hot water sets the stain and makes it harder to remove. Dab hydrogen peroxide on white fabrics. If the stain persists, soak overnight in the solution of non-chlorine bleach and warm water.

✔ **Chocolate: Rinse immediately with cold water.** If stain persists, soak overnight in the solution of non-chlorine bleach and warm water.

✔ **Grass: Apply a stick stain remover to grass stains immediately.** Let sit overnight. Wash as usual. Or pretreat overnight in non-chlorine bleach mixed with water.

✔ **Gravy: Rinse thoroughly in cold water as soon as possible.** If the spot is dry, soak in cold water for several hours. If stain remains, apply liquid dishwashing detergent directly to the stain. Squeeze the detergent into the stain so that it gets between the fibers. Let sit overnight. Rinse thoroughly in cold water, and then wash as usual.

✔ **Ink: Apply stick stain remover to ink stains as soon as possible.** Gently work stain remover into the fabric. Let sit for several hours before washing. Launder in cold water.

✔ **Juice: Pretreat with liquid dishwashing detergent or stick stain remover.** Wash as usual in hot water. Repeat pretreatment and laundering if necessary.

✔ **Ketchup: Rinse the stain in cold water immediately.** Soak the garment in cold water for several hours. Launder in cold water. If the stain remains, use stick stain remover, let sit overnight, and launder again.

If you want to dress your kids in designer duds for discount prices, look online at auction sites such as www.ebay.com. Search for the size and label you want, and you just may stumble upon a landslide of great fashion deals. Many of the clothes in these auction sites are new, too. You can also score brand-name clothing and accessories at consignment stores. Check in the phone book under consignment stores or thrift stores.

## Caring for clothing so it lasts

Small, stubborn stains can ruin an otherwise perfect piece of clothing. Finding simple ways to take care of grass stains and spilled spaghetti sauce can prolong the wearability of a garment.

This sounds too simple, but remember to use bibs to protect your baby and toddler's clothing from food spills. New babies don't spend much time playing outside in the dirt, so most soiling on their clothes comes from food spills and spit up.

Buying a high quality commercial stain remover for my kids' heavily soiled laundry saves quite a bit on the cost of having to replace stained clothing. Usually the stain removers in stick form work better for me than the spray-on ones. Just be sure to treat the stain as soon as you find it and allow the stain remover to sit on the stain and start working before you wash the clothing item.

Avoid "Dry Clean Only" labels if you're trying to save money!

# Requiring Kids to Cover the Extras

You, as the parent or guardian, can take care of providing for your kids' *needs* — but let them buy their *wants*. You can buy basic clothing (such as underwear, school shoes, jeans, and coats) and other personal necessities (basic toiletries, for example), but the kids can buy extras (such as make-up, hair doo-dads, brand-name athletic shoes, CDs, and video games).

Spend only what you've planned for various basic items. Then if your kids want designer duds or other extras, they can make up the difference. This tactic is an effective way to help your child understand first-hand how over-priced and unnecessary these items usually are.

See Chapter 2 for ways to help your child budget his or her money. Also, see Chapter 8 for advice on saving on school-related expenses.

# Chapter 8

# Putting Kids through School While Protecting Your Pocket

*T*axes and school shopping — the inevitable price a family pays for being alive in this day and age. Even people who've opted out of the back-to-school rat race and chosen to home school their kids still have to deal with the high cost of curriculum, paper, pencils, art supplies, and workbooks. What's a frugal parent to do?

In this chapter, I share how to meet the basic needs of your children on a limited budget. Whether you're dealing with finding money in the budget for school supplies, sports equipment, prom attire, graduation activities, or college tuition, you find ideas and tips to help. (In Chapter 7, you find information on saving money on school clothes.)

## Saving on School Supplies

Do you cringe when the school hands out the supply list for each of your children's classes? Do you wonder what your taxes pay for because you seem to be spending more and more on things that used to come as part of the package we call "education"? Well, I can't account for where your tax money is going, but I can help you curb at least some of the expenses that inevitably come when the school bell begins ringing loudly through the neighborhood.

For starters, do your kids ever tug at your sleeve persistently, giving you the pleading puppy look, and whine, "I've just *gotta* have the folder with the cute kittens (boy band, alien monsters, or whatever)! *Please*?" I have just the solution: *Don't* take the kids with you to the store! Go school supply shopping during your regular errand run. If you're alone, you can actually shop directly from a list without your kids sucking you into every impulse buy imaginable. Here's a list of additional tips that help you save big bucks on school supplies:

✔ **Check around your house for supplies you already have on hand.** Your kids may have squirreled away an extra pair of scissors into their dresser drawer or under their bed. And you may find more pencils, pens, erasers, markers, crayons, and rulers lying around in the junk drawer than you'll be needing at home for at least half a century.

✔ **Wait until a few days after school actually starts up to stock up on the majority of your back-to-school supplies.** Just buy the bare essentials — enough to get your child through the first week or two of school — and then hit the stores when they put all the back-to-school items (pens, pencils, lunchboxes, folders, backpacks, and so forth) on sale to make room for Halloween and Christmas display items.

✔ **Find expensive backpacks for a fraction of the original price a week or so after school begins.** The selection may not be as varied, but if money's a serious issue, a limited selection is better than no backpack at all. But remember, investing more money upfront in a high-quality backpack can save you money over the long haul because you won't need to replace it as often.

✔ **Check the local dollar store for bargains on school supplies.** Dollar stores are especially handy for good prices on paper, pencils, pens, scissors, tissue boxes, and folders.

✔ **Reuse extra promotional folders and binders you accumulate from the office, bank, or supermarket or from nicely packaged sales pitches for condominiums in the Bermuda Triangle.** Spruce up the folders with stickers or squeeze-on paint from the craft store for a personalized look.

If your child insists on a trendy folder with pop stars on the front rather than the plain bargain folder or the folder with the promotional logo from Dad's workplace, have the kids pay the difference for the fashionable folders themselves.

✔ **Don't hesitate to reuse last year's school supplies.** If your child still loves her pink, flowered lunch box or backpack, don't run out and buy a new one if the old one's still functional. Also, you can combine half-empty bottles of school glue to make one "like-new" bottle filled to the brim.

> ✔ **Watch for mail-in rebate forms and instant coupons for basic school supplies.** Office supply stores routinely run specials on such items as three-ring binders and pocket folders.
>
> ✔ **Look for special promotions on new products.** For example, designer pens may be available for pennies once discounts are taken.

 Get next year's school supply list as early as possible so that you can watch for sales throughout the year, rather than wait until the last week before school starts when prices are the highest. Keep the list with you whenever you go shopping, even to garage sales and thrift stores.

# Saying "Thanks!" without breaking the bank: Teacher appreciation

Giving tangible — and often expensive — gifts to your children's teachers at the holidays and the end of the school year is becoming more expected. But if money's tight, showing heartfelt appreciation can mean going broke. The following are simple suggestions for thoughtful and inexpensive teacher appreciation gifts (for Sunday school teachers, school teachers, and classroom aides and volunteers):

✔ Make homemade fudge, bread, cookies, candies, or whatever your specialty is and package them in decorative cookie tins (bought at thrift stores), or simply wrap them in plastic wrap or foil and tie with a seasonal ribbon.

✔ Donate a book to the local library in the names of the people who helped your child during the year. Make a card for each person thanking them for their input into your child's life and telling them about the donation in their name.This idea is especially frugal because it thanks more than one teacher or aide at a time.

✔ Cut a bookmark from posterboard and personalize it with hand-colored and -lettered expressions of thanks from your child. Laminate it, punch a hole at the top, and attach a colorful ribbon on the end.

✔ Write a letter or card from you and your child telling what you enjoyed about the year or how much you appreciate the teacher's input into your child's life.

✔ Pot a small start from one of your houseplants in a thrift store coffee mug or tea cup.

✔ Have your child write a poem about his or her teacher.

Remember, giving a teacher appreciation gift isn't a competition among parents to see who can give the best, most expensive gift to the teacher. The gift is an expression of thanks for those who have given of themselves and their talents to your child day after day after day.

# Finding Frugal Educational Resources

To the surprise of many people, not all true education happens within the walls of schools and tutoring centers. Before your children were officially in school, you casually taught them language and grammar, basic math, personal hygiene, and character development — all without the benefit of workbooks, teachers, or official curriculum. Exposing children to a wide range of people and experiences not only expands their social horizons, but also enables them to learn about the world around them.

## Homework: Finding inexpensive methods with quality results

Sometimes parents find their kids in need of a little extra attention on certain skills, but the teachers don't necessarily send homework or any specific instructions on practical ways to help the child improve in those general, and sometimes vague, academic areas like listening and communication skills. In this section, I share ideas for inexpensive — and often free — educational activities to share with your kids. By using a few of the following inexpensive ideas, many families can save substantially on the cost of extra tutoring or expensive classes.

### Listening skills

To increase your child's listening skills and powers of attention, try reading out loud to your kids for half an hour, three or four times a week. Yep, I mean reading out loud to all of them, even to a disinterested, scowling teenager.

Find a book that's interesting to everyone. If one child is studying a particular time period at school, read a book on that topic at home. Reading it aloud improves your child's listening skills and at the same time adds a deeper dimension to his or her studies and brings the time period alive in a richer way. Or maybe read a book their favorite movie is based on — read the original version of Dickens' *A Christmas Carol* during the holidays, or take a journey on the *Nautilus* with Captain Nemo in *20,000 Leagues Under the Sea*.

Choose books that don't talk down to your children. Young children have the capacity to listen to fairly advanced reading levels, well beyond what they can actually read for themselves. If your children are reading *Go, Dog, Go!* to themselves, try reading something like

*Charlotte's Web, The Hobbit,* or *Black Beauty* out loud as a family. Check out Chapter 10 for tips and ideas for finding inexpensive books for your family's read-aloud times.

## Composition skills

An easy way to regularly practice composition, as well as handwriting and spelling, is to keep a journal. Keep your eye out for blank books at thrift stores and garage sales, or simply use an inexpensive spiral-bound notebook purchased during seasonal "back-to-school" sales.

- **Personal journals:** Personal journals can be a diary of your kids' daily happenings, or a record of their thoughts and feelings, or even a place to record those "Ah, ha!" insights about life that we all have from time to time.

- **Vacation journals:** Another type of personal journal is the vacation journal. Each evening as the family is winding down for the night, have everyone write down a brief paragraph about what happened that day. You can even make a fun vacation journal out of picture postcards. Collect postcards at each place you visit and have the kids write a brief paragraph, or even just a sentence, about what they did at that place. Punch a hole in the corner of each postcard and bind them into a small book with the fastener or string. The kids now have a visual and written record of their vacation, plus an inexpensive souvenir or keepsake from their trip.

- **Nature journals:** A simple way to add to your children's understanding of science and nature is to have them keep a nature journal. Using a blank artist's sketchbook, the child draws a picture of any plant or animal seen in its natural environment. Don't worry if your children aren't artists, just ask them to try to draw what they see without worrying about how artistic the sketch is.You can help inspire your kids to keep a nature journal if you do it too. Try it, it's fun!

- **History journals:** If your children need a better grasp of history, try putting together a history journal or a Book of the Centuries. This concept is equally beneficial whether your child's a history buff . . . or a history duff. Each page in the journal lists a different century and as the children come across historical information — whether at school, at home, in the newspaper, on television, or just in their personal reading time — they make a note about that fact on the appropriate page of their notebook. For example, on the page for the 1800s they can write: Civil War, 1860–1865. Record inventions, wars, famous people, explorers, or whatever else grabs their interest. Eventually they will have a personalized time line of history.

## Home schooling

For a variety of reasons, many parents are choosing home education as an option for their kids. But sometimes the high expense of purchasing complete curriculum with all the required books, lab equipment, and other supplies is more than a little daunting for families on a tight budget. If you home school your children, you may find the following tips handy:

- ✔ Instead of buying a full-service curriculum (complete with an overrated teacher's manual and designer counting beads), purchase a math workbook that covers all the math topics for your child's current grade level for less than $10 from a teaching supply store and use homemade math manipulatives (beans, macaroni noodles, pennies).

- ✔ Buy books for nearly pennies at used bookstores, garage sales, antique malls, and bargain stores.

- ✔ Take full advantage of the library's vast, *free* resources. Reading an entire book on whales or penguins provides a lot more information than quickly reading a couple of paragraphs or even a full chapter about the same subject in a textbook.

- ✔ Get a copy of the educational guidelines for your child's grade level from a local school. Once you see what's being covered at the school, you can actually put together your own curriculum with free library books and a few field trips. Be sure to read the section in Chapter 10 on finding inexpensive family field trip ideas.

- ✔ Join a local home school support group. Even if you're not active in the group, you still hear about used curriculum sales and fairs.

- ✔ If you home school more than one child, look for curriculum and workbooks you can use year after year with multiple kids.

- ✔ Contact local schools and ask if you can purchase books or curriculum no longer in use.

For more inexpensive and easy-to-apply home education ideas, check out *Home Education Magazine* (online at www.home-ed-magazine.com). It's available through many libraries and has a wealth of home schooling tips and inspiration for parents looking for inexpensive options for their home educational efforts.

## *Making use of low-cost tutoring options*

Many community colleges have students available for tutoring others. Usually the students tutor other college students, but find out if the college has a community program that makes tutors available for school-age kids.

Neighborhood high school kids always seem to be looking for a little extra spending money and may be interested in tutoring a younger child in a favorite subject area — maybe in math, spelling, reading, or even sports.

If you're a math whiz and your friend down the street is a former Spelling Bee champ, consider exchanging tutoring services with each other if you both have children in need of tutoring in the other's strong subject.

# Budgeting for Sports and Other School-related Activities

Do you pull out the checkbook more times than you ever thought possible to pay for sports activities and hobby-related fees? We want our children to lead active, healthy lives — but we'd also like the family budget to remain healthy, too.

One of the easiest ways to cut back on expenses for hobbies and sports is to limit the number of activities for each child. Life is full of choices and the occasional compromise, so you aren't going to hurt your child when you say, "Sorry, but you only get to choose one outside activity per season this year." Thinking through options and making choices builds character. If you have more than one child, even one activity per child adds up to a lot of shuttling kids to various places around town. The more driving you do, the higher the overall cost of the activity for your family's budget. Car-pooling can really help save you time and money. Check with the parents of your children's friends to see if they'd be able to car-pool with you, especially if the activity involves more than one trip each week for practices or classes.

## Buying and renting equipment

Many of today's extra-curricular activities involve purchasing team uniforms, special equipment, or expensive musical instruments. If money's tight, consider choosing sports activities based on the amount of equipment they require. Track and wrestling need very little, while football demands a lot of expensive protective gear if it's not provided by your team or school.

You can find good quality used equipment if you scrounge around a bit, though. Ask if your child's school or local sports association has a lost-and-found box you can browse through. Often things have been sitting in the box for years, or a time limit exists for holding items. Some lost-and-found boxes give items to charity if they're not claimed in 90 days. Well, step right up and offer to be the charity that gets that old tennis racket in three months.

Another frugal option is a used equipment exchange program. One of my kids needed a new pair of ballet slippers, but because we'd faced several major unexpected financial setbacks that month, we couldn't afford the new shoes right away. The owner of the dance studio showed us to the exchange box where we sorted through slippers and found a perfect pair in my child's size in exchange for her outgrown pair.

Has your kid ever insisted he's going to be a famous drummer when he grows up and two weeks later lost all interest in music — just after you bought that expensive drum set? Until you're certain your child is talented or interested long term in a particular sport, activity, or musical instrument, borrow or rent the necessary equipment. Why spend $100 for sports equipment that sits unused in the back of a closet somewhere?

Check the classified ads in the local paper for used sporting goods and instruments. A friend of mine who recently moved to Europe parted with a well-cared-for, high quality violin for a fraction of its original price, so don't assume that *used* means beat-up or poor quality. Follow through on a few ads and you may find a terrific bargain.

Garage sales, thrift shops, and consignment stores are also excellent places to hunt for used sports equipment. See Chapter 16 for more ideas on secondhand shopping.

## Budgeting for fees

Don't forget to include room in your family budget for dues and fees for various school-related activities. If you forget about the fees, you may find yourself strapped for cash when all the dues need to be paid at once.

If money's tight and resources are limited, check to see if your local sports organization or parks and recreation department has any scholarships or low-income programs available for students. If you live in a major city, contact local professional sports offices or service clubs (women's clubs, Rotary, Kiwanis, Eagles, and so on) in search of suitable scholarships and subsidies.

Some schools and sports programs offer reductions in fees if the parent or guardian offers to volunteer and help coach or do some behind-the-scenes work for the team or the class. A friend of mine volunteered several hours each month at her daughter's dance studio. She did basic bookkeeping and cleaning chores in exchange for free tuition for her daughter's advanced dance classes.

## Affording all the trips

Students often have many opportunities to travel during their high school years. Whether they're involved with cheerleading, choir, sports teams, church youth groups, or band competitions, at some point your child's probably going to ask to participate in a group trip of some sort. These trips can be fun, educational, and unfortunately, very expensive!

Set up special bank accounts for your children just for saving for student and youth group trips. Have them set aside a little bit from any money they receive throughout the year for birthdays, holidays, and odd jobs. You can also hold a family garage sale and have your teens do the work and then keep a percentage of the proceeds for their special trip fund.

If your high school student wants to participate in the senior trip to Mexico at the end of the year, tell her she needs to start saving for it now.

Those trips can be great fun, but they are still "extras" the kids should pay for themselves out of gifts, allowances, babysitting, or part-time jobs. Plus, saving money and working toward a financial goal is excellent training for adulthood.

For more information on allowances and budgeting ideas, read Chapter 2.

## Casual learning through real-life situations

Don't underestimate the power of casual learning through real-life situations. Do you have a friend who does pottery as a hobby or as a business? Maybe he'd be willing to let your child come over and observe the process and help a bit. Watching and helping an artist at work becomes an instant art class for the price of gas to your friend's studio. Is Grandpa a carpenter? Ask Gramps to spend some time with his grandkids teaching them to use basic tools and maybe even build a birdhouse or sandbox together. Wow! An instant woodworking class and family togetherness all wrapped up in one frugal package.

# Protecting Your Budget during Prom and Graduation Season

The end of the school year brings additional expenses for many families, especially those families with a graduating high school senior. Between formal attire for the prom and all those "essential" graduation items like class rings and yearbooks, parents can easily feel overwhelmed financially.

## Funding a frugal prom

Kids heading to the prom these days often want to rent limousines in addition to the usual expenses of prom dresses, tuxedos, flowers, and dinner. If your child feels he absolutely *needs* the limo experience, he can save money by going in financially with a group of friends. Piling into the back of a limo with a group rather than just you and your date is still a lot of fun and much more frugal. To be honest, though, I have a hard time understanding the need for a limo in high school. The most frugal thing of all is to just say, "No!" to the whole extravagant rigmarole from the start. Your mileage may vary.

To save on the cost of formal wear, your daughter and her friends can exchange prom dresses with each other from one formal dance to the next. If your daughter won't be caught dead (or alive!) in a prom dress worn previously by a friend at school, visit local consignment stores and look for high-quality, gently-used formal wear that none of her friends will recognize. If your teenage son has reached his full height and attends formal functions regularly, look into the cost of buying a tux rather than renting one several times each year. Just a few dances' worth of tuxedo-wearing can easily make up for the price of buying one.

Another way to save on the pomp of prom is to start with a home-cooked dinner instead of paying out the nose for dinner at a fancy restaurant. When I was in high school, a group of my friends decided to save money by preparing dinner ourselves at a friend's house. We all brought food and dressed in our formal wear. We used the fine china, crystal, silver, and candles for atmosphere. Then we piled into several cars to head for the dance — and had a memorable night for minimal cost.

## Saving on graduation-related expenses

High school graduation brings all sorts of additional expenses to the family budget. Graduation catalog companies want you to believe that every graduate needs an expensive class ring, several hundred printed graduation announcements, and all the other bells and whistles.

To prepare for the expenses of graduation, start saving a small amount of each paycheck at the beginning of the school year, but don't feel like all the expenses need to fall on your shoulders alone. Have your child start a special graduation fund (perhaps in her junior year) to help defray some of the costs or to buy some of those "extra" items all her friends are ordering, like the class ring or imprinted name cards. Or ask the grandparents if they want to give the child her class ring for a gift.

---

### Finding frugal grad gifts

When graduation announcements begin to fill your mailbox, consider the following simple and inexpensive suggestions sure to please even the hardest-to-shop-for graduating teen:

- ✔ Bucket or basket filled with everyday "stuff" for life in the college dorm: stationery, envelopes, stamps, pens, blank book or journal, calendar, shampoo, toothpaste, dental floss, soap, batteries, and washcloths. You can purchase many of these items on sale or at the dollar store.

- ✔ Gift certificates: bookstore, coffee shop, music or grocery store, video rental.

- ✔ Assorted school supplies (if the grad's heading to college): three-ring binders, notebooks in various sizes, pens, highlighters, paper clips, stapler.

- ✔ Collection of kitchen supplies (if he's moving out on his own for the first time): hot pad, kitchen towel, measuring cups and spoons, stirring spoons, spatulas, small all-purpose cookbook. Package the items together in a large mixing bowl or colander wrapped in plastic wrap and tied with ribbon. Many of these items can be found inexpensively at thrift stores and dollar stores.

- ✔ Magazine subscription for his favorite hobby or personal interest.

---

Save on graduation announcements by making your own by hand or on the computer. If you know an artist or someone who can do calligraphy, perhaps he'd want to make your child a hand-lettered announcement as a graduation gift. You can then photocopy it onto high-quality paper for an elegant — yet incredibly inexpensive — announcement alternative.

Borrow a cap and gown from an older sibling or neighbor. Most graduating seniors want to save only the tassel from their cap for a souvenir — you can order a tassel from the graduation catalog and add it to the borrowed cap.

If you want to have a party to celebrate your son's or daughter's achievement, invite extended family and friends for a casual get-together at your house or converge at a local park after the graduation ceremonies. To save money, make it a potluck meal, a backyard barbeque, or simply serve dessert and beverages.

# Combating the High Costs of College

One of the most expensive parts of raising children is also one of the most important: a college education. But with creative financing, scholarships, and student loans, higher education can be within the financial reach of frugal families everywhere.

Attending an out-of-state college can nearly double tuition fees. Sticking close to home and attending an in-state college saves substantially compared to going to school where you can't prove residency.

## Earning college credit early

Each year your child is in college requires general expenses (such as room and board fees) in addition to tuition. So if she can cut down on the time she actually spends completing her degree, she saves money. One way to shorten a college stay is to get college credit through programs like Advanced Placement or CLEP testing. For more detailed information, go to www.collegeboard.com.

### Advanced Placement

The Advanced Placement (AP) program often involves classes taken in special high school AP programs, but prospective college students can also study for AP tests on their own. AP tests cost around $80 per subject, but if the student receives a passing grade on the exam, many colleges give full credit for the class, which can mean hundreds to thousands of dollars in savings depending on the costs of the college. If a student receives enough AP credits, some colleges even let the student enter college as a sophomore, skipping the freshman year altogether. Write to the colleges your child is interested in attending and ask for their Advanced Placement policies. AP tests are conducted each spring, usually in May.

### CLEP tests

CLEP tests allow students to receive credit for what they already know, whether learned through classes, life experience, or work-related activities. You can usually find a college's CLEP policies in its general catalog, or write to the colleges directly and ask for their policies on awarding credit for CLEP test results. CLEP tests are usually administered throughout the year and cost about $50 per exam.

### Other scholarship and testing programs

For up-to-date information about scholarships and tests, talk to your child's high school guidance counselor near the end of the child's sophomore year. Many scholarship and testing programs (such as the National Merit Scholar program) begin testing in the student's junior year, so you want to make sure you don't miss any testing opportunities. Don't wait until your child's senior year to start investigating tests and other scholarship options. Many of these programs provide substantial financial assistance for qualifying students.

When your child's still in high school, look into programs with your school district and the local community colleges. Our state has a program called Running Start where qualifying high school students can take college-level courses at the local community college. The local school district foots the bill, and at the end of their high school years, the students can have as much as a full year of college already completed and paid for by the school district.

# Benefiting from financial aid

Don't let a lack of surplus money in your family's bank account keep you from considering higher education for your children. The financial aid office at your child's college can help put together a package of aid to meet your child's needs for tuition, books, and living expenses. Financial aid packages often include money from scholarships, loans, and programs that pay tuition in exchange for services rendered.

Submit your application materials for financial aid as early as possible because many programs work on a first-come, first-served basis.

### Scholarships

College financial aid departments can point your student toward private and public scholarships. Some scholarships are offered only to students with parents or family members in a certain club or organization, but other scholarships are open to all high school seniors. Still others are limited to applicants who meet certain criteria according to race, talents, area of study, academic proficiency, and so on. Apply for as many scholarships as you qualify for. Every little bit helps when you're dealing with an expense as large as four years of college tuition.

Many scholarship contests that require essays and projects end up with only a handful of submissions, which greatly increases each individual's chance of winning. So put in the extra effort — it pays off.

### Loans

Scholarships are essentially gifts that don't need to be repaid, but student loans must be repaid with interest. Many students are able to afford college costs through a combination of loan options, usually either loans directly to the student or loans to the parents. Depending on the level of financial need, some student loans defer the interest until after graduation. Parents can also go through their bank or regular loan sources for more flexible repayment plans, but usually government-funded programs offer much better rates than private loan companies. For more information on the types of loans available to college students and their families, go to www.finaid.org/loans/.

### Service programs

Involvement with the military and ROTC programs can provide college tuition assistance for students who are inclined toward military service. Explore this option even if your child isn't planning on spending most of his career in the military. Future doctors, for example, can bypass much of the debt associated with a medical degree by trading training for a few years in the Armed Forces.

Also, the Americorps program helps with college tuition in exchange for commitments of various lengths to work for the program. The Americorps worker receives a small living allowance, health coverage, valuable work experience, and tuition credits to either pay for college or repay student loans. Service opportunities within Americorps include working for organizations like Habitat for Humanity, the Red Cross, or even helping tutor academically challenged kids in an elementary school. The program is open to U.S. citizens 17 years and older regardless of economic need. Check out Americorps online at www.americorps.org for full details.

## Attending community college

An easy way to save money on college expenses is to get a two-year degree from a community college. Not only are the tuition costs less at a two-year school, you can usually find a community or junior college close to home so that the student can save money on commuting and residential costs by continuing to live at home.

If your child plans to get a four-year degree, attending community college is a good way to reduce college expenses for the first two years before she transfers to a four-year university.

Be sure to think about what four-year school your child wants to attend so that you can verify ahead of time that classes taken at the community college level will transfer to the four-year college or university. You're not saving money if you have to pay tuition for a class twice because the university has different requirements and makes the student repeat a course or two.

If your child plans on paying his own way through school, by attending a community college for a couple of years and becoming a student who's no longer dependent on his parents' support, your child not only saves money on tuition, he may also find himself eligible for student loans otherwise blocked because of a parent's higher income. Be sure to weigh the financial benefits of qualifying for better loans versus the parents' losing the ability to claim the child as a tax credit.

## Working while in college

If your child is going to pay her own way through college, she has several options for working and going to school at the same time.

One thing to take into account is the energy level of the student. Some kids thrive on multi-tasking and handling work and school at the same time. Others need more time to thoughtfully focus on their schoolwork in order to succeed. If your child needs time to focus, suggest she alternate two quarters of full-time work with two quarters of full-time school. It may take a little longer to complete a degree, but it can be an excellent way to earn a college degree for the student who doesn't have the energy reserves to tackle both a job and school at the same time.

If you're footing the bill for your child's college tuition, books, and lodging so that he can focus on studying through the school year instead of working, consider making it a requirement that he works full time during the summer, saving all the money he makes to use for spending money during the school year. He needs to budget for clothing, extra food, entertainment, trips, and so on. His spending is easy to figure: he can spend what he earns.

Finding a regular job at a college can provide some tuition-related perks. A friend of mine worked part time in the engineering library at her university throughout her college years. Not only did she earn a regular hourly wage for the job, but she also received free tuition for one class per quarter.

## Taking summer classes

Another tactic is to take classes each summer to cut the years spent in college from four years to three. You won't save on the actual tuition costs this way, but you can avoid paying an extra year of room and board. Rather than paying for that extra year at school, your child can be out working and paying for living life in the real world.

---

# Heading back to school

Returning to school after joining the workforce is increasingly common. If you're looking for money-saving ideas for your own college career rather than your child's, here are a couple easy ideas.

Adult learners beginning their college years can take advantage of Advanced Placement and CLEP testing, as well. You receive college credit for your life experiences and time you've spent studying on your own.

Many companies offer tuition reimbursement to their employees. Several nurses I know started their college career by going to school to become an LPN (licensed practical nurse). Then they started working for an employer that paid tuition credits for nursing staff to complete their two-year RN (registered nurse) degrees. Eventually they went on to complete a four-year bachelor of science in nursing, and the only part of their education they paid for out of their own pocket was the one-year LPN program at a community college.

Colleges themselves often offer free tuition to employees. A man I know started working full time as a cook at a very expensive, private college, and found out that one of the benefits of working at the college was free tuition for a class or two each quarter. He ended up going back to college part time and completing a long-abandoned degree — for just the cost of books and supplies! Many colleges also offer free tuition to the children of employees — something to keep in mind if you're looking for work.

---

# Chapter 9

# Looking Good and Feeling Good on a Tight Budget

*B*ecause into every life a little deodorant and prescription medicine must fall, it's important to find ways to save money in this area before toothpaste and soap clean out your bank account. Here's a chapter with frugal ideas for those most personal regular expenses. You also find ideas for saving on exercise so you can keep your budget and your body healthy and fit.

## Saving on Toiletries and Personal Hygiene Products

Cleaning your teeth, washing your hair, shaving your face. Gotta do them, right? But if you think your favorite brands of personal care products don't have frugal alternatives, stay tuned. You can glean an idea or two for saving pennies on every dollar.

### Cleansing your body on a budget

Making your own toiletries saves money. For example, brushing your teeth with baking soda works great and is cheaper than buying brand-name pastes. Baking soda not only cleans your teeth, but it also freshens your breath! Think about that open box of baking soda on the back shelf of your fridge. What's it there for? Absorbing odors! So if it works for your fridge with all the atrocious odors brewing there, baking soda is bound to work wonders on a little dose of morning breath. (***Note:*** If you don't think it tastes all that great, make a paste by mixing peppermint oil and baking soda.)

Here are few more simple and frugal home alternatives for expensive toiletry items:

- ✔ Wipe on rubbing alcohol with a cotton ball as a substitute for deodorant. You can also try using witch hazel in the same way (allow to dry thoroughly before dressing) or baking soda (dusted on underarm with a powder puff or cotton ball).

- ✔ Use a mild solution of salt and water for mouthwash (about four parts water to one part salt). The salt water rinse and gargle keeps your mouth clean after eating and kills some of the bacteria that lead to bad breath.

- ✔ Substitute cheap, bought-in-bulk hair conditioner for shaving cream. A large container of conditioner is considerably less expensive than even the most inexpensive cans of shaving cream. Plus you only need to add one item to your shopping list instead of two.

Or if you want to try your hand at making your own frugal body cleansers, you can find recipes on the Internet for bubble bath, facial masks, lotions, you name it. Check www.luxurylane.com/thelibrary/tocrecipes.htm and http://thegreenguide.org/diy/pc.php for more ideas.

If you're not interested in making homemade body cleansing products, at least watch carefully for sales and coupon specials at your local stores. Buy several tubes of toothpaste or a couple bottles of your favorite shampoo when it goes on sale. And give generic products a try.

## Finding frugal make-up

Wearing make-up can be incredibly expensive, especially if you think you have to use certain brand names or home party products if you don't want your face to fall off or end up looking like Frankenstein's mother. But if money's tight, you can still look good without selling your first-born child in exchange for a tube of designer lipstick.

Try inexpensive store brands and "look-alike" brands you find in many drugstore chains. A make-up artist told me that the expensive department store brands usually just have more expensive perfumes added to them. Now, I've got nothing against the nice folks working the make-up counters in expensive stores, but their job is to sell you their expensive products, so keep that in mind.

The expensive mall brands and department store cosmetics do have good annual promotions where you buy one item and then receive a reusable tote bag of make-up freebees like mini-lipsticks, blush, mascara, lotions, perfume, and so on. Although I wouldn't normally spend $15 for a tube of under-eye concealer, I may do it if I could get all these additional items at no cost.

Inexpensive sources for cosmetics include:

- ✔ Discount, drug, and dollar stores
- ✔ Clothing stores in the mall
- ✔ Beauty supply stores
- ✔ Garage sales (Read on before you discredit this idea.)

Some of you are probably groaning at the idea of buying cosmetics at garage sales. "Eww! I'm not about to use somebody's used cosmetics!" Well, I'm not talking about buying used make-up. I shudder even thinking about it. I'm suggesting you keep your eye out for unopened, brand-new boxes of cosmetics from some of the popular in-home party cosmetic companies. Some cosmetic sales representatives sell their unsold surplus and merchandise from last season for dirt cheap at garage sales.

Here are a few simple cosmetic tips that save money and stretch make-up a wee bit farther:

- ✔ Mascara can double as an eyeliner if you use an eyeliner brush.
- ✔ Use a dark color of eye shadow (brown looks nice on nearly everyone) as eyeliner.
- ✔ Lipstick can double as cream blush for your cheeks — and as an added bonus, it perfectly matches your lip color!
- ✔ Regular liquid foundation can double as eye shadow primer.
- ✔ Apply foundation with your fingers rather than a make-up sponge. The foundation lasts longer because the sponge absorbs a little bit with each application.

## *Discovering cheap acne treatments*

Many teens and adults spend untold amounts of money on over-the-counter or as-seen-on-TV acne treatments. Although the following frugal alternatives probably can't replace prescription acne treatments for severe cases, you may find these alternatives are just as effective at taming a minor breakout as many items on your drugstore's shelves.

✔ **Desitin diaper rash medicine or zinc oxide cream:** Apply a dab directly to the blemish and leave on overnight. Avoid the eye and lip areas. Zinc oxide cream can usually be found under various brand names in the sunscreen aisle of your local store.

✔ **Tea tree oil:** Apply to the blemish. You can use it under make-up.

✔ **Fresh garlic:** Rub a cut clove of garlic onto blemishes and oily areas. (Also repels vampires and amorous spouses.)

✔ **Paste of baking soda and water:** Apply directly to the blemish and leave on overnight or for half an hour during the daytime.

✔ **Olive oil and salt paste:** Use as a gentle scrubbing wash in place of soap or harsh abrasives. Use an astringent afterward to keep your skin grease-free and discourage breakouts (see next point).

✔ **Hydrogen peroxide:** Apply with a cotton ball over oily areas as an astringent and oil-control measure. Avoid eye area. Hydrogen peroxide doesn't dry out skin like rubbing alcohol or witch hazel.

✔ **Glycerin soap:** Use in place of expensive acne washes for face, upper back, chest, and other acne-prone areas.

## Cutting the cost of caring for your hair

Not many things are worse than a really bad hair day. But how can frugal consumers keep their hair looking great and their wallets from getting remarkably thin at the same time? Read on for some simple tips and ideas:

✔ Mix half the amount of shampoo you usually use with equal parts warm water, and then lather as usual. Most shampoos work just as well when they're diluted with warm water.

✔ Use ½ cup of vinegar mixed with 1 cup warm water instead of a fancy store-bought rinse for shiny and soft hair.

✔ Wash your hair in cool (and therefore cheap) water to keep your hair (and your electricity bill) healthy.

Trimming hair isn't really that hard. You can find videos and books on simple haircutting techniques (try *Haircutting For Dummies* by J. Elaine Spear and published by Wiley). Cutting your own hair can save you a bundle, especially if you or one of your children wears bangs that need to be trimmed regularly. Or if you're not brave enough to cut hair yourself, find a talented "hair" friend you can barter services with . . . and save big! You can also save big by doing at-home perms and coloring your hair yourself, or with the help of a friend.

## Saving on feminine products

Okay. This is one of those embarrassing topics nobody likes to talk about in public. So, men, listen up. If you're one of those guys who would drop dead from embarrassment if you had to pick up sanitary napkins or tampons for your wife, skip ahead to the next section of this chapter, *quickly!*

Okay, now that the guys are gone, ladies, don't you just hate forking over all that money every month for something that just gets thrown away? Believe it or not, you can find alternatives, but they're probably not for everyone. Someone who doesn't want to wash diapers for her baby because they're too "icky" probably isn't going to be thrilled at the idea of washing her own cotton sanitary pads or rinsing out a rubber menstrual cup. But for people seriously interested in saving money and the environment, these products are excellent.

You can buy cotton menstrual pads that are comfortable, come in different sizes and absorbencies, and are completely washable and reusable. The pads can be reused for around three years before needing replacement. When you think about how much you spend on those monthly boxes of pads and tampons, you can save substantially on your toiletry budget over the course of several years. The reusable pads aren't right for every circumstance — swimming, for instance — but work well for normal wear. The average price I've seen for a pack of three pads is about $25. For more information, go to www.eco-logique.com or www.gladrags.com.

Tampon users may be interested in reusable menstrual cups. They're bell-shaped "cups" made of natural gum rubber and can be worn all day, even when sleeping or swimming. Not only are they economical, but they also last for as long as ten years. For more information, go to www.keeper.com.

# Health Isn't a Luxury — It's a Frugal Essential!

If you eat well, drink lots of water, and get plenty of exercise, your skin looks better (so you can wear less make-up), and your general health improves (so you have fewer doctor bills and prescriptions). But do you need to run out and buy expensive health foods and join an exercise club in order to be healthy? Nope.

## *Eating to live, not living to eat*

The foods you put into your body should be healthy. You know that, I know that. But how many times have I polished off a bag of cookies just because I didn't want them to go to *waste* — so I let them go to my *waist* instead. Silly me.

To avoid temptation, seal that opened bag of cookies and put it in the freezer until you have company. Or if you make up a big batch of homemade chocolate chip cookies, eat one or two now while they're warm and wonderful, and then freeze the rest in zip-top bags. When you want one of the cookies for a snack in a day or two, you have to thaw it first. Any delay between thinking about food and actually eating it can help ward off temptation.

If you've made more food than you can reasonably eat at one meal, don't finish off the extras out of some misguided sense of frugal duty. Eating extra doesn't save you money, and it may end up costing more when you have to pay for a weight loss program down the road. See Chapter 6 for ideas on using leftovers in creative and appetizing ways.

Watch for sales on fresh fruit, raw vegetables, and low-fat crackers. Feeding your kids a small handful of grapes for a snack is much cheaper — and healthier —than an expensive candy bar. Or for the most frugal snack around, pop a big bowl of popcorn with a sprinkling of salt (no butter or margarine).

If you don't have much time to prepare meals, falling victim to the call of convenience foods is easy to do. To keep on the frugal track, double or triple the healthy meals you cook and stick the extras in the freezer for those nights when you're just too busy to cook from scratch. Keep bags of chopped vegetables in the freezer. Be sure to check out Chapters 4 and 5 for more information on grocery shopping and preparing inexpensive meals and snacks.

Here are few more simple ways to save on healthy food expenses:

- ✔ Fresh fruit, vegetables, and dry beans are all relatively inexpensive if you watch for sales and buy in season.

- ✔ Cook with less fat instead of buying expensive low-fat products. Sautèe meat and vegetables in fat-free chicken broth or apple juice instead of oil. Or sprinkle cooked veggies with fresh herbs instead of seasoning them with butter.

✔ Think of meat and cheese as flavoring rather than one of the main ingredients in your meal. For example, a sprinkling of grated cheese over the top of your meal goes much farther — frugal-wise and health-wise — than pouring on a cheese sauce.

✔ Make your own low-fat baked goods by substituting apple-sauce for the oil in cakes and other home-baked items.

Not only does the food we eat determine our level of health, but also the beverages we drink. Take water, for example. It's not really a miracle cure for what ails ya, but it's definitely a step in the right direction. Drinking plenty of water keeps your body hydrated, keeps your skin moist and fresh, and even fills you up a bit when you're feeling hungry. Serve water to drink instead of milk, sodas, or juices. It's the cheapest — and healthiest — beverage of all! If you regularly purchase bottled drinking water, consider investing in a water filtration and purification system or a water purifying pitcher. Keep your eye out for these filters at discount stores or special sales. A filtering system easily pays for itself over a relatively short period of time.

## *Exercising for a healthy life*

As far as exercise goes, choose an activity you enjoy or else you won't stick with it. If the idea of getting your hair wet and changing out of a wet swimsuit is the last thing you want to do in the morning, an early morning swim probably isn't the right choice for you. But what about the same swim after a long, hot day at work? Try different activities and times of the day until you find a combination that fits you and your schedule. A few simple — and frugal — exercise ideas:

✔ Walk around the park early in the morning when nobody else is out except the bunnies nibbling the grass. Or find a friend to walk with you several times a week if you don't like to walk or jog alone. If no humans are available, consider getting a dog — or just borrow one from a friendly neighbor. Now that I think about it, lots of people will *pay* to have someone walk their dog daily — this could be a money-making proposition if you play your cards right.

✔ Put in your favorite aerobics video after the kids leave for school, or just turn on the CD player to your favorite dance tunes and let loose. Dancing is great aerobic exercise . . . and free too!

✔ Ride your bike (stationary or regular bike) or start running instead of paying for an expensive aerobics or exercise class.

✔ Grab a couple of one pound cans of tomatoes or beans from the pantry to add a little conditioning to your arms. Carry the cans with you while you walk around the local park, or while you're doing your aerobic video or dance routine. If you want heavier weights, fill two ½-gallon plastic jugs with water (about 4 pounds each).

✔ Shoot baskets for an hour with your teenager, challenge your spouse to a game of tennis at the local municipal court, or set up the badminton net in the backyard. Basketballs, tennis equipment, and badminton sets can be bought for next to nothing at garage sales and thrift stores.

✔ Invest in your own exercise equipment (weight bench, free weights, and exercise bike) instead of buying an expensive membership to the local gym. As a busy mom, I never seem to find time in my day to go to the gym, but if the exercise bike and weight bench are right there staring at me all day, I'm more apt to actually complete my workouts on a daily basis. I find it helps if I keep the exercise equipment near the television so I can schedule my workout with the morning news and take care of two priorities at once.

Check for inexpensive exercise equipment at garage sales or in the classified ads. The best time to look for these items is in the spring (around April or May) when people are realizing their New Year's resolutions to work out didn't work out.

✔ Teach aerobics or yoga. Some health clubs give discounted memberships (or even free memberships) to their employees, so if you've ever wanted to teach aerobics or yoga, this could be a great way to get healthy and stay financially fit at the same time. Also, many businesses give discounted health club memberships to their employees as part of the benefits package. Consider joining a smaller, less expensive health club rather than the huge one with all the bells and whistles (pool, sauna, Jacuzzi, and so on) that you pay for but may never use. If your local health club offers a free one month trial membership, take 'em up on it!

✔ See if the studio your child takes dance lessons at offers free or discounted classes for additional family members. One of my friends has two daughters taking Irish dance lessons. The studio offers free classes for any family members in excess of two paying students, so my friend started taking an adult Irish dance class for free. Great exercise, lots of fun . . . and free!

✔ Walk up the stairs instead of using the escalator. Park in the spot farthest from the grocery store's front door. Look for ways to do things that use the most energy.

# Saving on Medical Expenses

Unexpected medical and pharmacy bills can take a huge bite out of the family budget. When our first child was born eight weeks prematurely, our out-of-pocket medical expenses for newborn nursery care skyrocketed. Even though you can't possibly plan for all emergencies and contingencies, here are a few things you can do to cut back on regular medical-related expenses.

## Keeping a close eye on bills

Remember to keep careful track of all your medical expenses and look over every itemized bill in detail. One time my daughter had surgery and the surgeon accidentally billed us twice for the main surgical procedure, which added an additional $800 to our total bill. When we pointed out the error to his office, they happily corrected it. Be sure to follow up on corrections like that, though. Sometimes the paperwork gets lost in the shuffle and you need to remind the office more than once to take the charges off your bill.

Keep calm when you're haggling with doctors or hospitals over disputed amounts. They'll often negotiate and lower the amount due, especially if patients are assertive, yet courteous. Keep written documentation of every phone call, letter, and bill related to the disputed charges. Be organized, confident, and polite, and the situation will probably turn out all right.

If you belong to an HMO or PPO, make sure that every doctor and specialist working on you is part of your medical plan. Don't assume that just because you're in a plan-approved hospital that you're being treated by a plan-approved doctor, anesthesiologist, or nurse. A friend told me she once fought a $400 bill for over a year — the emergency room was plan-approved but the doctor on call that night was not. It took a while, but eventually they wrote off my friend's $400 bill.

## Looking into payment plans

If you're facing after-insurance charges that you can't pay for all at once, call the billing office of the doctor or hospital and see whether you can make some sort of payment arrangement. You may be surprised just how much help you receive. I called the hospital about a surgical charge I couldn't afford to pay, and somehow in the conversation I discovered that I was eligible for a couple of low-income food programs. Before I knew what hit me, the billing department wrote off my entire hospital bill. So don't be afraid to say that you're having difficulty meeting your financial obligations. Doctors and hospitals are often quite willing to accept payment arrangements or make generous allowances for their low-income patients.

## Coordinating insurance benefits

If you and your spouse both have medical or dental insurance coverage, be sure to coordinate benefits between your insurance companies for any medical services. Usually you have a primary insurance carrier that needs to be billed first, and then, if you or your children are also covered under your spouse's insurance, be sure the secondary insurance company is billed after the first insurance has paid its portion. When insurance plans can coordinate benefits like this, you often don't have to pay much of anything out of pocket.

## Finding less expensive prescriptions

Pharmacy expenses are one of the most difficult medical bills to budget for in many families. Even with insurance coverage, out-of-pocket expenses can add up substantially over the course of an extended illness or a course of several antibiotics. Here are some simple ways to reduce pharmacy costs:

✔ If you can buy a larger amount of medication at once, you may save a bit of money. Each time you have a prescription filled, the pharmacy adds administrative charges. By ordering a full month's supply of your medication rather than one week at a time, you can save three service fees for filling the prescription.

✔ Pharmacies vary in their prices for different medications. Before filling your prescription, call around to several pharmacies and ask how much your particular prescription costs to fill.

✔ Don't forget to ask your doctor to prescribe the least expensive or generic version of your medication.

✔ If you don't have prescription coverage, tell your doctor so and ask whether over-the-counter medications are available that are just as effective as the prescription versions.

# Chapter 10

# The Family That Plays Together, Stays Together: Frugal Family Fun

* * * * * * * * * * * * * * * * * * * * * * * * * * * * * * * * * * * * * * * * * *

## In This Chapter

▶ Discovering the fun of family field trips

▶ Sharing simple pleasures with your family at home

▶ Finding inexpensive resources for reading addicts

▶ Dining out in style

▶ Affording vacations your entire family enjoys

* * * * * * * * * * * * * * * * * * * * * * * * * * * * * * * * * * * * * * * * * *

*W*ith today's two-income families and busy schedules, families struggle to find the time to be together. But setting aside time in your busy schedules for play is more than just a fun break in the routine — you're creating lasting memories. And don't think you have to spend a lot of money to create that feeling of family togetherness. Fun doesn't have to equal expensive. Sometimes simple and cheap is actually more fun than extravagant and overpriced.

In this chapter, I share simple ideas for inexpensive family entertainment. Whether you want to explore free community art festivals, enjoy a special dinner on the town, or hit the open road for a fun, family vacation, you can find plenty of frugal ideas in this chapter.

## Enjoying Family Field Trips

Probably one of my family's all-time favorite activities is the Family Field Trip. No, I'm not suggesting you crowd your family into a hot bus and head off to tour the local pickle factory. My family's field trips are often educational in nature, but they're also just plain fun.

A meaningful family field trip can be simple, like taking a leisurely walk down a local nature trail and watching a pair of red squirrels do aerial acrobatics while gathering hazelnuts from the tips of the branches. Or extend the field trip and follow the path of Lewis and Clark across the United States for a long — but relatively inexpensive — educational family vacation. (I give advice on saving on travel expenses later in this chapter.)

## Choosing an event the entire family enjoys

Sitting down at the kitchen table with your family to plan an outing can be a fun activity in itself, and planning together which events to attend also assures that everyone is interested in the activities you choose. Advance planning also gives everyone time to get excited about the upcoming outing. But those spur-of-the-moment ideas instigated by a parent can be loads of fun, too.

The weekly "What's Happening?" section of the newspaper and monthly issues of regional parenting magazines — often found lying around for free in libraries and bookstores — provide a never-ending variety of activities appealing to our entire family, from preschoolers to adults. Also, your local library may offer classes, readings, and live performances for kids. Check your library's bulletin board for notices about family-friendly activities and attractions.

The following list of field trip ideas can be the beginning of a brainstorming session for your family. Be sure to visit www.fieldtripping.com online for further tips and ideas.

| *Industry* | *Businesses* |
|---|---|
| Manufacturing plants | Grocery stores |
| Metal works | Newspaper offices |
| Train depots or airports | Restaurants or caterers |
| Wood-products or paper mills | Television or radio stations |

| *Historical* | *Cultural* |
|---|---|
| Civil War reenactments | Concerts in the park |
| Local historical societies | Cultural festivals |
| Museums | Family service projects |
| Pioneer cemeteries | Art galleries |

| *Nature* | *Just-for-fun* |
|---|---|
| Dairy or vegetable farms | Drive-in theaters |
| Local nature centers | Kite-flying |
| Tide pools and beaches | Local parks |
| Zoos and aquariums | Tourist towns |

## Getting ready to go

My kids and I take a lot of spur-of-the-moment field trips, but I find it helps if we do at least a little bit of planning beforehand. We don't want to find ourselves in the mountains, raring and ready to take a nature hike, and then discover that the area we chose is about to be hit with the worst thunderstorm in three years.

Here are a few suggestions to follow before leaving home.

- ✔ Check the gas level in the car or van.
- ✔ Gather some inexpensive snack supplies and drink bottles.
- ✔ Bring along some extra cash.
- ✔ Confirm driving directions.
- ✔ Check on admission prices.
- ✔ Ask about the availability of inexpensive restaurants or picnic grounds.
- ✔ Look at the weather report for your destination so that you can dress appropriately.
- ✔ Check your destination's Web site for unanticipated park closures or hour changes. Also look for any "online only" coupons.

# Having Fun in Your Own Backyard

The family activities highlighted in this section not only are fun and cost next to nothing, but they also help build family relationships because you spend time together pursuing enjoyable pastimes.

## Reviving the lost art of storytelling

Much to my amazement, my kids actually enjoy hearing stories about my childhood. I always thought I was boring them, so I didn't share much about my childhood escapades, but when I started hearing requests for the same stories over and over again

("Tell the story about the bear sitting by the fence, Mom!"), I realized that entertainment can be as inexpensive as a dramatic retelling of a solitary horseback ride in the mountains or a trip to the park when my bike chain broke. Don't worry about your skill, or lack thereof, in the art of storytelling. Your kids just want to spend time with you, hear your voice, and get to know you better through the tales you tell.

My kids also love hearing bedtime stories about themselves when they were younger or just general family history. When your family contains such varied characters as the World Champion Clam Eater, several big game hunters, an Alaskan bush pilot, soldiers from three different wars, and large poverty-stricken immigrant families from the Depression, you never lack for stories to tell. I bet if you think about it, you'll find a few long-forgotten family characters just waiting to live again in your children's bedtime stories.

## Discovering the games people play

If the power goes out for several hours — and the television, video games, and Internet access with it — the activity level in many homes screeches to a halt. But now imagine candles lit throughout the house and everyone gathered together on the living room floor in front of the fireplace playing board games or card games. Sounds like fun, doesn't it? Sort of peaceful and friendly. Well, you don't have to wait until the power goes out — family games can be enjoyed whenever you want some inexpensive entertainment and time together.

Institute a family game night. Set aside time two or three times a month to pull out the old classic board games from the closet shelf. My son recently had an overnight birthday party where the boys stayed up all night playing board games. I just piled all the games in a corner of the living room, provided snacks, and let the boys play whatever they wanted. They had a blast! No reason not to do the same thing with the family now and then. Don't just wait for special occasions or birthdays to have fun with the old games.

If you don't have a closet full of board games, you can acquire them inexpensively at garage sales and thrift stores. If someone asks what to get you or your family for a gift at the holidays, suggest a favorite board game you've been wanting to play at home.

Speaking of old games, do you remember Charades? How about Spoons? Twenty Questions? Hide the Thimble? Spotlight Tag? Rummy? Crazy Eights? Board games aren't the only family-friendly games to play on a family game night. Delve into the recesses of your mind and try to remember the games you played as a kid. Those games may be old to you, but they're *new* to your kids!

## Playing "Hide the Thimble"

"Hide the Thimble" is a great game to play with any age group, or even mixed ages at a family reunion or holiday party. To play, one person in the group is "it" and everyone else leaves the room. "It" places a thimble (or some other small, but distinct object) somewhere in plain view in the room. Then the other players rejoin "it," and the game begins. As the players look around the room, they silently sit down on the ground as soon as they spot the thimble, being careful not to indicate where they saw the thimble. As each player finds the thimble, they sit down until only one player is left standing. The first person to find the thimble is "it" the next game and gets to hide the thimble for the others to find.

# *Rekindling the joys of an open campfire*

Some of my fondest childhood memories involve campfires, friends, stories, and songs. If you aren't a camping family, you can still enjoy a campfire in your own backyard. Check for burn bans and ordinances in your area, and if you get the "all clear" from the powers-that-be, build a small fire pit in an open corner of your backyard. You can buy enclosed, portable fireplaces that can be used in the yard or even on a patio or deck. Although these outdoor fireplaces may be a bit pricey upfront, they can be well worth the investment if your family enjoys spending time around an open fire.

If anyone in your family is musical, an evening campfire is a great opportunity to tune up the ol' guitar. But even without instruments for accompaniment, just singing some old folk songs around an open fire can make for some wonderful family bonding opportunities. Don't let a lack of singing ability keep you from having a hootin'-howlin' good time. Just sing a few songs, let everyone tell a favorite story, roast marshmallows or hotdogs, and you've got fun memories to last a lifetime. If your mind goes blank about what to sing around the campfire, keep your eye out for old cassettes, songbooks, or sheet music of folk music sung by Burl Ives, Pete Seeger, or Peter, Paul, and Mary.

 If outside fires aren't an option but you have a fireplace in the living room, you can build a fire on a cold winter night, turn off the lights, gather together on the floor with some warm blankets, and do the song-and-story routine in your own living room.

## Frugal family fun with old photos

We all have boxes and drawers full of old photos. For a fun and frugal afternoon activity, ask the kids to help you put the photos into albums or inexpensive scrapbooks. Not only are you passing on family history (you can tell the tales as you arrange the photos), but you're cleaning out the drawers where the photos are stored.

If scrapbooking is a favorite hobby, or one that interests you but you thought it was too expensive, here are some simple ideas for saving money:

- Start with the essentials like a variety of pretty, acid-free papers, a pair of quality scissors, and photo-safe adhesive. You don't need every tool and doo-dad available.

- Shop your home for potential scrapbooking supplies before running out and buying things. I'm sure you've got decorative ribbon, buttons, fabric scraps, and wrapping paper stashed away in your closets.

- Check the Internet for poems you can add to your scrapbook. The Internet is also a good place to find sample page layouts.

- Check for after-holiday sales at craft stores and other retail outlets for seasonal stickers, decorative ribbon, and fancy papers. Also, check online auction sites like www.ebay.com for inexpensive scrapbooking supplies.

- Share scrapbooking supplies with a friend. A woman I know has regular scrapbooking get-togethers where a bunch of her friends bring all their own supplies and then work side-by-side at the dining room table, making use of each others' fancy scissors, hole-punches, markers, and fun extras.

## *Making frugal music*

If your family plays musical instruments, grab the instruments and have a family jam session. Play some favorite songs together or take turns performing for each other. This isn't the time to critique technique or tell your children they need to practice more. Just loosen up, let your hair down, and have a great time! You can invite another musical family or group of friends over to play with you. This is especially fun around the holidays with appropriate seasonal music. Your non-instrument-playing friends and family can provide vocals, or simply hand them a tambourine, a rattle, or a couple of rhythm sticks. Most people — even totally unmusical folk — can beat sticks together in time to the music. If you don't have musical instruments, be sure to look for them at garage sales and thrift stores during your regular travels.

## *Enjoying movie favorites*

Don't forget that old musicals (*The Sound of Music*, *Singing in the Rain*, *Camelot*, *South Pacific*, and so on) and favorite movies from your own childhood are probably "new releases" for your kids. If you're a classic movie buff, be sure to share your favorite flicks and movie stars with the kids. I was surprised to find my children love old musicals nearly as much as I do, and my teenage daughter and I can watch Spencer Tracy movies together all weekend. Visit the classic movies section of your local video store, check out a stack of your old favorites, cook up some popcorn, and have a fun and frugal time together.

Most movie rental stores offer older movies for a much cheaper price than the new releases. Or check out churches and libraries where you can often borrow movies for free. If you have cable television, keep your eye on the movie listings on the various stations. You can record movies early in the week to watch on the weekends. Keep several blank tapes around for recording movies. Movies taped from the television are not only free, they also save you a drive to the video store or library. To make watching a video at home even more fun for the younger kids, have the little ones draw marquee posters to display throughout the house and build excitement about the big show. You can even set up a "concession stand" and the kids can serve popcorn and drinks in exchange for play money. Little fun touches like this can make even the most frugal night at home an adventure!

## Free frugal fun for a month

Set aside one month a year as a free month, and during that month, every activity you do as a family must be completely free. No video rentals, fast-food meals, amusement park fees, or camping costs. But don't just sit home and watch the grass grow. Brainstorm about ideas you can do together that are both fun and cost nothing. Check the newspaper for free activities, ride your bikes, visit the library, go to a park to play ball, or invite some friends over for a night of cards or board games. Use your imagination. Let your motto be "Creativity rules!" This idea not only saves money during the "free" month, but it also provides the opportunity to discover new activities your family enjoys. After all, "free" is the best price of all in any frugal dictionary!

During the course of an average month, if your family normally rents five videos ($20), goes out to eat at a fast-food restaurant four times ($75), goes camping over a long weekend ($25 or more, depending on where you stayed and what food you brought), and visits the zoo ($40), you'd save an easy $160 during your "free" month.

# Financing a Reading Addiction

Whenever I'm asked what my favorite hobbies are, reading always finds its way to the top of my list. Not only do I enjoy reading for pleasure and information, but I also love reading aloud to my children or listening to my husband read to our whole family.

Because we've lived on a limited budget for years, I'm really good at finding bargain books. The biggest problem with my book fetish, though, is not having enough room for book storage. Hey, maybe I can sell some of my extra books back to the bookstore or exchange them for store credit!

## Finding books at the bargain sales

I've developed what I call book radar. When I enter a thrift store for the first time, my antennae go up and I scan the shop for bookshelves. If I pass a yard sale and see piles and boxes of books stacked in the yard, I always pop out of the car and browse through quickly, looking for any hidden literary gems. Library sales are also irresistible. Call your local library and ask about when they hold the library book sales.

My favorite resource for classic books and interesting reading material is estate sales. Often the estates belonged to older people whose collections include books they got when they were young. Hard-bound classics are often in abundance at these sales. Because most people shopping at estate sales are looking for antique furniture and decorative items, I usually don't have too much competition for the books. (See Chapter 16 for more information about estate sales and secondhand books.)

## Browsing used bookstores and exchanges

Used bookstores are an excellent resource for the book addict. Many used bookstores accept trade-ins of your old books, so you can often accumulate credit with the store to purchase more books later. One of our local stores sells books for half of the original selling price. When you trade in books, the store gives you book credit for half of what they sell it for, or one-fourth of the original price.

You can even make a little money with this if you're on the lookout for quality books in your yard sale and thrift store travels. I once found a large, high-quality art book at a garage sale for only $2, but after bringing it home, I decided it wasn't quite what I was looking for. I took it to the used bookstore, and they gave me one-fourth of the original selling price of the book — and because it was originally a $60 book, I came home with $15 in my pocket. After subtracting my $2 investment, I made a $13 profit from just one book!

## Taking advantage of inter-library loans

An excellent frugal resource for books is the local library. Not only does the library give me free access to my choice of thousands of books, but the reference librarians can access the inter-library loan system and locate books for me from almost anywhere in the United States. Some libraries don't participate in the inter-library loan system — and others charge a nominal fee for the service — but inter-library loans are an excellent way of getting books without shelling out $10 to $20 for a new book you want to read.

Before investing in the purchase price of a new book, always try to find it at the public library first. That way you can see if you really want to add the book to your home library or not.

# Saving on Fine Dining

Dinner out in a nice restaurant doesn't have to become a vaguely remembered activity from before you undertook a frugal lifestyle. By following the simple suggestions in this section, families and couples can enjoy an occasional dinner out for a small price tag.

## Seeing through suggestive sales

The wait staff at restaurants commonly suggest specific drinks, desserts, and other expensive extras to intentionally run up your meal tab. Appropriately enough, this technique is called *suggestive sales.*

In a lifetime long ago, I was a dining-room supervisor at a hotel restaurant. Upper management held regular training classes for the new wait staff to help them learn effective suggestive sales techniques. "Would you care for a piece of hot apple pie a la mode to go with your after-dinner coffee, sir?" Not only did they suggest after-dinner coffee that may not have been ordered otherwise, they also enticed the diner with a specific dessert idea. And then notice the a la mode suggestion — they mention ice cream on your pie because it not only tastes better, but adds more money to your total dining bill.

The most important thing to keep in mind when ordering in a restaurant is that anything "extra" or suggested by the waiter is going to add to your bill. If you really want ice cream on your slice of pie, fine. But if you're only saying yes because what the waitress suggested suddenly sounds delicious, you've succumbed to suggestive sales. Keep your radar alert when someone starts suggesting additional things to eat, drink, or garnish a meal.

## *Avoiding overpriced drinks*

Ordering water to drink is one easy technique to save money when you go out to eat. A simple cup of coffee can cost at least $2, and sodas, milk, and juice for the kids are usually more than that. Drinking water can often cut $10 or more from the cost of a typical family's meal. To make the water special, ask for a lemon or lime wedge.

Some people think going out to eat just isn't any fun if you have to drink water instead of soda or a glass of wine. But for my family, a $10 difference in the cost of the total meal can spell the difference between affording an evening out at a nice restaurant (albeit with water to drink) and just staying home for frozen pizza again. Personally, I prefer to give up a few drinks in order to experience the greater luxury of actually getting out of the house occasionally for a nice meal.

If the nicer drinks are essential to your dining experience, you may need to plan your meals out in restaurants less frequently to allow for the higher expense of added drinks.

## *Choosing dining times wisely*

Ask around to see if any of your local restaurants have reduced-rate menus on certain days or during particular hours. A popular Seattle restaurant chain has a special late-afternoon menu on weeknights to attract a pre-dinner crowd on off-days. By choosing from their special early dinner menu, we can get a four-course seafood dinner (including drinks) for around $30 for the two of us (including tip). Not a bad deal (especially because the restaurant has some of the best waterfront views in town). Over the years, my husband and I have celebrated most of our "just-the-two-of-us" dinners (birthdays, anniversaries) at this restaurant.

Dining out for lunch rather than dinner is another way to save substantially. Many restaurants have luncheon items for about half the price of the same item on the dinner menu.

Keep your eye out for advertisements and coupons for local restaurants in the weekly advertising circulars that come in the mail and the newspaper. Many places offer half-price appetizers (which are sometimes large enough to make a light meal for two people with a dessert) during "Happy Hour." Or you may find an ad for buy-one-get-one-free dinner specials. Some restaurants even advertise free meals for kids during certain hours or on particular days of the week.

Also, always ask for the restaurant's special of the day. It's often $2-$5 cheaper than the rest of the main menu items.

# Vacationing in Big Style with a Small Price Tag

Many families with limited means feel that a vacation isn't something they can afford. But a frugal family getaway is possible! This section explains how to plan ahead for a vacation, save and budget your resources wisely, and find less expensive alternatives than the more traditional airfare/hotel/theme park family trips.

## Saving for a family getaway

Finding money in the family's budget for a trip — large or small — can be challenging, but not impossible.

If you cut back on various smaller activities during the year, you can pocket the money you save and put it into your vacation fund. For example, instead of going to the theater for a first-run movie and spending $60 for tickets, popcorn, and drinks for the whole clan, rent a newly released video, pop your own popcorn, and have ice water or bargain cola to drink. The total for the evening now may be only $5 instead of $60. Take the money you just saved, put it in a special account — or even a hidden box in the back of a drawer — and you're $55 closer to your vacation savings goal.

Here are some other ideas for saving a little here and a little there to fund a family getaway:

- ✔ **Watch movies on television.** If you normally spend $10 on video rentals each week, watch a movie on TV and put the savings into your vacation fund.

- ✔ **Save all your loose change in a jar.** Every night, dig through your pockets, purse, and car for change. I know a woman who funds her family's vacation every year just from the change she's saved during the year. The family plans their vacation based upon what they can afford from the change jar. Maybe a camping trip to a local campground, a car trip to Yellowstone, a trip to visit relatives back East, or a even couple days at a major theme park. And all from loose change. Amazing!

- ✔ **Have a yard sale.** A one-day yard sale can often net an easy $100, but if you have a lot of stuff, consider having your garage sale over the course of four or five days. I know families who've made over $1,000 from one large multi-day garage sale. Collect castoffs and clutter from friends and neighbors. They'll probably be happy to pass on their junk to you rather than have to cart it to the dump themselves.

- ✔ **Sell some clothing at a consignment store.** Many consignment stores pay cash upfront for gently used, like-new clothing in current styles. Everything from baby gear, maternity wear, designer fashions, and sporting goods can find a new lease on life through consignment sales. See Chapter 16 for more information on consignment stores.

- ✔ **Babysit.** It's not just for teenagers anymore. Are any of the neighbor children in need of afterschool daycare for a couple of hours?

- ✔ **Work a part-time job during the school year.** A woman who works part time at the elementary school across the street from me uses her earnings for generous and often exotic vacations with her family during the summer. The hours she works at the school coincide nicely with the hours she has available while her own kids are in class each day.

- ✔ **Eat at home, skip the drive-through.** When you're seriously tempted to run out to the drive-through for a quick lunch or dinner, take the money you would've spent, put it in the vacation bank, and then fix something quick and cheap like peanut butter and jelly sandwiches, soup, or macaroni and cheese.

- ✔ **Cut back on "extras" to jump-start your vacation savings.** Maybe do away with cable television, dry cleaning, or professional carpet cleaning through the fall and winter to save for a nice summer vacation.

> ✔ **Tally up the money you save using coupons at the grocery store each week.** Sock that amount away in your vacation fund.
>
> ✔ **Wash your car yourself rather than take it through the auto-mated car wash.** The price difference goes into the vacation fund.

# Traveling on a few dollars a day

All travel seems to have the same basic expenses: food, accommodations, and fun activities. The following section discusses ways to save money on these basic travel and vacation-related expenses.

Traveling in a group can often get you accommodation discounts. Try taking a vacation with a couple of other families or your in-laws. Rent a big house at the ocean and have everyone split the cost. Stay at a lodge in the mountains and have it all to yourselves for a fun family reunion in the snow.

### Choosing frugal travel times

If possible, take your vacation during off times. For example, the months of May and September (in the Northern Hemisphere) are especially good times to travel because they're not as hot as July or August, they're not the prime tourist season, and the weather is usually nice. Save money, avoid crowds, and keep your sanity. What a deal!

Be aware that "off times" in your area may not be "off times" at your destination. The winter weather may be horrible in your small town in the mountains, but thousands of other travelers will be escaping their winter weather and heading to Hawaii, so it definitely won't be an off vacation time in Maui. Holidays and regular breaks from school (winter and spring break, summer vacation from school) are also usually expensive times for travel.

Many resorts offer a schedule of rates, showing their prime and off seasons. To maximize your money and enjoyment of available perks, make your reservation for the week just before the prime time starts or right after it ends.

Also, when picking a destination and time of year to visit, you may want to make sure the dates you choose aren't during local festivals or events, which usually run up hotel rates and make sightseeing a nightmare (unless you actually want to participate in the festival or event, of course).

# Saving on souvenirs

Bringing something tangible home to help you remember your vacation is always fun. My family collects ornaments from our various trips so that as we decorate our Christmas tree, we remember our vacations over the years. Usually the ornaments are simply inexpensive items like seashells, jewelry, or small toys hung with a string. Here are some other simple and fairly inexpensive souvenir ideas:

✔ Picture postcards, ticket stubs, or colorful brochures that you can add to your scrapbook or travel journal when you get home

✔ Bracelet charms of local landmarks, common animals, or major industries of the area

✔ Free paper placemats or coasters from restaurants

✔ Seashells or rocks

✔ Pressed leaves or flowers

✔ Local newspaper clippings or headlines with the date and name of the paper

✔ A calendar with photos of local attractions

✔ Family photographs taken at different landmarks or fun local activities

✔ Maps (city, state, country, region). If you travel often, keep a "map journal" of all the places you've been. Highlight the area you stayed and any attractions you visited.

By traveling on certain days, you may find discounts on airline tickets and hotels. Call around and check online to see when the cheapest departure dates are, and then plan your trip accordingly. See Chapter 15 for more money-saving transportation ideas.

## Looking for affordable accommodations

Accommodations are often one of the most expensive parts of any vacation. The following section contains money-saving options for finding accommodations and making reservations.

✔ **Camping:** Ah, camping . . . the all-American travel option. It brings to my mind images of sandy hotdogs, mosquitoes, and rocks under my sleeping bag. But camping also reminds me of fun, laughter, and saving money! If you have a tent or a trailer, you can often pull into a campground almost anywhere and find a spot to sleep for about $12 per night for the whole family. (**Remember:** National forest campgrounds are usually much cheaper than camping in a national park.) Also, many campground chains have special discount passes that are valid at various locations.

Another benefit of camping is being able to bring your own food along. You cut the cost of eating every single meal in restaurants while you're traveling. Be sure to get a nice camp stove and plenty of fuel, and take some time to practice setting up the stove, lighting it, and cooking on it before you take to the road.

✔ **Hotels:** If you plan to stay at a hotel, be sure to ask about special prices or seasonal deals when you call to make a reservation. Depending on when you're traveling, ask about:

- **Sunday night specials:** Sunday nights are often slow and hotels offer cheaper rates to encourage customers to stay.

- **Christmas shopper rates:** Hotels near downtown shopping in big cities sometimes offer special rates for people coming to town to shop for a day or two.

- **Super Bowl package deals:** If the hotel has a lounge with a big screen TV, you may find a great deal complete with accommodations, food, and beverages in the bar.

- **Anniversary, honeymoon, or birthday specials:** Some resorts and hotels offer packages including accomodations, food, entertainment, and a special celebration cake or dessert.

Call during the day when the office staff are on duty. They are more likely to know what special discounts or rates the hotel is offering. Nothing against the night crew, but they're often left out of the loop a bit because they're not physically present when the powers-that-be are working. Consequently they aren't necessarily up to date on current offers.

Call the hotel directly for your reservations. Those toll-free numbers for national chains don't know about any current updates at the hotel itself. The hotel's staff are the ones who know about the cancellation an hour ago or the planned construction that will make rooms on the east side of the hotel "a bit noisy" during your vacation.

If you're feeling adventurous, you can always travel without reservations. When you're ready to settle in for the night, stop at a hotel with a vacancy sign and make an offer on a room. If business is slow, they just may take it!

✔ **Home swaps:** Working out a casual house swap with friends or family who live in different cities or countries can be a great way to get a vacation somewhere else in the world for no more than the cost of airfare and food.

Are you thinking, "But my house isn't nice enough for a house swap"? Well, all you need is someplace clean and roomy enough for the family you're swapping with. If you have a second vacation home or cabin, it may be an ideal "swap" location because it's just sitting vacant for large portions of time. For more information on house swapping, visit www.homelink.org or do a Web search for house swapping.

✔ **Timeshares:** If you travel often, buying the right to use a condo or home during particular weeks of the year can be a good money-saving idea. (***Remember:*** If you buy a timeshare from the owner instead of from the resort or developer, you save substantially.) A timeshare is usually a condo with kitchen facilities, so you can shop at the local grocery and buy easy-to-fix foods that save big bucks over the cost of restaurant meals.

Timeshares often sound good upfront but they limit the places you can go on vacation. Also, in addition to your monthly payments on the timeshare, you may have to pay yearly maintenance fees that can get more and more expensive every year. On the up side, some organizations coordinate trading timeshares with other people around the world.

---

# To tent or to trailer

Which is better: A tent or a tent trailer? Obviously, a trailer is the right answer if you're talking about comfort, but the better choice actually depends a lot on your financial situation. We've found a tent to be the ideal frugal place to lay our pillow at night. If you have friends or family with a tent trailer, perhaps you can borrow or rent it from them inexpensively. Sleeping on the hard ground every night can be a little rough on the body, so if you don't have a trailer, consider investing in air mattresses or thin foam pads. The foam pads are nice because you don't have to blow them up when it's time for bed, and they don't puncture and go flat. Just roll them out under your sleeping bag, and it's sweet dreams for everyone.

### Finding frugal food while traveling

Don't eat all your meals in restaurants. Here are some ideas for
restaurant alternatives:

- ✔ If your hotel or motel offers a free breakfast, take full advantage of it.

- ✔ If you have a huge breakfast, eat lightly at lunch. Maybe just a
  piece of fruit and some cheese and crackers or an energy bar.

- ✔ Visit a local supermarket and pick up the ingredients for a
  picnic in a local park or even on a bench on the sidewalk.
  Make your own sandwiches, grab a bag of chips, and buy
  whatever soda is on sale.

- ✔ Because restaurants are usually more expensive at dinnertime, plan your main restaurant meal for lunchtime instead.
  The menus are similar but the cost is greatly reduced. Then
  choose a lighter, less-expensive dinnertime option.

- ✔ Carry some simple snacks with you so that you're not
  tempted to buy expensive snacks when your stomach starts
  rumbling. A small plastic bag of raisins, granola bars, or beef
  jerky is a lot less expensive than a $5 snack at a fast-food
  joint, convenience store, or local restaurant.

### Planning for fun, not flash

One of the most important ways to save money on vacation is to
under-plan activities. You don't have to see *everything*. Three major
activities per area or per city is a good average. Or no more than
two major activities per day (one in the morning, and then another
after lunch or in the evening). Spend the remainder of your time
just hanging out and wandering around. Or go swimming in the
campground or hotel pool. Taking time to stop and smell the roses
while traveling gives you a chance to enjoy "being" there rather
than being a blur of activity roaring by. A vacation should leave you
rested and refreshed, not aching for a vacation from your vacation!

Instead of planning your trip around expensive tourist spots, plan
around cheap — or free! — activities: hiking, walking on the beach,
flying a kite, making sand castles, having a campfire, star-gazing,
fishing, crabbing, or swimming.

Don't make shopping in the malls or tourist towns one of your
main activities. Just by staying out of the shops, you save big
money on your trip.

## Don't gamble your vacation savings away

If you're vacationing in a gambling hub like Las Vegas, Reno, or Atlantic City, set a daily gambling limit. As with other budgeted activities, spend only that amount and no more. If you tell yourself you can gamble $20 on Friday, spend that amount only — and then *stop!* Consider gambling an entertainment expense rather than a way to recoup your vacation money.

A friend and her husband went to a horse track just for the fun of it. They budgeted a maximum amount they could each spend for the entire day, and then they just had fun checking out the horses, watching the races, and collecting their winnings (or not, which was usually the case). The experience of a day at the racetrack was enjoyable, not all that expensive, and they didn't feel bad for not winning because winning was never their goal.

## *Staying at home for the time of your life*

Looking for a fun vacation close to home? Well, just stay home! No, I don't mean stay inside the four walls of your house day after day. Get out and see the sights outside your own backdoor! I often take for granted all the tourist spots around me. Most large cities have some sort of tourist attractions or something people from out of town always want to see first. But how often do people who live there actually go to the tourist spots? I can't even remember the last time I went to the observation platform at the top of Seattle's Space Needle or drove to Paradise on Mount Rainier, even though those are two of the main activities that attract visitors to Seattle.

Gather tourist brochures and contact the local Chamber of Commerce just like you'd do if you were visiting another area for the first time. Make out a daily itinerary of activities and destinations, get up every morning, have a quick breakfast at home before you leave, and then go out on the town from morning 'til night.

By staying at home and sleeping in your own bed, you save money on transportation costs (airfare, car rentals, and so on), lodging, and at least one of each day's meals. By saving big bucks on the more expensive aspects of a vacation, you free up money for doing fun things like riding a ferry, visiting the art museum, going to the zoo, or eating lunch at an open-air market. Also, you can lower your stress levels by being better rested. No collapsing in a strange bed after 9 hours of driving, only to rise 6 hours later to hit a theme park for 12 more "fun-filled" hours. Plus, if the kids bicker, you can threaten to take them home . . . and mean it.

# Chapter 11

# Frugal Holiday Fun
# Year 'Round

- - - - - - - - - - - - - - - - - - - - - - - - - - - - - - - - - - - - - - - - - -

### In This Chapter

▶ Planning for the holidays

▶ Celebrating annual holidays on a tight budget

▶ Enjoying birthdays without breaking the bank

- - - - - - - - - - - - - - - - - - - - - - - - - - - - - - - - - - - - - - - - - -

*H*olidays come around at the same time year after year, but somehow they always sneak up on me. I used to ask myself every year, "Why, oh why, am I so surprised it's Christmas again? It never changes. I should've planned ahead." Sigh. It's easy to reprimand yourself in the middle of the holiday rush. The trick is learning to think year-round about those regularly occurring events so that you can stock up during sales throughout the year on gifts, decorations, wrapping supplies, cards, and party favors.

In this chapter, I share ideas for saving money during various annual holidays such as Christmas, Halloween, Easter, and birthdays. By examining personal attitudes and priorities surrounding yearly holidays, you can more easily control festive spending sprees.

## Finding the Path from Insanity to Blissful Celebration

Does thinking about holiday celebrations send you running for cover, looking for a safe hiding place for your checkbook and credit cards? If so, you're not alone. Many people find themselves unwillingly caught up in a holiday spending spree of unbelievable proportions, especially during October, November, and December.

Holidays that originally developed as celebrations of life, spiritual beliefs, and simple pleasures now lead us to worship that dreaded modern god: Consumerism. There's got to be a better way!

The following sections examine some simple ways to add joy back into various holiday celebrations that have become full of consumer-driven insanity and frantic living.

## Exploring holiday priorities and attitudes

Most people don't want to incessantly acquire more stuff, but they honestly don't know how to find a better way to observe traditional holidays.

Take time to examine your own expectations and true desires for each holiday season. For example, decide how many gifts to give your children at Christmas or Hanukkah, how important it is for you to spend the 4th of July with all the extended family (49 cousins and all), and whether the Easter bunny should bring a whole pile of gifts this year or just a few colored eggs. The sooner you start thinking about these things, the more easily you can make changes in your spending patterns, celebration plans, and time commitments.

In order to get a strong sense of what's important to everyone in your family about each holiday, have each family member spend a little time a month or two before the big day thinking about the perfect holiday. Then sit down together as a family and answer the following questions:

- What do you want to do to celebrate?

- Where do you want to go?

- Who do you want to invite to share it with you?

- What do you want to eat?

- What role do you want gifts play in the festivities?

- Do you want to be indoors or out?

These questions don't have a right or wrong answer. They are just an opportunity for each individual to see what his or her deepest desires are for each holiday your family celebrates annually. Share your dream holidays with each other. Discuss practical ways to incorporate some of the shared ideas into your current holiday traditions.

Children often internalize the marketing messages around them and believe that holidays equal extravagant gifts and lavish decorations. If the family is running madly from one holiday activity to another for weeks on end, a small child can feel overwhelmed and lost in the shuffle. A pile of presents can become a substitute in their minds for what they really want: time with you. As a parent, you have the opportunity to provide your children with deeper, more enduring holiday celebrations. By focusing on things like family togetherness and traditions, gifts can end up taking a back seat in the festivities.

## Budgeting and setting limits

Budgeting for birthdays and other gift-giving occasions can put a big dent in the family coffers. My family just passed birthday season around our house. More than half of us all have our birthdays clumped together within weeks of each other. Do you have times of the year like that where you seem to be buying a gift every week? These times can be a real bummer for the budget. If you have regular gift-giving occasions every year, figure out the number of these occasions, multiply by the amount you want to spend on each gift, and then add that number into your family's yearly budget. Divide the total by twelve if you want to know how much your regular gift budget is for each month.

To keep from overspending, limit yourself to a specific dollar amount or a set number of people to buy gifts for. For example, you may decide not to spend more than $10 on birthday gifts for each of your five nieces this year, or to limit holiday gift giving to just your immediate family. Maybe you can decide together with your significant other not to buy expensive gifts, flowers, or candy on Valentine's Day and make your own homemade gifts or cards instead. Or agree to cook a nice meal together on your anniversary instead of eating at a fancy restaurant.

## Putting yourself into planning mode

I probably sound like a broken record if you're reading this book from cover to cover, but in order to save money on anything, you need to plan ahead. (Panic nearly always pushes people into paying top dollar.) Saving money on gift-giving at the holidays is no different. Start thinking about gift ideas (such as birthday presents and Father's Day gifts) immediately after Hanukkah and Christmas. Most stores start marking down all gift items to a fraction of their original price on December 26. Stock up! And then throughout the year as you find sale-priced gift items, stock up! For example, if the power saw your husband asked for but didn't get for Christmas goes on sale December 26th, buy it and give it to him as a birthday gift in February.

Keep a box just for storing future holiday gift items for your immediate family as you stock up during the year. You may want to label the box "old blankets" so the kids (or hubby!) don't peek.

The day after every major commercial holiday (Easter, Mother's Day, Fourth of July, and so on) you can find drastic markdowns on all holiday-related items such as decorations and gift-wrapping supplies. Floral wrapping paper on sale after Mother's Day can be used to wrap birthday or wedding gifts. Plain red paper from Christmas can be used at Valentine's Day. Just make sure the items don't have holiday-specific labeling. Giving a birthday gift wrapped in paper that proclaims "Happy Mother's Day!" may not go over quite the way you'd hoped.

---

# Exploring alternative gift ideas

Rather than buying more items to clutter up our family's and friends' homes, many people are starting to give alternative gifts that are more in keeping with their personal priorities and the spirit of each season. Be careful of the feelings of others, though. Some people would rather receive a cheap and tacky store-bought knick-knack than a gift acknowledgment from a charity. Know your friends and family so that you can lovingly give a gift from your heart to theirs that they appreciate.

Some alternative gift ideas are:

✔ Donate your time, energy, or resources to a charity in your friend's name. Then drop him a nice note telling him that you donated your time as his gift.

Be sure you're donating to a cause your friend or family member believes in and cares about. One of my friends received a gift acknowledgment from a political action group he never would've supported himself. A friend had given the gift, but instead of feeling blessed and honored by the gift, my friend felt a bit angry and used. It was almost an anti-gift.

✔ Organize a canned food, clothing, or toy drive in your neighborhood, school, or place of worship. Send a note to the gift recipient telling her you've donated your time in this way.

✔ Write a long, heartfelt letter to your friends and family members.

✔ Give a gift of time: visit a shut-in, check in regularly on your elderly neighbor, spend time baking with your nephew, take your niece to the park.

✔ Put together a homemade coupon book of personalized jobs you'll do for the recipient: mow the lawn, give a back rub, take him shopping, and so on.

For additional frugal gift ideas, see Chapter 18.

# Cutting Back without Settling for Less Celebration

When I think of holiday over-spending, I usually think of the December holidays and all the expensive gifts, activities, and decorations. But the other holidays can take a huge chunk out of the family's yearly budget as well. For example, Halloween is often considered the second-highest consumer buying time after the Christmas and Hanukkah season.

Is it possible to have festive holiday celebrations without dipping into savings or running up a credit card balance? I think so. The following sections examine some ways to do just that. Use these ideas to jump-start your creativity and see where your imagination takes you!

## Will you be my Valentine?

Take advantage of after-Christmas sales to stock up on red and white items for decorations and treats for Valentine's Day. A friend of mine buys bags of red-and-green holiday candies after Christmas, and then she sorts the colors into two separate bags — the red candies for Valentine's Day and the green ones for Saint Patrick's Day.

If you're looking for creative yet frugal ways to say, "I love you," to your sweetheart, see Chapter 17.

## Here comes Peter Cottontail! Easter decorating and gift ideas

I love the Easter season: warm spring weather, newborn bunnies, freshly cut tulips, and little girls in new dresses and Easter bonnets. If only those store-bought springtime goodies, like Easter baskets for the kids and decorations for our home, weren't so awfully expensive. But with a little creativity, you can enjoy the season frugally.

### Decorating an Easter Tree

I like to make an Easter Tree to decorate a corner of the living room. I get a nicely shaped branch (there aren't any leaves yet at this time of year) with multiple smaller branches, and cut it to the size I want. Then I spray-paint the branch white, and after the paint's dry, I place the thick end of the branch into a bucket filled with sand. I decorate the tree with a string of white Christmas lights and hang small Easter ornaments I've collected over the years at garage sales. My kids like to make their own ornaments out of homemade clay or baking dough. My youngest traces seasonal cookie cutters (eggs, bunnies, flowers) onto construction paper, and then she colors in the shapes with markers and glitter pens. Punch a hole, add a ribbon, and it's good to go.

### Making inexpensive Easter baskets

I look forward to giving Easter baskets to my children, but I really don't enjoy the high prices of those expensive premade baskets in stores. So I make my own and fill them with treats that I accumulate throughout the year — crayons, bubbles, chopsticks, stickers, and little cookies and candies.

But even homemade baskets can get costly when you start adding in the costs of plastic grass for filler, the basket itself, the candy, and assorted trinkets and toys. I've found that setting a spending limit helps. I try to fill each basket for under five dollars, and then have fun being creative enough to keep within my basket budget.

Quality wicker baskets can be reused year after year (a nice tradition in itself) and at other times during the year for decoration or for storing small items. You can also reuse the decorative grass from year to year. But if you don't want to invest in wicker baskets, check out the following list for inexpensive basket alternatives:

- **Paper bags:** Decorate with pictures or stickers of bunnies, eggs, or flowers.
- **Easter bonnets:** If you're going to purchase an Easter bonnet for your daughter, turn it upside down and fill it with goodies.
- **Inexpensive, colorful plastic sand pails:** Include a shovel and sand mold.
- **Plastic storage containers:** Reuse to store toys, games, socks, or childhood treasures.
- **Novelty pillowcase:** This is an especially good choice if you're giving a large gift or stuffed animal that may not fit well in a traditional basket.

Finding a frugal basket is half the battle, but now you need to fill it frugally. Here are some simple ideas:

- **Plastic eggs that can be refilled every year:** The week after Halloween, many stores have bags of candy on sale for half price (or less). I purchase several bags of family favorites at these bargain prices, and then put the unopened bags in the freezer. Frozen candy keeps just fine until you're ready to pack the plastic eggs at Easter. Also, bags of fake bugs, dinosaurs, plastic rings, and tiny dolls make great egg fillers, and you can often find them at dollar stores for a dollar a bag.

✔ **Homemade candy, cookies, and crispy rice treats:** Color with pastel food coloring and wrap individually in colored cellophane. You can even mold the crispy rice treats with your hands into egg shapes.

✔ **Sidewalk chalk eggs:** Mix together 1 cup plaster, ½ cup water and several drops of food coloring. Pour the mixture into empty egg carton sections. When dry, peel away the carton and hot glue two sections together at the center to form a complete egg.

✔ **Homemade coloring books:** Find simple Easter-related clip-art on your computer or on the Internet, and print the pictures out in black and white for homemade coloring sheets.Or print out several and staple them together for a custom-made coloring book. For a collection of high quality, artistic coloring pages (including many Easter-themed pages), go to `http://familycrafts.about.com/library/blcolorbk.htm`.

✔ **Audiotapes of you reading their favorite books aloud:** This is a fun and much appreciated gift your kids can treasure for years to come. Be sure to include a signal for the child to turn the page if they'll be reading along with you. These tapes may even become treasured family heirlooms. A woman I know still has tapes of her grandmother reading aloud from 30 years ago.

# Easter ideas for older kids and teens

Even older kids appreciate finding something left by the Easter Bunny, but sometimes cute little egg-shaped toys and candy chicks aren't grown-up enough for their maturing tastes. Here are a few easy ideas for the older set:

✔ **A make-up container:** Include sample sizes of soap, perfume, lip gloss, and nail polish.

✔ **A fishing tackle box:** Add a few lures, hooks, bobbers, or other fishing supplies.

✔ **A personal popcorn bowl:** Put a bag of gourmet popcorn and a gift certificate for a movie rental inside.

✔ **A new purse:** Throw in some lip gloss, eye shadow, a key ring, or any other small necessities.

# Honoring Father's Day and Mother's Day

Probably the single most popular gift parents receive on these holidays from their grown children is a long, chatty phone call. Someone told me recently that Mother's Day is the busiest day of the year for long distance phone calls. And Father's Day is the busiest day for *collect* calls. Hmmm . . . if that's true, I probably owe Dad a phone call or two on my own dime! But if you live close enough to actually reach out and touch your mom or dad in person, what can you do to brighten their day? Read on for some frugal gift ideas!

## Celebrating Dad

If you're looking for something fun and meaningful for Dad to help celebrate his day, consider the following inexpensive gift ideas:

✔ Share one of his favorite hobbies with him for the day. Take him fishing on his favorite lake or river or play a round of golf at an off time when the course fees are cheaper.

✔ Relieve him of some of his chores. Mow the lawn, clean the gutters, trim the trees, weed the yard, or spread bark.

A lot of dads just don't get enough time to visit with their kids, so the opportunity to be together is a welcome treat.

## Celebrating Mom

I asked the mothers around me what they wanted to receive more than anything else from their families for Mother's Day. I was surprised that almost all of them gave some variation of wanting time: time to themselves, time for pursuing personal hobbies, time for a quiet, relaxing bubble bath (without someone banging on the door, desperately needing Mom's attention), quality (and quantity!) time to spend with their family, or time to enjoy life without pressures, deadlines, expectations — or meals to fix.

Here are a few additional ideas these women gave of gifts they'd love to receive for Mother's Day (but usually never do):

✔ A whole day to do whatever they want whether it's shopping with friends, reading a stack of magazines, getting lost in a good book, or lounging in their pajamas until noon.

✔ A manicure, spa treatment, hair appointment, or facial.

✔ A professional massage (or even just a foot rub from a loving husband).

✔ Dinner out at their favorite restaurant with all the kids on their best behavior, or dinner alone with Dad and the kids safely at home with a babysitter.

✔ A long, uninterrupted nap.

# Enjoying frightfully affordable Halloween fun

Halloween costumes don't have to scare the living daylight out of your budget. Even a simple homemade gypsy or hobo costume can be loads of frightening fun, especially if the children design it themselves. Be sure to check thrift stores — and even your own garage, attic, and closets — for supplies. You don't need to buy expensive costumes. Part of the fun of the holiday can be seeing what creative ideas you and your kids can come up with from things around the house.

## Frugal costume ideas

The following inexpensive costume ideas can be made from things found around the house or at thrift stores:

✔ **Ghost:** This is an old standby, but still a hit with the younger set. Use a permanent marker to draw some details on a sheet, like spider webs or fake blood stains. If you add an old chain or two to drag on the ground and tie a large white handkerchief around the top of the child's head and under his jaw, you've created Jacob Marley from Dickens' *A Christmas Carol.*

✔ **Tacky Tourist:** Hawaiian shirt, sunglasses, hat, camera, layer of white sunblock on the nose (just use white face paint), large bag or purse, and maps or tourist brochures peeking out of a few pockets.

✔ **Soldier or Hunter:** Camouflage clothing, green and brown face paint splashed on randomly, a canteen, backpack, compass, or whatever you have around that can complete the look.

✔ **Ladybug:** Dress your child in a pair of black leggings or tights and a plain long-sleeved black shirt. Remove the arms from a large red sweatshirt (bought at a thriftstore or garage sale) and pin, glue, or draw large black dots all over and a stripe down the middle of the sweatshirt. You can also fashion antennae with black pipe cleaners.

✔ **Dalmatian:** Begin with a white sweat suit, then pin on black spots made from either felt or construction paper. Make black floppy ears from construction paper or black felt and attach to a headband or a white baseball cap.

- ✔ **Rock Star:** Throw on anything glittery or wild; things don't have to match. Spike or over-tease the hair, maybe spray on a little temporary hair paint, add some over-sized jewelry, a pair of dark glasses, and you're all set!

- ✔ **Birthday Gift:** Take an old box big enough for your child to "wear" and cut a hole in the top of the box for her head and two holes in each side for her arms. Wrap the box with gift wrap, attach a ribbon, and tie curled ribbon or a big bow in her hair. Cute, simple, and very cheap!

- ✔ **Tooth Fairy:** If your child has an old pair of fairy or angel wings from a previous costume or Christmas pageant, add a fluffy, cute skirt and blouse, and then tie old toothbrushes all over her clothes with dental floss. You don't have to use real toothbrushes, though. To save money, cut toothbrush and large tooth shapes out of paper and decorate with markers. You can also make the fairy wings out of aluminum foil fashioned over wire coat hangers that you've shaped into wings.

- ✔ **Professional "Whatever":** If you or someone you know wears a uniform at work, let your child dress up as that person. Possible ideas include a doctor, a nurse, a baker, a cook, a waitress, a lumberjack, an athlete, or a junior executive.

- ✔ **Scarecrow:** Use an old flannel shirt with holes in it, old ragged jeans, and a straw hat, and then tie or stitch a bit of decorative straw-colored raffia to the shirt and pants openings.

- ✔ **Mummy:** Attach ragged strips of cloth ripped from an old white sheet to a white T-shirt and pants. Or wrap the child lightly in surgical gauze if you find some on sale or at the dollar store.

You can adapt different colored sweat suits to become almost any type of animal you can imagine: a pig, cow, unicorn, or kitten. Just attach any extra finishing pieces (spots, stripes, arms, tails, horn) to the sweat suit, add any required head gear (horns, antennae), and your little goblin's good to go!

If you're due to buy your child new pajamas, purchase ones that double as costumes like super heroes, animals, or princesses.

### Keeping the "treat" in trick-or-treat

When the neighborhood goblins show up at your door, how can you keep from forking over the family farm in treats and goodies?

- ✔ Put the treats in a big bowl or basket, and then pass the candy out yourself rather than letting the kids grab their own. That way you can limit them to one or two small candies rather than a large handful — some of those preteen ghouls at the door have mighty big hands!

✔ Candy bars keep well in the freezer for several months, so if you see a sale during the summer on bags of favorite treats, stock up in anticipation of Halloween.

✔ Buy trick-or-treat candy your family enjoys, so if you have any leftovers, you can add it to your kids' lunchboxes or use for occasional treats.

✔ Give alternative treats rather than the traditional candy and gum. Many dollar stores have bags full of inexpensive toys and plastic figurines for a dollar or less.

### Decorating to greet the ghouls and ghosts

I know many families who spend nearly as much on their Halloween decorations each year as they do on December holiday décor. One way to save in this area is to grow pumpkins and ornamental gourds in your backyard. Your kids will get quite a thrill watching their very own pumpkin plant grow a future jack-o'lantern or the filling for the family's holiday pie.

I have friends who grow corn in their garden every year, so I always ask for a dozen dry corn stalks after the growing season is finished to use for decorating my front doorway. I also string white Christmas lights around the front door and among the corn stalks and the pumpkins and gourds scattered on the ground. Then I throw handfuls of colorful autumn leaves around the entryway to add more seasonal color.

# Keeping a costume box

Designate a box in the garage for storing potential costuming material and props you stumble across throughout the year. Then have a contest to see who can make the most creative costume out of the contents of the box. Potential costume materials include:

| | |
|---|---|
| old sheets | an old suit |
| aluminum foil | a bathrobe |
| boxes | pieces of felt |
| old clothes | chains |
| large white shirts | jewelry |
| newspaper | hats |
| Army surplus | construction paper |

We also like to make our own decorative scarecrow out of old clothes stuffed with wadded up newspaper. The scarecrow's head is just a plain brown grocery bag stuffed with newspaper with a face drawn on with markers. We set the scarecrow in an old wooden chair next to the front door, and he acts as the doorman, greeting the ghouls and goblins. One year, we made a whole family of scarecrows using children's clothing and baby items for the scare-kids. We set the scarecrow-family all together on a hay bale, and they looked great!

By decorating in a general autumnal décor rather than a specifically spooky look, we can keep the adornments in place throughout October and November. It saves on Thanksgiving decorations, too. I frequently hear from parents of preschoolers how much they appreciate the well-lit, cheerful, and inviting décor at my house each Halloween.

If you want to add a bit of spooky atmosphere to entertain the trick or treaters, have your kids make their own audiotape of scary sounds. Let them get creative looking for squeaky doors to record on tape. They'll love making their eeriest howls, evilest laughs, and yowling like a banshee.

## No Charlie Brown Thanksgiving, please!

Thanksgiving is one of my favorite holidays. Not only does our family spend quality time together without the distraction and expense of gifts, but we also focus on the good things in our lives and establish our family's priorities. This can lead to saving money down the road as we shift our focus to people, activities, and relationships rather than the accumulation of stuff, stuff, and more stuff.

I've found that a sure cure for my children's greedy gimmies, or my husband's and my "I'm-so-broke" blues, is to focus on being thankful for the many good things in our lives. Yes, even in the middle of hard times, you always have something to be thankful for. Whether you keep a gratitude diary or a Thanksgiving jar throughout the year (both are described in the "Keeping a record of thankfulness" sidebar in this chapter), or just spend time around the Thanksgiving holiday to focus on the year's blessings, thankfulness is a valuable trait to develop in yourself and your kids.

# Keeping a record of thankfulness

A *gratitude diary* is an excellent way to focus on the good things in life — instead of just seeing the negative things that happen to all of us. Grab a blank book or small spiral notebook and list at least two things you're grateful for each day. Some days you may write pages full of excitement and gratitude. Other days, you may have to work a little harder to think of things to be thankful for — but even acknowledging that you woke up this morning still breathing can at least turn your attention to things you have to be thankful for in your life.

Another way to keep a record of things you're thankful for is to keep a *Thanksgiving jar.* A family in our church keeps a jar in their kitchen throughout the year. Whenever anything fun or noteworthy happens, they write it on a slip of paper and stick it in the jar. By Thanksgiving Day, the jar is filled with assorted happenings that they read aloud as a family on the holiday itself. It's a wonderful chance to remember and rejoice over the important events from the previous year — everything from a visit with Grandma to a neighbor's new baby to little Suzy learning to ride a bicycle.

### Feeding the family without starving the bank account

Probably the single greatest expense of the Thanksgiving holiday is preparing all the food for the family and friends converging on your house. To save money, suggest that each person or family group attending the festivities bring one food item that represents their favorite part of the Thanksgiving meal. Have people tell you in advance what they're bringing, though, or you may end up with three different versions of sweet potato casserole.

Watch for sales on whole frozen turkeys throughout the year and don't hesitate to buy your holiday bird earlier in the year if you find a great price. Turkeys keep well in the freezer for several months.

I like to make as many side dishes as possible ahead of time and store them in the freezer for the big day. Some of my favorite Thanksgiving items to freeze ahead are candied yams and, believe it or not, mashed potatoes. The mashed potatoes separate a bit in the freezing and thawing process, but if you stir them well as they're reheating, they recombine beautifully.

For other ideas on saving money on your Thanksgiving dinner, check out Part II for general food-savings ideas that can be applied anytime of year, holiday or not.

### Decorating a Thanksgiving Tree

Making a Thanksgiving Tree is one of our favorite family traditions and helps us focus on the good things in our lives. Here are the easy instructions to make a Thanksgiving Tree of your own:

- ✔ Cut a tree trunk and bare branches out of a large sheet of black craft paper.

- ✔ Tape the tree to the dining room wall or some other spot in the house seen easily and regularly by family members.

- ✔ Cut out individual leaves from craft paper in autumn colors (red, orange, yellow, brown).

- ✔ As you think of something or someone you're thankful for, write the item, event, or person's name onto one of the leaves.

- ✔ Tape the leaf to the tree branches.

If you really want to get fancy and reuse the Thanksgiving Tree from year to year, cover the tree and leaves with clear adhesive paper. You can use a dry-erase marker and wipe off the leaves after Thanksgiving so that your family can start fresh again with next year's Thanksgiving list.

We always try to put the Thanksgiving Tree in place by mid-November so our family has at least a full week to add leaves to the tree. By Thanksgiving Day, the tree is full with the names of people, events, and things we're thankful for.

At a teacher's supply store, I saw a large poster of a turkey with large individual tail feathers that could be written on, cut out, and attached to the bird. You can use a Thanksgiving Turkey in the same way as the Thanksgiving Tree mentioned previously. Cover it with clear adhesive paper before cutting out the turkey and tail feathers, and it can be reused year after year.

## Keeping Christmas and Hanukkah from breaking the budget

The December holidays are huge money-makers for the retailers of the world. They're also huge debt-makers for the shoppers of the world as they try to finance their "dream holiday" — a Christmas or Hanukkah filled with vast arrays of food, gifts, and expensive activities. But "holiday giving" and "frugal living" don't have to be polar opposites if you follow the easy ideas in this section.

# Dealing with mandatory office gift exchanges

Those mandatory office gifts can really cause havoc during the winter holidays. Who really needs another $5 coffee mug or snowflake-shaped candleholder? I know I sure don't.

Mix things up this year — have everyone who participates in the annual office gift exchange donate the designated gift amount to a local charity or food bank. Or if people really want the fun of giving something their fellow office workers can use and enjoy, try a Christmas ornament exchange instead of buying general gifts. Ornaments are gifts that keep on giving every year when you trim the tree. Mark the ornament with the date and your name so the recipient remembers who gave the ornament, and when.

Or have a White Elephant exchange — everyone picks out a funny, useful, or completely goofy item that's lying around unused and unloved at home. (White Elephant exchanges are more of a gag gift exchange and a time to laugh together than an actual "gift" exchange per se.) Don't we all have a few of those completely tacky touristy-type joke gifts hiding in a box in the garage or back of a closet somewhere that we just don't have the heart to throw out because Aunt Lula-belle brought it specially to us from the Islands? You can give that poor unused item a new lease on life.

A fun office gift idea, which also contributes to the community, is a childhood toy exchange. You draw a name out of a hat, and then purchase a new toy you think the person would've wanted to receive or play with as a child. Be sure to set a spending limit (a reasonable amount for each participant to spend is $5-10 per gift). After everyone has the fun of seeing what someone in the office thinks he or she was like as a child, donate the toys to a children's charity or a homeless shelter.

Check out books from the library about holiday celebrations in other countries. Many of these traditions include simple decorations like greenery from your yard, homemade decorations, candles, homemade Advent wreaths, and inexpensive food decorations.

## Creating homemade wrapping paper

My kids and I like to make our own wrapping paper out of brown paper grocery bags, inexpensive kitchen sponges (the softer, the better), and craft paint. Use scissors to cut the sponges into simple holiday shapes (snowmen, trees, stars). Cut open the paper bags and spread them flat on newspapers with the plain insides of the bags facing up. Dip the sponges into red, green, or white paint and then sponge-paint randomly over the open paper bags. After the paint has dried completely, use the paper for wrapping your holiday gifts. Tied with inexpensive brown twine, this makes a rustic and beautiful gift-wrapping idea — plus it's a fun holiday family activity, too.

### Decking the halls with inexpensive décor

A few strategically placed decorations can have a dramatic effect without sending you into debt. A seasonal decoration on the front door, a tree in the living room, a centerpiece on the dining table, and a few fragrant candles scattered around the house can set the mood just as well as — and definitely less expensively than — animated Santas dancing in every window.

A stack of multi-colored craft paper from the supermarket can provide hours of decorating fun for the entire family. Cut out ornaments, fold paper snowflakes, decorate boxes, and make paper chains. These may seem like simplistic projects, but young children love making colorful paper creations.

Here's another inexpensive decorating idea my family enjoys: If you have evergreen trees in your yard, cut off a few branches about two to three feet in length. Tie the thick ends of the branches together with strong cord and make your own holiday swag for the front door. Decorate with a big red bow and a couple of jingling bells if you have some around the house.

# Celebrating Birthdays on a Budget

Birthdays are a fact of life, and whether you are planning the parties or coming up with frugal gift ideas, birthday celebrations can put a real crimp in any frugal family's budget.

Family birthdays can be as simple as having your extended family over for cake and ice cream. Just spending time with those you love is often enough to make even the simplest birthday celebration special.

## Cutting gift costs: Keeping a birthday box

The single most helpful thing I've done to cut down on the cost of gifts for my kids' friends is to keep a Birthday Box (this is a different box than the one described earlier in this chapter because the gifts kept in the Birthday Box are for friends, not immediate family members). I fill the Birthday Box with gift items (such as toys, books, and clothes) and assorted birthday cards, wrapping paper pieces, and gift bags I've purchased throughout the year during clearance sales. I also add in things I find new and still in the original wrapping at thrift stores and garage sales. When party invitations arrive in the mail, all my family has to do is go "shopping" in my closet, rather than making an expensive trip to the mall or toy store.

Before I started keeping the Birthday Box, I was easily spending about $15 per gift for my children's friends, including wrapping paper, ribbon, and a card. Now the cost per gift is closer to $2 — a much easier sum on my poor budget, for sure!

## Hosting a frugal birthday bash

Hosting a birthday party for your significant other or one of your children can easily become a huge financial expense. By the time you add in the cost of decorations, food, games, and party favors, you can spend over $100. And if you hire an entertainer, look out! Credit card debt, here we come!

The best advice I can give on this front is, once again, to keep everything simple. Here are some examples:

- ✔ Print out your own invitations on your computer.

- ✔ Bake the birthday cake yourself rather than pay the big bucks for the local baker to do it for you.

- ✔ Collect party favors from thrift stores or garage sales. Or make party favors out of pictures of the party guests having fun at the party. Use a camera that takes instant photos, or a digital camera you can immediately hook up to your computer to print out photos, and make picture frames for the photos using cardboard decorated with ribbon.

## Catering to the kids

From decorating the cake to entertaining the bunch, frugal birthday fun can be had by all for a small price if you plan ahead and get creative. Here are some ways to cut corners without crimping on the fun:

- ✔ Have the kids do a fun activity as they're arriving at the party. Here are a couple ideas.

    - **Gift bags:** Give the kids brown paper lunch bags and let them decorate their own gift bag with crayons, markers, and stickers.

- **Festive fedoras:** Give the kids paper plates, pieces of cardboard, colorful construction paper, ribbon, and assorted odds and ends — and let them go to town making and decorating their own party hats. Even making folded paper hats out of the comic section of the newspaper can be lots of fun.

✔ Bake birthday cupcakes instead of a layered cake or sheet cake; then let the kids decorate their individual cakes themselves, using sprinkles, candy, licorice whips, and so on. They'll actually be happier eating something they had a hand in creating. If you make a layer cake, remember that kids are just as happy with candies and sprinkles on their cake as they are with their favorite cartoon characters elaborately drawn in icing.

✔ Make your own party favors: homemade play dough, bubbles, even small bags with a colorful string and a handful of beads for a do-it-yourself necklace or bracelet. Cookie cutters, sunglasses, lip gloss, or nail polish from the dollar store or thrift store make great party favors, too.

✔ Choose a children's picture book to read to the kids. After the story, have everyone choose a character from the story, use face paint to make each other up as that character, and then act the story out. The face painting itself makes a great party favor.

✔ Schedule a tour at a local factory or restaurant — it's fun, educational, and usually free.

# Chapter 12

# Celebrating Special Occasions, Frugal-Style

In This Chapter
▶ Finding creative ways to celebrate frugally
▶ Planning wonderful weddings
▶ Creating special baby or bridal showers with what you have on hand

**Y**ou're helping your best friend plan her wedding and she's working with a limited budget, or your boss decides you get the "privilege" of hosting a dinner party for the department heads and their guests. Dinner parties and weddings aren't usually the most frugal activities, but by planning ahead and anticipating needs, your budget can still stay on track throughout these festivities. This chapter helps you plan wisely for all those fun and frugal special events, including hosting your own parties and get-togethers.

## Planning a Frugal Party

The simplest and most important trick for saving time, effort, and money on a party is to plan ahead. And the best way to plan ahead is to make a party planner — a small notebook or three-ring binder used to keep track of all the big (and small!) details of your event. The notebook also helps you stick to a predetermined budget. Start putting together your planning notebook at least a month in advance if you have enough forewarning about the event. The planning notebook can also be used for spur-of-the-moment get-togethers to ensure you don't forget any important details, but you just have to adjust the time frame accordingly.

Use notebook page dividers to separate your party notebook into the following six sections:

- ✔ Basics (date, time, and location)
- ✔ Budget
- ✔ Guest List
- ✔ Menu
- ✔ Preparation Lists
- ✔ Decorations

Within each section of your handy-dandy party notebook, include a timeline of the steps needed to accomplish everything for that aspect of your party. Yep, everything! Break each section down into the weeks, days, and hours before your event (for example: "send invitations three weeks before the party," "set the meat out to thaw the morning of the party," and so on). Details tend to be overlooked in the party-prep rush, but you'll be on top of everything and your whole shindig will come off without a hitch if you plan ahead. Planning may seem like a lot of work, but believe me, you save time, energy, and lots of money in the long run.

## Getting down to the basics

The Basics section of your party notebook lists the details of your party: the date, time, and location. Include a page with detailed instructions to the party location and draw or print out a simple map if necessary. You don't want your guests wandering aimlessly around town looking for your house! You can find printable street maps and driving directions online at www.mapquest.com. When you're ready to prepare your invitations, all the information you need is easily accessible and in one place.

 To save money on invitations, print your own cards or flyers on your computer, or make your own cards with inexpensive card-stock and rubber stamps bought on sale at the craft store. You can save on postage by hand-delivering invitations to neighbors or people you see regularly. Also, e-mail invitations are acceptable for casual parties, plus you hear back from your friends more quickly than with traditional phone or mail RSVPs.

## Preparing a budget

Party budgets get out of control easily, so take the time to set a budget before you start shopping. Be sure to list both the items you need to buy and an estimate of what you can afford to spend on each item. Keeping that set amount in your mind goes a long way toward keeping your party from breaking the bank. Keep a running total of the expenses in your planning notebook as you shop and prepare so that you can gauge your spending and know when you need to cut corners to keep on budget.

Impulse buys are as common in party planning and shopping as they are in the cookie aisle at the grocery store. Always shop from a detailed list. Otherwise, you may give in to temptation and blow your budget — those corn-shaped corncob holders would be a hit at the barbecue, but are they necessary?

Check out the following budget-saving ideas:

- ✔ Use the good china and silverware (if you have it) instead of buying paper plates, disposable tableware, foam cups, and so on. You have a bit more cleaning up to do — you can't really toss the fine china in the trash as you're clearing the room — but using the nice dishes, silver, and glassware brings a touch of elegance to your gathering . . . and saves big money, too!

- ✔ Bake the cake yourself or serve sliced homemade snack cakes (pumpkin bread, zuchinni cake, and so on) instead of ordering a personalized cake from the grocery store.

- ✔ If you entertain frequently, invest in some high quality cloth napkins in a neutral color that you can use again. Using cloth napkins is much less expensive and better for the environment than purchasing paper napkins over and over again.

- ✔ For a simple decoration, set up a bulletin board or two. Pin up photos and memorabilia covering events in the life of the guest of honor — or maybe photos of your latest vacation. The bulletin board makes a nice conversation piece.

- ✔ For inexpensive entertainment at an outdoor party, set up a croquet game. Even young children can join in the fun with the adults.

## Generating a guest list

What's a party without guests? Nothing much to write home about. Include the following details in the guest list section of your notebook:

- ✔ Guests' names
- ✔ Mailing addresses

✔ Phone numbers

✔ RSVP record of who's coming and who's not

✔ Any special dietary requirements

Save money on your party plans by inviting as small a group as possible. (For example, if you're planning a baby shower for a friend, do you really need to invite her entire high school graduating class?) Tightening your guest list helps you save money by having to prepare less food and send out fewer invitations.

## Making up the menu

Write down everything you plan to eat and drink at your party — from beverages to appetizers to desserts. An important thing to remember when planning your menu is "know your guests": know their likes, dislikes, and any special needs.

Aim for a simple, balanced menu. Don't overspend on food by serving three appetizers, three meat choices, four side dishes, three kinds of bread, and three desserts. A simple snack or appetizer, salad or soup, vegetables, and a main course followed by a simple dessert make a nice, well-rounded meal. You can usually even skip the salad and soup course altogether.

Foods don't have to be expensive to be tasty. Keep the following budget-saving ideas in mind as you plan your menu:

✔ Add fresh herbs from your garden as a garnish to dress up less-expensive recipes.

✔ A delicious homemade or inexpensive store-bought chutney adds flare and flavor to a simply prepared meat like chicken or ham bought on sale.

✔ Focus the meal on a healthy chef salad or hearty homemade soup to save on the expense of meals prepared around expensive meat items.

✔ Cook homegrown vegetables dipped in olive oil on the grill or under the broiler for a delicious and inexpensive change of pace.

✔ Serve food the guests help prepare themselves such as a salad bar or a baked potato bar so the food prep becomes part of the activities, saving on entertainment costs.

## The most frugal party of all: Potluck!

Depending on how many people are coming to your shindig, have them each bring a food item. You can assign things ("Bob, you bring a vegetable," "Sue, you can bring a main dish," and so on) or just truly take potluck and eat whatever everyone decides to bring. You may end up with five green salads, four desserts, and nothing else, though, so a little planning goes a long way for a successful potluck meal. If a lot of people are coming, divide them up according to last names and have A-G bring main dishes, H-P bring salads or vegetables, and Q-Z bring desserts. The host of the party can supply the beverages, eating utensils, plates, and napkins.

For a smaller, casual dinner gathering, you can ask your guests to bring the various ingredients for whatever you're planning on serving for the meal — perhaps a can of olives, a couple of apples, or half a pound of spinach — and then everyone can pitch in together in the kitchen to chop, peel, grate, and cook the dinner. A glass of wine or juice, some fun music, a group of good friends, and you have a great party that even the kids can be a part of.

 Don't try a new recipe for the first time at a party. Use tried and true favorites that you're comfortable preparing. Recipes that you can make ahead of time, freeze, and then thaw and reheat on the party day are especially convenient.

## *Putting your preparations down on paper*

This section of your notebook includes detailed lists of the step-by-step pre-party preparations. Planning ahead helps you avoid overlooking details that can cause you expensive last-minute trips to the store for forgotten items. Include information about when you want to do each step. Stretching the preparations steps out over the course of the entire week before the party prevents you having to stay up until 3 a.m. the night before folding napkins or scrubbing the kitchen floor. Plan and write out individual preparation lists for these topics:

- ✔ Cleaning and preparing the house and yard
- ✔ Checking for party-related supplies and equipment (such as plates, forks, and food items)

- ✔ Shopping
- ✔ Decorating
- ✔ Cooking

## Decking the halls

When it comes to decorations, simpler is often better — not to mention, cheaper! Too many decorations can overwhelm your budget and also make a crowded room look too busy. A seasonal wreath on the door, a few candles scattered around the house, and a flower arrangement on the table can be all you need to make the house look festive.

Think through every room guests may use and then decide whether you want to include special decorations in each room. Be sure to consider table and food service décor, room decorations, the yard, front door, bathroom, and so on.

Think cheap, not chintzy! Being frugal doesn't have to mean being boring. Be creative with the things you have on hand, or borrow from others. The following items make easy and frugal centerpieces:

- ✔ Candles
- ✔ Fresh fruit and vegetables
- ✔ Flowers or flowering branches from your yard
- ✔ Pine cones and pine branches
- ✔ Colorful autumn leaves
- ✔ Sea shells
- ✔ Grape leaves

Avoid using potted flowers for the table centerpiece because the potting soil can sometimes contain small bugs. You don't want bugs visiting Aunt Bertha's retirement bash, believe me!

For evening parties, your guests will love these elegant, inexpensive lighting ideas:

- ✔ Set lighted candles in safe locations around the house.
- ✔ Line your front walkway or the edge of your backyard with inexpensive luminaria: small brown paper bags containing about an inch of sand in the bottom and a lit votive candle.
- ✔ If you have torches gathering dust in the garage or attic, they can add a festive look to your yard.

✔ Pull your strings of tiny white Christmas lights out of storage. String the lights around doorways, through your flowerbeds, or entwine them in trees and bushes.

# Here Come$ the Bride

The cost of weddings can often run as high as $20,000 these days and the budget-conscious bride and her parents always appreciate any ideas for saving on the clothes, food, and decorations. Here are some ideas that are frugal to the max; others are simply ways to cut back a little on those expensive wedding traditions. But remember, it's your wedding. You don't have to do it the way tradition — or modern habits — dictate. Be a rebel, if you want. It's okay.

Avoid everything you see labeled "wedding." For example, generic invitations that don't have the word "wedding" splashed all over them are much less expensive than official wedding invitations. Prom dresses at a department store can make beautiful bridesmaid dresses, and sometimes you even see white and lacy ones that can make lovely bridal gowns for a more casual wedding.

## Planning saves you money

During the early planning stages of the wedding, give some thought to the big decisions that affect the final bill of the wedding itself. For starters, decide what type and size of wedding you can afford. If you want to save money, consider a more casual wedding. Exchanging your vows and cutting your cake before a few close friends and family members in your home can be much less expensive and just as special as getting married in a church and having a large reception at a banquet hall. Get creative — plan to marry where you met or at a favorite getaway spot, someplace that has special meaning for you and your fiancé(e).

Consider non-traditional dates and times when planning a frugal wedding. You can save by planning the wedding and reception at a time other than the popular Saturday afternoon and evening time slots. Have the wedding on a Friday evening, Saturday morning, or Sunday afternoon — these times still work with most guests' schedules, and you can often reserve a church or reception hall for a less expensive price during these "off times." Picking an off time also allows you to save on food bills. Plan the wedding so that the reception falls in the mid-afternoon at tea time. That way you only need to serve simple, lighter fare rather than a full dinner or luncheon. Or consider having an evening wedding with a dessert-only reception.

Limit the guest list to close friends and immediate family. Fewer people means less food, less work, fewer invitations, and less money spent.

After you determine the type and size of wedding you want to have, set up a budget for each wedding-related expense. An easy way to keep up with the planning and the budget is to set up a wedding planner notebook along the same lines as the party planner notebook in the previous section of this chapter. Keep all the same categories except add a section on attire and photography. Flowers come under the decorations subheading. Read on for great ideas on saving big bucks on every wedding-related expense!

## Saving on invitations

The following list provides great tips to help you save on wedding invitation expenses:

- ✔ Order invitations from an online catalog. They're much cheaper than ordering through a stationery or wedding supply store. To get you started, check out: www.bestinvites.com, www.invitationfactoryoutlet.com, and www.discount-invitations.com.

- ✔ Make your own invitations. If you have nice handwriting or know how to do calligraphy, you can design your own cards and make copies on good quality paper at the print shop. Handwritten invitations are personal, elegant, and frugal.

  You can even design nice-looking invitations on your home computer. The choices are limited only by your imagination, plus you can even personalize invitations to close friends and family.

  If you're planning on creating your own invitations, look into the etiquette of how to word invitations and what to include. For ideas, go to www.wedalert.com or www.verseit.com.

## Playing dress-up

Whether your wedding is a traditional church wedding and you wear a long flowing gown, or an alternative celebration in the park and you have flowers in your hair and bare feet, probably the single most important decision for the bride is "What am I going to wear?" This section gives some simple ideas to save on attire for the bride, groom, and wedding party:

✔ Rent the wedding gown rather than buy it. Check with the local tux shop to find out about local rental businesses that cater to the entire bridal party.

✔ Purchase the sample wedding gown off the rack in the bridal shop. Sample bridal gowns and bridesmaids' dresses are usually sold at discount prices.

✔ Borrow shoes from a friend. Some people collect shoes like they're going out of style! If you have one of those friends who happens to wear the same size as you, the chances of her having shoes that match your dress are probably pretty good.

✔ Check for specials at various tuxedo rental stores. Some even offer free limousine service with tux rental, or a free tux rental for the groom with a minimum number of tuxes rented for the wedding party total.

✔ If your friends know how to sew and are willing to do so, they can make their own bridesmaid dresses. A friend of mine had her mother make all the bridesmaid dresses for her wedding. Considering she had nine bridesmaids, they saved a bundle by purchasing fabric and trim in bulk.

✔ For an informal wedding, have the men in the wedding party wear suits they already own — in the same color — to avoid tux rental. The bridesmaids' can also wear dresses they already own in a specified color.

## Finding frugal flowers and decoration options

Flowers and decorations can break your budget more than any other item. Here are some ideas for saving on flowers and décor:

✔ If you have a florist in the family, or like working with flowers yourself, you can save a bundle. Contact local greenhouses to see what seasonal flowers you can buy — perhaps even at a discount if you're buying a large quantity — to arrange into bouquets and floral decorations for the church and reception hall. You can also make the bouquets yourself from silk flowers purchased inexpensively at a craft store.

✔ Use the wedding party bouquets as decorations at the reception. The bride's bouquet can be the centerpiece of the head table or a decoration on the buffet table. Each of the smaller bridesmaid bouquets can be used as centerpieces at other tables. Guests enjoy getting an up-close look at the flowers, too.

✔ Balloon bouquets are much less expensive than flowers. Choose balloons in white or in colors that match the bridesmaids' dresses.

✔ Greenery (pine boughs, ivy, leaves) entwined with small white Christmas lights is beautiful, especially during the December holidays. Tie ribbon bows (in the wedding colors) amid the greens and you save on the cost of flowers.

✔ Focus the floral decorations at the front of the church where the guests look most of the time. Pew candles and pew flowers are pretty, but can add substantially to the overall flower budget.

✔ Use flowers from your own yard. One of my friends decorated her reception with sweet peas she and her mother grew at home.

✔ Have bridesmaids carry one or two long-stemmed white calla lilies or roses instead of an expensive bouquet of professionally arranged flowers. Tie with ribbon to match the wedding colors.

✔ Use fresh tulips. These look elegant displayed one or two at a time in tall glasses bought at the dollar store. They are much less expensive than a full-blown flower arrangement.

✔ Decorate the reception tables and buffet with framed photos of the bride and groom's families. Include baby photos of the bride and groom, plus wedding photos of their parents. Have copies made of the original photos so you don't risk losing or damaging someone's precious heirloom.

✔ Candles and greenery placed on top of mirrors make beautiful and inexpensive centerpieces.

✔ If you love Christmas decorations, consider having a wedding in December. Many churches decorate the sanctuary with beautiful trees, swags, and altar décor, and you can save your decorating budget for other things.

## *Hiring photographers, musicians, and singers . . . oh my!*

Hire a professional photographer only for the formal portraits. At the reception, place disposable cameras on every table for guests to take their own candid shots and group pictures. The photos may be lower quality, but the relaxed smiles caught on film by a friend are priceless!

# Forget the engraved beer mugs

One easily overlooked expense incurred by the bridal couple is giving gifts to the wedding party. Family and friends participate in a wedding out of love for you, not out of a desire for a gift, so don't feel obligated to break your budget by providing expensive gifts for the bridesmaids, ushers, singers, DJs, and servers at the reception. An inexpensive alternative to the usual gifts is to give a special photograph (framed or unframed) of the attendant or helper with the bride or groom. With a nice note thanking the person for his help on the bride and groom's special day, this gift becomes a treasured keepsake.

If you want a professional photographer in addition to the candid shots taken by guests on disposable cameras, call the head of the photography department at a local university and ask for a referral to a few trustworthy and talented students who may be interested in taking wedding photos for minimal pay. Be sure to look at samples of the student's work before negotiating a contract.

Find out whether any of your friends or family can sing or play an instrument. You can probably find the talent you need for a price you can afford among your circle of acquaintances. Usually friends are willing to offer their talents to a friend for free, or for a minimal fee. Calling a local university and asking about talented music students looking for performance experience is another money-saving trick.

## *Saving on the reception*

The reception with all its food and fun can quickly add up to a substantial chunk of your wedding budget. But you can cut corners, save money, and still have a memorable reception. Check out these ways you can do just that:

- ✔ If you plan to serve a catered meal, have a buffet rather than a sit-down dinner. Caterers usually charge considerably less for a buffet because they don't have to provide as many people to serve the food.

- ✔ If your goal is to have fun — and not necessarily to impress the Queen — have a potluck meal for the reception. Ask friends and family members in town to bring a hot dish to share.

Potluck receptions are much more friendly and less imposing. You can also ask guests to bring the recipe of the dish they bring to the reception so that the newlyweds have a collection of tried-and-true recipes as a souvenir of their reception.

If you have a potluck reception, remember you still need to provide beverages, plates, utensils, and coffee pots. Also, be sure to station a helper in the reception hall to receive the foods people bring in before the wedding ceremony.

✔ Borrow chairs, tables, and table settings from friends and family. Have friends act as hostesses for each table at the reception. They are in charge of decorating the table and providing the china and silverware. The table hosts can also supply their own table and chairs for the reception table, if they have a set that's easy to transport. Set a theme ahead of time, such as Victorian-style decorations or a springtime garden, and the tables will blend together even though they don't match exactly.

✔ To save on a professionally decorated, multi-tiered wedding cake, contact the culinary arts department of a local community college. Many schools are willing to provide a cake that's baked and decorated by their advanced students at a relatively minimal cost, providing you take care of delivering the cake.

✔ Do you have a friend or younger sibling whose favorite pastime is playing CDs and creating party mixes of music? Well, chances are, you've found yourself the perfect DJ for your reception. Rent a sound system, explain to your DJ what sort of music you want played, and then let her spin the discs to her heart's content.

✔ Provide basic beverages such as punch, coffee, and tea, but have a no-host or cash bar set up for people who want something a little stronger to drink. This way, the guests wanting to celebrate with expensive mixed drinks, wine, or beer can pay for their drink tab themselves.

# Showering the New Bride or Baby

Bridal and baby showers don't need to be huge events with sit-down luncheons and white tablecloths. As with any party, the simpler, the better. Many of the party planning ideas from earlier in this chapter can be adapted and used for planning both baby and bridal showers for friends and loved ones.

# Decorating for showers on a shoestring

Instead of running out and purchasing table decorations, see what you already have on hand or can borrow from friends or family. For a recent baby shower I hosted at my house, I borrowed porcelain dolls and a few small stuffed teddy bears from my daughter's room, and I picked flowers from my yard. I also brought out my grandmother's lace tablecloth, fine china, and silverware and then filled in any extra spaces on the table with inexpensive candles and lacy items. The shower was cute, festive, old-fashioned, and didn't cost me more than the price of a few candles.

Another small — but nice — addition to the baby or bridal shower decorations is to matte and frame the shower invitation and set it on the table as part of the centerpiece. Give it to the guest of honor as a gift after the shower. You can purchase precut mattes inexpensively at many frame shops and find frames in dollar stores and secondhand outlets. Glue on a bit of ribbon or some dried flowers if the frame is too plain for your gift-giving taste.

# Showering with frugal gifts

If any of the guests like to quilt (and it seems like every group has at least one avid quilter these days), making a quilt together can create a memorable keepsake for the new bride or new mom. Give each guest a square section of the quilt fabric and have her decorate it in a way that's meaningful to her. Make sure everyone signs her name with a fabric pen on her square. Sew on buttons, bows, ribbons, beads, or whatever strikes your fancy. If any of your guests don't feel at all artistic, she can simply use a fabric pen and write out a favorite quote or verse. Someone else can add a small decorative flourish to the square later, if needed. You really need to plan this project ahead of time so that the person who sews the quilt together has enough time to collect the finished squares from the guests. Perhaps include the squares in the invitation with instructions for mailing the squares to the quilter when the guests are finished decorating them.

You can also have each guest bring a page telling the guest of honor how special she is, or offering a few words of wisdom for the bride- or mom-to-be. Tell your guests to feel free to share funny stories or goofy advice, too. The pages can either be simple letters or intricately decorated scrapbook pages. Have someone bind them all together into a memory book.

A reader of my e-mail newsletter hosted a baby shower for a relative who was having her third child. The mother-to-be didn't really want a shower, but the hostess believed that every baby needs to be celebrated. So she went forward with the party plans but with a simple twist. Each guest brought her babies' outgrown items rather than new items. Then they all sorted through the baby items together and found things the mom could use for her new baby. And instead of party games, the guests went around the room and shared one special quality of the mom they hoped she passed on to her baby. Everyone had a great time, and the party was meaningful, but also casual, low-stress, and low-cost.

# If I could save time in a capsule

A fun gift for a newborn or newly married couple is a time capsule. On the day the child's born, or on the day of the wedding, save the following items:

✔ **A local newspaper and a national paper:** Save at least the front pages, but even the entire paper will be of interest twenty years from now. The types of classified ads, the weather forecasts, and stock market reports will all be interesting. And the sports page may even become a collector's item, depending on the future of the players featured on the front page that day.

✔ **Photographs:** Include pictures of the house where the baby's family lives (the front of the house, the yard, and the baby's room) or pictures of the new couple's first house or apartment. Also include photos of family members (siblings, parents, grandparents, cousins) and family pets. Finally, be sure to include a picture of the baby just home from the hospital or the new couple at — or a few days after — the wedding. When they open the capsule, they'll enjoy remembering what they looked like way back when.

✔ **Letters from friends and family:** Ask family members and friends to write a paragraph or a short letter to the baby describing from their perspective what the first day of the baby's life was like. Or ask friends and family members to write words of wisdom or share memories with the new couple.

✔ **Videotape of baby's first day or the couple's wedding:** Bring your own video camera to the wedding and reception to film the day from a casual perspective that will provide lots of laughs and precious memories on a future anniversary. For a new baby, include numerous shots of the baby (eating, sleeping, being held by various family members), plus short interviews with Mom, Dad, siblings, grandparents, and anyone else on hand during baby's first day. Maybe even a few words from the midwife or doctor, too.

Seal the items in a moisture-proof container. If you have one of those food sealing machines, this is an excellent way to use it. Wrap the time capsule and include instructions for the baby or couple to open it at some predetermined point in the future. Perhaps on his eighteenth birthday, or the couples ten-year wedding anniversary.

# Part IV
# Enjoying a Frugal Home and Hearth

The 5th Wave — By Rich Tennant

"...and don't tell me I'm not being frugal enough. I hired a man last week to do nothing but clip coupons!"

# In this part . . .

*E*ver hear yourself muttering, "Rats! The washing machine is broken again! Do we replace it or keep having it fixed?" Much of a family's income goes toward maintaining and paying for various items around the house. Lucky for you, this part shows you how to evaluate purchases, maintain your home and vehicles, and cut back on utility-related expenses so that you can stretch the family income at home. In this part, you also find information on caring inexpensively for household pets and shopping secondhand to live within your means.

# Chapter 13

# Saving Money around the House and Driveway

*E*very time I turn around, I seem to need to make another trip to the store. We need more dish soap . . . we need more laundry detergent . . . we need to replace a light bulb. But I've found I can save money on those trips and even cut down on how frequently I spin that revolving door at the hardware store. In this chapter, you find a hodge-podge of easy house and yard-related ideas for saving on cleaning supplies, basic household upkeep, cars, pets, carpet care, auto maintenance, and home decorating ideas.

## Cleaning . . . Always Cleaning

Sometimes I feel like I'm always cleaning my house. But I often wonder, if I'm *always* cleaning, why isn't my house *always* clean? Probably because five people, four cats, a lizard, umpteen fish, and half the neighborhood children either live here or traipse through on a regular basis. (Actually, the fish probably aren't doing much to mess up the house — although, now that I think about it, I'm the one in charge of cleaning their aquarium, so I guess the fish fit under the "cleaning" category, too.) Finding ways to save money on frequently used cleaning products is a necessity in my busy — and often crowded — home.

## Saving on paper products

Paper products such as dinner napkins, paper towels, and toilet paper can add up to a significant amount of money over time. You can buy them in bulk to save a bit — a pack of paper towels or a few extra rolls of toilet paper don't go bad stacked in the garage or at the back of closet shelves. And generic and dollar store brands of toilet paper, napkins, and paper towels usually work just fine and are often a lot less expensive than brand-name paper products. For other money-saving tips for household paper products, try the following ideas:

- ✔ **Tear off just enough paper towel for the job at hand.** I learned this trick from a frugal friend. I have a tendency to always rip off an entire sheet without thinking whether or not I actually need that much. Maybe using only half a paper towel doesn't save the big bucks, but the little things can add up to major savings over the long haul.

- ✔ **Use reusable rags instead of paper towels to clean up spills.** Keep a stash of rags handy. You can make rags from remnants of old T-shirts and other stained or ripped clothing doomed for the garbage. Or get the small white kitchen towels sold in packages of 12 for a couple of dollars. I can use them again and again and ill-treat and bleach them all I want.

- ✔ **Limit how much toilet paper you use each time.** Ask your family to limit their toilet paper use as well. My friend asks her kids to use no more than five toilet paper squares each time. Because they're good kids who usually do what Mom says even when she's not looking, I can imagine her kids sitting there counting out their allotment of toilet paper squares everyday. I don't obsess about toilet paper squares, but it really is a good idea to give your family (especially young kids) a general idea of the appropriate amount to use. In a family with multiple kids, overuse of toilet paper can be a bit annoying, as well as expensive.

- ✔ **Use cloth napkins instead of paper napkins at mealtime.** You can buy cloth napkins or make them yourself. My grandmother always kept a large number of cloth table napkins and assorted napkin holders in a drawer by the table. When mealtime rolled around, we grabbed our personal napkin holder and its accompanying napkin and then reused the same cloth napkin all day. At the end of the day, Grandma just tossed all the dirty cloth napkins into the washing machine to wait for the next load of laundry. Thrifty!

# Considering low-cost cleaning supply alternatives

Why spend your hard-earned cash on a broom closet full of cleaning supplies you don't really need? Window cleaner, bathtub scouring powder, furniture and chrome polish, room deodorizer, and disinfectant can all be replaced with three inexpensive and commonly available household products that I consider essential for all household cleaning:

- ✔ White vinegar
- ✔ Baking soda
- ✔ Bleach

 Many people also add ammonia to the list, but because ammonia combined with bleach and some other cleaning products produces a toxic, or even deadly, gas, I avoid using ammonia all together (I'm also allergic to ammonia).

Not only do alternative cleaning supplies save money, but they also keep harmful chemicals and harsh cleaners from building up in your home. A healthier house . . . a healthier pocketbook. Hey, that sure sounds good to me!

 One of the most important tips for economically using cleansers around the house is to allow the cleanser plenty of time to work. You use more cleanser and elbow grease if you start wiping immediately. Let the cleanser sit on stubborn stains or dried-on food for about ten minutes before attempting to wipe it up. You'll be amazed what a few minutes can do to even the most obnoxious dried-on food.

## White vinegar

Full-strength white vinegar is an excellent cleaning option that kills many germs, bacteria, and molds. I keep a spray bottle of full-strength vinegar around the house at all times. It's handy for spraying countertops, toilet seats, doorknobs, and even cutting boards. Vinegar helps deodorize, and you can use it in your wash and get the same results as costly store-bought detergent additives.

Here are a few easy ideas for cleaning around the house with vinegar:

- ✔ **Basic cleaning**
  - Wipe down the inside walls and shelves of your refrigerator with a mixture of vinegar and water. Or use

full-strength vinegar if something went bad in the fridge and you're trying to remove stubborn food odors.

- Leave a cupful of vinegar in the toilet bowl overnight. In the morning, scrub with a toilet brush.

- Use vinegar mixed 50/50 with water to mop vinyl flooring. Don't use on wood or imitation wood flooring, however.

- Use vinegar for degreasing stovetops, ovens, pots and pans, and overhead kitchen exhaust fans.

- Use full- or half-strength vinegar for cleaning windows, mirrors, chrome, and tile. (Polish your windows with newspapers and you cut down on the lint left behind from cloth towels or paper products.)

- To easily clean the microwave oven, heat half a cup of white vinegar in a microwave-safe bowl or mug on high for three minutes. Let the vinegar sit undisturbed for about fifteen minutes, then remove the vinegar container and wipe down the inside of the microwave with a sponge and clear water.

- Use full-strength vinegar in the rinse-aid container of your dishwasher.

✓ **Deodorizing**

- Pour a cupful of vinegar down the kitchen drain once a week and wait for at least half an hour before rinsing. Ice cubes made from vinegar can be run through the garbage disposal to freshen it, too.

- If your kitchen is smelling a bit strong from cooking fish or burning something on the stove, wipe down your countertops with full-strength vinegar. The vinegar not only neutralizes the smell, but also makes your counters sparkling clean.

- Pour a small amount of vinegar directly on the carpet where your pet had an accident. Let the vinegar sit and dry to remove the odor.

✓ **Laundry**

- Use about one cup of white vinegar and a quarter cup of baking soda (in addition to your laundry detergent) in place of store-bought bleaching products to whiten and brighten your clothes. You can even use this combination on white and colored clothing without presorting if you wash in cold water.

- Add half a cup of white vinegar to the rinse cycle or pour it into the machine's fabric softener container to remove any leftover soap residue from the clothes. The clothes will smell clean and fresh. I always worried we'd walk around smelling like a pickle factory if I added vinegar to the rinse cycle, but I discovered that by the time the clothes dry, the vinegar smell is gone.

### Baking soda

Baking soda doesn't only come in little boxes in the cooking aisle. You can find bulk containers in the baking supplies aisle of the supermarket or at warehouse stores. Baking soda is fairly inexpensive normally, but when you buy it in bulk, it's really a household-cleaning bargain. Baking soda works well for the following cleaning needs:

✔ **Basic cleaning**

- Mix baking soda and water into a 50/50 paste for scrubbing bathtubs, tile, sinks, chrome, and pots and pans. Rinse thoroughly with water.

- Use a baking soda and water paste to gently clean vinyl dolls and toys.

- Put the greasy, blackened cooking rack from your barbecue grill (make sure the rack is cool) into a garbage bag, cover with water mixed with about a cup of baking soda, close the bag, and let it sit for several hours. When you remove the rack from the baking soda and water mixture, the cooked-on residue comes off much more easily.

✔ **Deodorizing**

- Sprinkle baking soda directly onto carpets, wait half an hour, then vacuum thoroughly. You can freshen upholstered couches and chairs the same way.

- Leave an open box of baking soda in the refrigerator and freezer to remove odors. Change every month or so.

- Add about one teaspoon of baking soda to a cup of water, stir, and use in a spray bottle with a fine mist setting for an easy and inexpensive air freshener to spray around the room.

- If stinky food has gone bad in one of your nice plastic storage containers, sprinkle the container with baking soda, close the container tightly, and let it sit overnight. Then wash and rinse as usual. The smell is gone.

- Sprinkle a thin layer of baking soda in the bottom of the cat's litter box (before adding the kitty litter) to help cut the smell. Fluffy will thank you, and this can also prevent the need for buying more expensive deodorized kitty litter brands.

✔ **Laundry**

- Add about a quarter cup of baking soda to the washing machine's rinse cycle as a fabric softener and odor remover.

- Use a paste made from a mix of 50/50 baking soda and water to pretreat spots before putting the clothes in the wash.

### Bleach

When it comes to killing germs and removing household mildew, you won't find a less expensive disinfectant and cleaning agent than common household bleach. Here are some simple cleaning ideas using bleach:

✔ Use bleach mixed 50/50 with water for removing stubborn stains and mildew from tile and grout.

✔ A 50/50 bleach and water mix can be poured into tea cups or coffee mugs with difficult coffee or tea stains. Allow to soak undisturbed overnight. The next day, pour out the bleach and water and wash the cup as usual.

✔ Mix one cup of bleach with one gallon of water for general cleaning and disinfecting, but be careful not to let the bleach mixture touch fabrics or anything that can have color bleached out of it (such as carpets, window treatments, clothing, and so on).

## Caring for your carpets

If you're like me and you need the carpet you have to last for several more years, keep the following cleaning and protecting tips in mind:

✔ Vacuum the carpet regularly. Removing dirt not only keeps the carpet looking clean, but also helps your carpet last longer by removing grit that wears away at your carpet's fibers.

✔ Place large entry mats inside and outside each door going into your house. It's amazing how much dirt gets tracked in from our shoes. Wash the mats at least twice a month.

   To really protect your carpet, institute a shoes-off-in-the-house policy.

✔ Protect your carpets from fading by keeping direct sunlight off them. Close blinds or draperies during the hours when the sun shines onto any portion of your carpet.

✔ Remove spots as soon as they appear. Spot removal cuts down dramatically on the need for an overall carpet cleaning. If you can work on the stain or spot right away, gently rub plain club soda into the fresh spot. Keep a general spray-on spot remover on hand to remove set-in stains that you can't get to immediately. Or you can rub plain white foaming shaving cream into dingy areas of the carpet and rinse lightly with water.

When your carpets need a thorough cleaning, clean them yourself with a rental carpet-cleaning machine. Check with your neighbors to see whether anyone wants to go 50/50 with you on the rental cost. You usually get to keep the carpet-cleaning machine long enough to do more than one carpet. You can really save money by using a solution of half white vinegar and half warm water in the machine instead of expensive cleaning solutions.

If you rent a carpet cleaner frequently, consider investing in one of your own. After a few cleanings, the carpet cleaner easily pays for itself in savings. To save even more, consider splitting the purchase cost of a carpet cleaner with a family member, neighbor, or close friend.

Be aware that some new carpets have guarantees that become void if you use non-approved carpet cleaning solutions; be sure to check before you use any homemade carpet or spot cleaners.

# Decorating on a Dime

I find great comfort in an eclectic decorating style. A little of this, a little of that, all brought together with a common color or theme. I'd rather be surrounded by individual items that please me than be trapped in an expensive room that can only have wood of a particular color or upholstery in a particular shade of periwinkle blue. Sometimes, though, I really want a matched set of furniture but can only afford garage sale prices. So what do I do? Well, just buy a can of spray paint . . . and go to town!

For a whole slew of helpful ideas on money-saving decorating, be sure to check out *Home Decorating For Dummies* by Patricia Hart McMillan and Katharine Kaye McMillan (published by Wiley).

## Finding inspiration

For frugal inspiration, I look at magazines like *Country Home* and *Victoria* to find decorating ideas I like. I don't run down to the local furniture store and recreate the magazine photos with expensive furniture and decorations, but I use the photos as inspiring examples of how to decorate with older, used furniture. Carrying a vision of a rustic country room or a Victorian-style bed and breakfast in my mind's eye helps me recognize the gems amid the trash at the thrift stores and yard sales. My living room may not ever make the cover of *Decorating Dreams,* but it looks nice and people are comfortable and relaxed in my home.

## Locating inexpensive home furnishings

One day when my grandfather was visiting, he said, "I finally figured out why I always feel so at home whenever I'm at your house — most of the furniture used to be in *my* house!" And it's true. Whenever my grandparents moved or bought different furniture, I was always first in line to offer a new home to their hand-me-downs. Many of their furnishings were quality items with classic lines that blended well with my penchant for Victoriana. I always tell friends my decorating style is "Early Grandma's Attic."

Decorating on a dime doesn't have to mean avocado green curtains and gold velvet chairs.

My favorite sources for quality secondhand furniture and home décor are:

- ✔ Garage sales
- ✔ Antique stores
- ✔ Auctions
- ✔ Clearance/salvage stores
- ✔ Grandma's attic

Sometimes I spy useable junk (that means treasures) piled in front of someone's house, waiting to be carted away by the trash collector. I've been known to boldly ask whether I can have that lamp, the old student desk, or the scratched headboard destined for the landfill. Most people are surprised someone wants their castoffs, and they're more than happy to give me their old things.

If you end up with a piece of secondhand furniture you can't fix, cover the imperfections. Toss a decorative cover (a quilt, baby blanket, table runner, scarf, or other fabric) across a scratched or damaged table. You can also lay a piece of trimmed fabric across a clawed-up seat cushion.

If you have a solid wood table with unsightly water rings, try removing the rings by making a thick paste of water and baking soda (about a 50/50 mix), and then gently rubbing the baking soda paste into the stain in one direction along the grain of the wood with a soft toothbrush covered with a wet washcloth. If this method doesn't work, you can always hide the water rings under a large vase of flowers or a lace doily.

You can save a few pennies with assemble-it-yourself furniture, especially for things like bookcases, desks, and children's furnishings.

## Simple is elegant: Finding frugal final touches

Think simple when you're contemplating window coverings. An understated window treatment of a valance and blinds can be elegant and usually purchased at a fraction of the cost of custom-made draperies. To save the most money, be sure to hang window treatments yourself rather than pay an expert.

For a cheery kitchen valance, find decorative kitchen dishtowels (checkered ones look especially cute), fold down two inches along the side of the towel and sew a pocket along the length. Thread a dowel or curtain rod through the pocket. You need to measure the width of your windows and length of the towels to make sure you buy enough towels for your window treatment.

Garage sales and thrift stores can be an excellent source of window treatments, especially for children's rooms. I regularly see curtains featuring the latest animated characters and pop music stars. If you like to sew, make curtains out of cute bed sheets you find at secondhand stores.

For your bedroom, buy a decorative curtain rod (on sale, of course) and simply drape a silk, lace, or flannel flat sheet that matches your bedding across the top. You may have to play around with the sheet to get the look you like, but a single sheet and a curtain rod are *much* less expensive than professionally designed and installed curtains — and you don't even have to be a seamstress or own a sewing machine.

If you're tired of the current look of your draperies or window treatments but don't really want to replace them yet, try adding a few extra touches. Tie back draperies with fancy cord or ribbon; string a swag of silk flowers or holiday greenery over the top of a valance. Simple changes like these can breathe new life into your room for minimal expense.

Household decorations and knickknacks are always in plentiful supply at garage sales and thrift stores. I found a large, framed and matted photo by a popular wildlife photographer for $5 at my neighbor's yard sale. The complete set of hardbound Harvard Classics gracing my fireplace mantle was only $6 through a "Friends of the Library" book sale. My favorite lace tablecloth was found in a box of donations a friend gave to my latest garage sale.

# Maintaining Your Home's Exterior and Yard

Taking care of a house and yard is time-consuming as well as expensive. The vast majority of home care costs are labor expenses. But if you can do the work yourself, you save big money over the course of owning a home. Caring for your home yourself can also become a favorite hobby. What seems at first like a chore becomes rewarding as the labor of your own hands provides you and your family with something of value.

For more ideas on caring for your home, read *Home Maintenance For Dummies* by Morris Carey and James Carey. For tips on maintaining your yard, pick up a copy of *Lawn Care For Dummies* by Lance Walheim and the editors of the National Gardening Association, or check out *Landscaping For Dummies* by Philip Giroux, Bob Beckstrom, Lance Walheim, and the editors of the NGA. (All these books are published by Wiley.)

## Caring for your home's exterior

When the outside of your house needs to be repainted or restained, you definitely save money by doing it yourself. For detailed information on finishing the exterior of your home, ask the experts at your local home and garden store, or go to http://doityourself. com/paintext/index.htm.

If you decide to do the house painting yourself, calculate your rate of pay after the job is complete. For example, if it takes you five days to paint your house, and you saved $2,000 by doing it yourself, you just paid yourself $400 per day! You also enjoy the personal reward of pointing to your freshly painted house and saying, "I did it myself!"

But if you're not a do-it-yourself person and are planning on hiring someone to paint for you, you may want to check into the cost of vinyl or aluminum siding that doesn't need to be painted. It often

pays for itself after just one or two professional painting jobs —
that you don't have to do or pay for.

Most exterior maintenance and improvement jobs are physically
taxing and often require special tools and knowledge. You may
want to have the work done professionally to save you time and
effort. Hiring a local handyman (they usually advertise in the newspaper) who can help with big projects (such as shingling) is usually cheaper than hiring a major contractor. You can also offer to
help the handyman with the work to cut the cost. A friend and her
husband hired a handyman to run electricity around their deck.
They asked if he'd reduce the price if her husband helped him with
the job. The handyman agreed without hesitation. It worked out
nicely — the job was done professionally, and her husband helped
cut the cost *and* learned about running electricity while working as
the handyman's apprentice for two days.

## Caring for your yard

I want my yard to look nice year 'round, but overspending is so
easy to do when buying plants for the yard and garden. Here are a
few tips for cutting back on the expense of new trees and flowers.

- ✔ Plant a low-maintenance landscape full of plants, bushes, flowers, and trees that grow wild in your local area. These usually
  require minimal watering and fertilizing.

- ✔ Plant a line of evergreens (or other large shade trees) along
  the side of your yard. When the trees mature, they will shield
  your home from the sun's blistering heat and also block blus-
  tering winter winds.

- ✔ Plant trees and bushes that take up a lot of room in the
  yard — they're often an excellent frugal investment. You can
  buy one potted rhododendron, for example, for about $15.
  Once it takes off, you don't need to plant much else throughout the year in that spot.

The fall is a great time of year to find excellent price cuts on
trees and bushes. But check first with the experts at your
local garden center or nursery to confirm the proper planting
season. A low price isn't a good deal if it's the wrong time of
year to plant the tree or bush — it may wither or die before it
has a chance to take root and grow.

- ✔ Plant perennial flowers rather than annuals to keep your yard-
  care expenses to a minimum. Perennials grow back every
  year, but annuals have to be planted fresh each year.

Many perennials can be started from cuttings off a friend's or neighbor's plant. If you know someone with a green gardening thumb, ask what he recommends. You may find yourself going back home with your car full of free perennial starts. For more information on growing perennials, be sure to read *Perennials For Dummies* by Marcia Tatroe (published by Wiley).

✔ Save on mulch by using a layer of wet newspapers beneath any bark or chips you use for mulching. The newspapers control weeds so you only need about half the amount of bark as usual. The papers also cut down on cats using your garden for a litter box. They can't dig deep enough to do their business, so they usually leave it alone.

✔ Start your own compost pile in a corner of the backyard instead of purchasing fertilizer or bags of expensive compost from the garden store.

# Discovering the Joys of Preventative Auto Maintenance

Preventative auto maintenance is the process of routinely checking and sometimes replacing parts and systems on your vehicle before the systems fail and cause expensive or dangerous problems. Human nature tends to overlook maintenance unless a problem occurs, but I'd personally rather be safe than sorry when it comes to the vehicle transporting my most precious cargo — my three kids. I think of regular maintenance as a form of health insurance for my car.

## Consulting the manual for maintenance schedules

Read your owner's manual for specific suggestions on basic car maintenance and schedules. The recommended maintenance schedule from the manufacturer is usually a little less stringent than that recommended by your friendly auto repair shop. Most auto mechanics want to see you back in their shop as soon as is reasonably acceptable to keep their paychecks coming in, so they're going to recommend you come by a bit more frequently.

The warranty on the automobile is usually tied to the upkeep recommended by the manufacturer, so be sure to at least follow the manufacturer's maintenance guidelines if your car is still under its initial warranty. Be sure to keep detailed records of all work on your car so that you can prove you've done the minimum maintenance in case you ever have a claim against the warranty.

# Keeping up on auto upkeep

Maintenance intervals depend on how heavily you use your car and under what kind of conditions. If you drive long distances, tow a trailer, drive with frequent starts and stops, spend a lot of time idling, live in a hostile climate (hot, dusty desert or severe winters, for example), or use your vehicle for commercial use, you need to check your car or truck more frequently.

For a basic outline of generally recommended services, check out your car's owner's manual (service schedules can vary quite dramatically from vehicle to vehicle) and then compare to the following schedule to come up with the best maintenance schedule for your vehicle.

- ✔ Inspect lights, tire pressure, and wiper blades — Monthly

- ✔ Replace wiper blades — Yearly

- ✔ Inspect air filter — Every other month (Replace air filter yearly)

- ✔ Inspect antifreeze/coolant levels — Weekly

- ✔ Replace coolant and flush system — Yearly, or 12,000 to 24,000 miles

- ✔ Check brake, power steering, transmission, and washer fluids — Monthly

- ✔ Check oil level — Every other fill-up, or at least twice a month

- ✔ Change oil and filter and lubricate chassis — Every 3,000 to 5,000 miles, or 3 to 4 months

- ✔ Replace fuel filter — Every 2 years or 24,000 miles

- ✔ Inspect engine, do computer scan and tune-up — Every 30,000 miles

- ✔ Check battery — Every tune-up (Replace battery every 3 to 5 years)

- ✔ Inspect engine belts and hoses — Every oil change

- ✔ Service automatic transmission — Every 2 years or 24,000 to 50,000 miles

- ✔ Replace belts (including engine timing belt when equipped) and hoses — 60,000 to 100,000 miles, or 5 to 8 years

- ✔ Rotate and balance tires; check wheel alignment and brakes — 6,000 miles or every other oil change

- ✔ Replace shocks — Every 2 years or 24,000 miles

- ✔ Check air conditioning performance — Every spring

## Performing routine maintenance yourself

One benefit of driving older cars is being forced to learn basic auto repair skills. We save substantially now that we don't pay exorbitant labor costs for simple repairs and maintenance.

If you have any good friends who like to work on cars, see whether one of them is willing to work side by side with you as you learn the basics. Even investing in a basic auto repair class through adult continuing education or your local community college can easily be reimbursed through what you save by not paying the high labor costs on car repairs.

Especially consider doing the labor yourself for simple jobs like:

✔ Checking and replacing the air filter

✔ Checking and replacing wiper blades

✔ Checking and refilling fluid levels

- • Antifreeze
- • Windshield washer fluid
- • Oil
- • Brake fluid
- • Transmission fluid

Keep a copy of *Auto Repair For Dummies* by Deanna Sclar (published by Wiley) handy at all times. This book more than pays for itself with the money you save in repair bills.

## Cutting down on wear and tear

A good way to save on car-related expenses is to cut down on the amount you drive. You save wear and tear on the car, spend less on fuel and oil, and have a car that lasts much longer. Teenagers used to ride their bikes if they wanted to go somewhere, but for some reason, Mom and Dad have become the family chauffeurs, driving the kids from soccer to ballet to the movies to Bobby's house — all day long. I realize parents often drive their kids to and from school these days because of safety issues, but there's nothing wrong with letting them walk home in the rain from time to time. The last time I checked, kids don't melt in water.

Another option is to make use of public transportation and commuter car pooling. Most metropolitan areas — and many smaller
areas — have bus, subway, or rail systems for commuters. For
more information on public transportation, see Chapter 15.

# Saving on Pet Costs

Little furry, scaly, or feathered friends can bring so much joy to
people's lives and even the most frugal family can afford to keep a
pet or two. Here are some easy ideas for saving money on your
leash-and-collar friends around the house.

## How much is that doggie in the window?

The best source for finding inexpensive pets is the "free pets" section of your local newspaper's classified ads. And don't forget the
local Humane Society. Sometimes the pound even includes in the
adoption fees a voucher for having your adopted pet spayed or
neutered at a local veterinarian's office.

Before you choose a pet, figure out what sort of pet you can afford.

- ✔ A dog may seem easy, but large dogs are one of the more expensive pet options. They eat a lot, often have grooming requirements
  and high vet bills, and can do a lot of damage to your personal
  property. Smaller dogs are often less expensive, although the
  really small ones are more fragile and have more healthcare needs.

- ✔ Cats are usually less expensive than dogs because they eat
  less and are often inside-only pets, which keeps their exposure
  to illness and injury to a minimum. Cats who go outdoors,
  however, usually end up in an occasional fight with a wandering tomcat and can incur additional vet bills.

- ✔ Reptiles, amphibians, and fish need special equipment (tanks,
  lights, heaters), but their food and vet bills are usually minimal.

- ✔ Gerbils, hamsters, rats, and guinea pigs need enclosures and
  food, but have virtually no vet bills, required immunizations
  and licenses, or expensive lighting to pay for.

## Saving on assorted pet supplies

Food, kitty litter, and pet toys can get expensive after awhile. I want to
take good care of my furry friends, but I often feel like they're eating

our family out of house and home. The following sections contain tips for cutting back expenses without cutting back on loving care.

### Finding bargains on feline foodstuff and canine cuisine

Sometimes you're better off to spend a little more upfront on quality pet food. Just as people who eat a poor diet get seriously sick later, pets need proper nutrition to stay healthy. I tried various generic dry cat food brands over the years, and each time my cats wound up chronically sick to their stomachs and generally ill. Now we invest in a higher quality brand, and our cats are healthier, more active, and seem happier.

Shopping around for bargain pet food prices can save you big bucks over the course of a year, especially if you have more than one pet to feed. Check around at various stores (pet, drug, grocery, and warehouse stores all carry pet foods); you may be surprised at the variety in prices. One store had our favorite brand for $13 per large bag, while the store across the street sold the same thing for only $8. Keep an eye out for coupons in the weekly circulars arriving in the mail or newspaper. Also, check online for mail order resources for your pet's favorite brand. You can also find recipes for homemade pet foods online, but I recommend you run any pet food recipes by your vet to make sure the recipe will truly meet your pet's basic nutritional needs.

Switching dog or cat food from week to week just to save a few pennies can cause havoc with your pet's digestive system. Recently we adopted a new pet from the local animal shelter and had to get him adjusted to a different food than he'd been eating previously. His stomach was upset for several days — and I had a lot of messes to clean up around the house. Ick! After you've discovered a brand of food your pet enjoys, thrives on, and digests well, it's best to continue having them eat the same brand.

### Getting the most from your grooming dollar

Ask around at different pet grooming salons and compare rates. They can vary greatly. If you can find a groomer who's just starting out in business, you may find an excellent bargain. Or groom your pet yourself, if possible.

### Saving on kitty litter

An ongoing cat expense is buying litter. You want Fluffy's litter box to be clean and fresh, but do you need to invest in high-priced litter? The expensive bags of clumping and scented kitty litter are nice but not really necessary. Try small bags of the cheapest varieties until you find a brand that meets your qualifications for kitty litter.

I know several people who make their own kitty litter from shredded newspaper. If you have a paper shredding machine in your home office, just feed your old newspapers through the machine, and then place a generous amount of the shredded paper in the cat's litter box (sprinkle ½ cup of baking soda in the bottom of the box first to cut the odor). Be sure to check the litter box regularly because you need to change newspaper litter frequently, possibly as often as every other day or so.

### Playing with your frugal cat or dog

Have you ever seen children at the holidays playing for hours on end with empty gift boxes rather than the expensive store-bought gifts themselves? Well, your favorite furry friend is also just as happy with something simple and cheap as with those cute — but expensive! — packaged pet toys in the store. Common objects found around the house are often just as fun for Fido or Fluffy, and a lot healthier for the pet owner's budget.

Check out the following cheap dog toys:

✔ Knotted socks, towels or lengths of rope

✔ Stuffed animals bought at yard sales and thrift stores

✔ Old, knotted panty hose for a tug-o-war toy

If you use stuffed animals as inexpensive chew toys, make sure Fido can't rip off and choke on any parts. Keep an eye on the condition of the toy and retire it if the stuffing is starting to come out. You don't want your dog eating the stuffing — it could be dangerous for his digestion if he ingests too much.

Here are some items that are sure to amuse your cat for pennies:

✔ A bag of craft pom-poms (purchased for less than a dollar at the craft store or dollar store)

✔ Paper crimped into a "bow-tie" shape with a long string tied from the middle

✔ A clean plastic lid from an old hairspray can

✔ Small stuffed animals sprinkled with catnip

## Taming those dreaded vet and pet med bills

Nothing is more detrimental to your pet budget than veterinarian bills. You want your pet to be healthy, but does that mean your kids have to go without shoes this month? The following ideas help you find ways to save on this pet expense:

- ✔ Call around to different vets in your area and ask for fee schedules. You may find a huge difference in the usual fees from one office to the next — even among vets in the same town. If you live in or near a rural area, check with the rural vets. Often their prices are quite a bit lower than the prices of vets in the city.

- ✔ Don't hesitate to tell your veterinarian that money is an issue and you can't afford to pay for the most expensive treatment options. Maybe you can set up a payment plan. Most vets want your pet to get well more than they want to make more money off you.

- ✔ Check with your local university to see whether it has a veterinary college. Ask to see the fee schedule and compare it to the fees charged by local vets.

- ✔ Ask for an itemized statement after each vet visit. Make sure none of the medications or procedures were double-billed. Vet offices make clerical errors occasionally, just like any business.

- ✔ Keep your eye out for advertisements for low-cost immunizations and spay/neuter clinics. You can also give your pet many of its vaccinations yourself, although you still have to go through a regular vet or immunization clinic for a rabies vaccine. Check online for do-it-yourself immunizations or ask at your local pharmacy.

- ✔ Flea and tick medications can often be purchased online at a reduced price.

- ✔ If your pet's veterinarian is willing to fax or mail in a prescription, you may be able to purchase heartworm and parasite meds online at a reduced cost. Check online at www.petmarket.com for more information.

If vet bills are eating your budget alive, you can actually purchase veterinary insurance for your pet. The policies vary greatly, but can often cut your out-of-pocket expenses by as much as 80 percent. Companies offer assorted options, and just as with human medical insurance, the coverage varies from company to company. You usually pay a monthly or yearly fee and also have a deductible and co-payment. Only you can decide whether the insurance premiums outweigh the current bills you're paying. If you have one healthy housecat, you may not save much in the long run. Do a search online for pet insurance. Be sure to find a company that's licensed in your state.

# Chapter 14

# Cutting Utility and Service Bills

So you've decided to become a frugal utility user and cut back a bit on your electricity, phone, and water use. Does that mean nothing but cold showers, dark rooms, and hot, miserable summers from here on out? No more warm, cozy winter nights? No more long-distance phone calls? No more evenings at home watching favorite movies? Hardly! Instead of living a Spartan life of shivers and shadows, pick a few ideas in this chapter to try. Every little bit helps, and if you combine a number of these ideas, you just may see a substantial downward shift in your utility bills and fees for other monthly services like cable and garbage pickup.

## Reaching Out to Touch Someone

Do you have any "phone friends"? You know, those people who live too far away to see regularly in person so your relationship stays alive through the wonders of the phone lines? I have several long-distance phone buddies who regularly add joy and quality to my life. I'd never want to end my phone calls to them just to save a few pennies on the phone bill. Even though calling long distance can get expensive over time, it's still cheaper than the gas and time I'd use to drive to their homes regularly. E-mail and traditional letter writing also help fill in some of the gaps created by long-distance relationships.

## Saving on phone bills

Keeping in touch over the phone lines is an expensive proposition, so finding ways to cut back a bit on the monthly phone bill is a welcome relief to many pocketbooks.

Check your statement from the phone company and make sure that you're not paying for extra services you never use or don't really need. If you have an answering machine, you probably don't need an additional voice messaging service from the phone company. If you have a voice mail service but no answering machine, consider buying one. Purchasing your own machine is often considerably less expensive over a period of time than paying the monthly fees for the voice mail service.

Here are some other ways to save on your monthly phone bill:

✔ Check to see whether your phone company offers a flat rate or a measured service plan that can save you money based on how often you call or on the times and days you usually use the phone.

✔ Put off making long-distance calls until evenings and weekends, when rates are usually lower. If you make a lot of long-distance calls, check around for calling plans that suit the amount of calls you make.

✔ Try not to use operator assistance for placing long-distance calls unless absolutely necessary.

Using one of those access numbers you see advertised on television ("Call this number and your first 20 minutes are only 99 cents!") can save a lot of pennies if you're careful. A long-distance friend and I use these numbers regularly. I call her and talk until my 20 minutes are up. I usually set my kitchen timer for 19 minutes just so I don't run over. Then we hang up, and she calls me back for 19 minutes on her 99 cents. This method easily cuts the cost of our phone calls to each other in half.

Many of these companies charge the entire 99 cents even if you only reach an answering machine and hang up right away. Try calling first on your regular long distance plan to see if the person you're calling is available (so you're only charged for 1 minute not 20). Then hang up and call back immediately on the 99 cent plan.

Another way to reduce your phone bill if you call friends and family out of state regularly may be to get a cell phone. Some cell phone plans offer huge amounts of free long-distance calls.

## Using e-mail to stay in touch

As long as you don't have per-minute service charges connected with your e-mail or Internet service, sending an e-mail is free. And what's a better price than that? Some people have a home computer but don't want or need complete Internet access. If you're one of these people, you can get e-mail-only services, often free of charge. Ask around at your local computer store or talk to your friendly neighborhood computer geek for current ideas for free e-mail-only services.

If money's really tight, sending an e-mail greeting card from an online card company is miles better than sending no greeting at all. (For a large collection of free e-mail greeting cards and messages, go to www.bluemountain.com.)

Another way to save on the cost of a stamp or a long-distance phone call is to make use of online video conferencing and instant messaging services. You can also set up meeting times with family and friends in online chat rooms or message boards to exchange greetings.

## Rediscovering the joys of letter writing

Since the advent of e-mail and more affordable long-distance phone service, letter writing seems to have become a thing of the past — as archaic as dinosaurs or Model Ts. But nothing can match the thrill of finding a hand-addressed envelope from a good friend or favorite family member sitting in your mailbox. (Clicking on your flashing e-mail card to see the dancing birthday ponies just isn't the same.) Sending cards and letters doesn't have to be much more expensive than the price of a first-class stamp if you watch for specials on stationery while you're shopping. I regularly find packages of beautiful note cards and stationery at garage sales and thrift stores for pennies. Dropping an inexpensive card or letter into the mail is still much cheaper than an extended long-distance phone call or paying a monthly service fee to an Internet service provider for e-mail access.

 If you don't have a long period of time to write a detailed letter to a friend, try carrying around a pad of stationery when you're out and about. Instead of being a source of frustration, a 15-minute wait in the doctor's reception area can be the start of a great letter. You can also use that time sitting in the van waiting for Junior to get out of school to keep in touch with far-flung family members. I keep a small pad of stationery, a couple of stamped envelopes, and an address book in my purse at all times so that I can use those waiting times throughout the week to frugally keep in touch with friends and family.

# Saving on Climate Control

The weather outside is frightful, but your utilities bills don't have to be equally as scary! Whether it's time to warm the house in the winter or cool it during the heat of summer, you find helpful tips on controlling the temperature of your house in the following section.

## Dressing for the weather

My first reaction to uncomfortable temperatures is to run for the thermostat. But I've found an easier and more energy-efficient way to deal with the extremes of heat and cold: Dress appropriately. Wear light-colored and lightweight, breathable natural fabrics in summer. Spend your day in a T-shirt, shorts, and sandals. In the wintertime, wear woolen clothes or dress in layers, perhaps by adding a fleece vest. By trapping air between the layers, you're actually using your own body heat to keep warmer. You'll also be amazed at what a difference a nice warm pair of socks can make on a cold day.

## Keeping your cool when the weather's not

If you can keep excess heat from entering your house in the first place, you've already won half the battle of trying to reduce your cooling bill. The primary source for heat inside a home during the hot summer months is sunlight absorbed through the roof, the walls, and the windows. Indoor appliances, especially in the kitchen and laundry room, give off heat, too.

### Insulating yourself against the heat

If you want to drop your cooling — and heating — bills dramatically, add insulation to your home. First insulate your attic floor, and then when time and money allow, add insulation to your basement, exterior walls, floors, and crawl spaces (in that order).

Insulation on the attic floor helps reduce the amount of heat absorbed through the roof and then through the ceiling of the house. Adequate ventilation under the eaves allows cooler air to enter and circulate throughout the attic. Install an exhaust fan in one of the attic windows (if you have them) to cut down on heat buildup under the roof. Even if you don't have a permanent exhaust fan installed in the upstairs window, you can set a temporary box fan with the air flow pointed outward to pull the hot air out of the house.

### Shading your house from the sun

One of the coolest options of all is shade. Trees on the south side of the house are always a good investment, but if you're not planning on living in your home for a long period of time, you may not personally reap the shady benefits from planting a leafy friend.

If your house isn't shaded by trees, install awnings over any windows that are exposed to direct sun during the day. Many awnings are removable and adjustable, so you aren't stuck with them when you don't need them.

### Filtering the sunshine: Covering your windows

Windows are a major source of unwanted heat during the summer months. Some easy ways to reduce the heat coming in through your windows include the following:

✔ Close the drapes during the hours of direct sunlight. I have a large south-facing window in my living room, and if I forget to close the blinds during the afternoon, the entire living area of the house heats up to a hotter temperature than that outside. Can you say, "Oven?" Ugh.

✔ Add reflective window tint to southern windows. This is a relatively easy job, but be sure to ask for instructions at your local home and garden center. Try covering one small window with reflective tint as a test. You'll find it's so easy that you'll probably be itching to redo all the windows on the south side of your house!

✔ Use bamboo window shades. By hanging old-fashioned bamboo shades on the outside of heat-producing windows, you create a bit of shade and a pocket of insulating air between the heat and the house. These shades can really make a big difference. They roll up with the pull of a cord, allowing you to keep the shades in place all summer but still have easy access to open windows during the rest of the day. Bamboo shades are fairly inexpensive and are made to last in the elements for years. Sometimes I even find them at garage sales. Shutters work well for this purpose, too.

✔ Keep window coverings closed in unused rooms. If you have bedrooms sitting vacant all day, keep the curtains shut so that the empty rooms don't heat up from the sun.

✔ Add reflective window curtain liners. Usually these have the reflective coating on only one side, so be sure to have the reflective side facing outward during the summer to keep the heat out of your house. Then during the winter, you can reverse the curtain liners to reflect warmth back into the room. The curtain liners are usually just a plain, neutral color that won't show through your draperies.

### Making efficient use of air conditioning and fans

Using air conditioners to cool your house during the heat of summer can be one of the most expensive appliance-related energy uses in your home. Save a bit on the cost by implementing some of the following ideas:

✔ If you use an air conditioner to cool your house, turn the thermostat up a bit higher than the temperature where you usually keep it. If you normally have it set for 72 degrees during the summer, switch to 78 degrees. When it's 95 degrees in the shade outside, 78 degrees still feels comfortable and not too warm.

✔ Use fans to circulate air. Moving air feels several degrees cooler than still air. An overhead ceiling fan works well for cooling the whole room, but even a small box fan or oscillating fan keeps the air moving.

✔ At the end of the day when the temperature outside cools down, turn off the air conditioning, open the windows, and place an outward-facing fan in a window to vent the hot air from the house. A vent fan in an upstairs window works best. Opening a downstairs window at the same time allows a full cross-breeze to develop throughout your home. The fan cools your house in a fraction of the time it takes if you only open the windows and let the hot air sit in the house. Only open the windows if humidity is low, however. Otherwise the air conditioner will have to work much harder to cool the humid air when you turn it back on.

### Reducing the creation of inside heat

The first line of attack in reducing your cooling bills is to keep the heat *outside* your home, but reducing the amount of heat you create inside your home is also important. Consider these tips:

✔ Use your outdoor grill more often to keep from heating up the kitchen. Some friends of ours bought a new outdoor grill with a griddle attachment and a small gas burner next to the large grill. Now they can cook breakfast, lunch, and dinner outside and never have to heat up their kitchen during the summer.

✔ Use small appliances rather than the stove and oven for cooking. The microwave, slow cooker, electric skillet, and toaster oven give off less heat and are more energy efficient than the range.

✔ Dry clothes in the dryer on the no-heat setting. Add a clean, dry towel to the dryer load to help absorb extra moisture from your clothes.

✔ Hang your washed clothing on a clothesline in the backyard or on the porch. You can find retractable clotheslines that fit in almost any small space. Or simply put your clothes on hangers and hang them over the shower curtain rod or on a line in the laundry room. I sometimes hang my clothes on hangers over the edge of the eaves on the back of my house on warm, breezy days.

✔ Use the no-heat drying cycle on the dishwasher. Don't open the door after the rinse cycle or you just add steam and more heat to the house.

✔ Take short showers to avoid a buildup of steam. Humid air always feels hotter than dry air, so use the exhaust fans in the bathroom during the summer.

✔ Darker colors absorb more heat, so if the outside walls of your house are dark, consider painting the house a lighter color the next time you redo the exterior of the house. Light-colored curtains reflect more heat back out of your house, too.

## Warming the house

It never seems to fail: Opposites attract. Some people love the brisk air and like to see their breath in the house. "It's so invigorating!" they say with glee. Meanwhile, their partners sit huddled with four blankets and a down parka in the corner of the room nearest to the roaring fire. "You weirdo," they mutter. "Brrrr . . . turn up the heat!" Well, you can both be happy and still save money on your heating bills by following the hints in this section.

### Staying warm without turning up the heat

The simplest way to save money on heating is to turn your furnace down a couple degrees. During the winter months, if you usually keep your thermostat set at 72 degrees, turn it down to 70. If you're used to 70-degree temperatures, turn the thermostat down to 68. Lower the temperature of your thermostat even further at night when you're sleeping. Toss on an extra blanket if you're still a bit chilled.

To keep your furnace running efficiently, have it inspected regularly and change the filters monthly during heavy use.

Consider these other ways to stay warm without running up your heating bill:

✔ If you heat with a wood-burning stove or fireplace insert, make friends with a builder. They often pay people to come and haul away the scraps of lumber around construction sites — a great source for free firewood if you don't mind a bit of work to collect it yourself.

✔ Close off the vents and doors in rooms that aren't in use for long periods of time. If you have a guest room that's only used occassionaly, you don't need to keep it heated until company comes calling.

✔ A ceiling fan set to push air down into the room keeps the warm air circulating to the lower regions of the house.

✔ Add some steam to the air of your house. Higher humidity keeps the air warmer. Here are a couple of simple ideas:

- Let steamy air from the bathroom escape into the rest of the house after a shower.

- Boil water on the stovetop.

- Keep a kettle or pan full of water on top of your wood-burning stove or radiator.

### Insulating against drafts

When we moved from an older 800-square-foot home into a new home twice as big, I expected our energy bills to double, as well. But much to my surprise, our gas and electricity bills were nearly half what they'd been in the smaller house. New houses are often built with energy-efficient features such as thermal-paned windows, well-insulated walls, and energy-efficient water heaters and furnaces. The whole experience reinforced the monetary benefits of well-insulating a house.

If you aren't in the process of having a new house built with all the energy-efficient bells and whistles, consider using some of the following ideas to increase the benefits of your home's current heating system.

✔ Add a layer of air between your windows and the great outdoors (the air insulates much better than the window glass alone). If you have storm windows, use them. You can also buy special sheets of plastic to stretch across the inside of your window frames. I personally don't like the look (I feel like I'm looking out of a fishbowl when I peer through the plastic), but it does insulate your windows.

✔ Use heavy curtains in the winter. Or buy reflective curtain liners. (See the section "Filtering the sunshine: Covering your windows," earlier in this chapter.)

✔ After dark, hang blankets or quilts in front of the windows for added insulation. Install a decorative towel bar or curtain rod over the top of your existing window treatment, and then simply fold a blanket or quilt over the bar.

- ✔ Open your curtains during daylight hours, especially on southern windows, for a bit of passive solar heating.

- ✔ Use weatherstripping or caulk around doorways and window frames. I've heard an estimate that, when all the various cracks and spots that lose heat in the average house are added together, you have the equivalent of a large 2- or 3-foot square hole in the outside wall of your house. Brrrr!

- ✔ Use a draft stopper at the bottom of outside doors. You can make one yourself, buy one inexpensively, or even just roll up a bathroom towel and place it next to the bottom of the door.

- ✔ Fill electric switch plates that are on outside walls with plastic foam or purchase plastic insulation that's already cut to size and made for this purpose.

- ✔ Remember to close the flue on your fireplace when you're not using it. Leaving a fireplace flue open is like having a vacuum hose hooked to your living room, sucking all the warm air right out the chimney.

## Cozying up

Even if you're trying to save money on heating costs, you don't need to sit and shiver when the weather cools off. Here are some simple ideas for staying cozy and warm this winter.

- ✔ To keep your bed warm on those oh-so-cold winter nights, place a hot water bottle between the sheets before you climb in. You can even use a 2-liter bottle filled with warm (never hot!) water, making sure to tape the lid shut to prevent leaks. An old sock filled with rice (not instant rice), tied shut, and then microwaved briefly until warm, works essentially the same way as a water bottle. You can even use the warmed, rice-filled sock as a hot compress for aching muscles. Add a bit of cinnamon and you've got an air freshener, too.

- ✔ Exchange your regular bed sheets for cotton flannel sheets during the winter.

- ✔ Keep a blanket or two as throws on the couch for snuggling when it's cold. Rather than running to the thermostat at the first shiver, get in the habit of grabbing a blanket.

- ✔ Happiness is a warm friend. Snuggle up on the couch and read a good book with your kids, your spouse, the dog, or a warm kitten. Sharing body heat really does keep you warmer. That reminds me. Where's my cat when I need him?

# Cutting Back on Electricity and Gas Use

Saving money on electricity and gas utilities can be as easy as making a few minor adjustments in your day-to-day life. Every penny and dime saved add up to a considerable amount of money day after day. The following tips, when combined together, can help cut your electricity and gas use considerably.

✔ Wash clothes in cold water. The majority of electricity used for washing clothes is used to heat the water. Save hot water washes for white towels, socks, and undergarments.

✔ Wash only full loads in the washing machine and dishwasher.

✔ You use less electricity to heat a cup of water in the microwave than on the stovetop. When you're boiling water on the stove, always keep the pot covered because water boils much faster in an enclosed pot. Or use a teakettle. Don't boil more water than you actually need to use, or you're wasting energy to heat water that's just going to cool off again or end up dumped down the drain.

✔ If you're preparing food and the recipe says something like, "Heat to a boil; then simmer for five minutes," don't simmer! Just heat it to a boil, cover the pan tightly, turn off the burner, and let the whole thing sit undisturbed for 5 to 10 minutes. It actually simmers and stays hot long enough to cook your soup, ramen noodles, oatmeal, or instant rice.

✔ Keep indoor lights off during the daytime. Position your desk near a window for adequate lighting.

✔ Turn off your computer, printer, scanner, monitor, and any other office equipment at night. Even when they're turned off, a lot of devices (TV and VCRs, for example) use electricity. Instead of trying to remember to unplug each device every night, plug them all into power strips that can be flipped off easily.

✔ If you really need to cut back on electricity use but like to keep an aquarium, choose fish that can tolerate room-temperature water so that you don't have to pay for heating their tank. See *Aquariums For Dummies* by Maddy Hargrove and Mic Hargrove (published by Wiley) for details.

✔ Find out whether your local energy provider has off-peak hours when electricity use is less expensive. If they do, do your laundry and run the dishwasher accordingly.

✔ Many power companies allow users to pay a flat rate every month of the year, so they don't have really high energy bills in the heat of the summer and dead of winter. If the total energy use is higher or lower than the amount paid over the course of the year, the extra amount will be charged or refunded accordingly the next year.

✔ If you have an outdoor pool or pond, circulate the water for only one hour per day. Set it on a timer so that you don't forget.

✔ Put a timer on your hot water heater so it runs for only four hours total each day during peak use times (morning showers, evening dishes, and children's bathtimes).

✔ Use a programmable thermostat in your house that you can set it for different temperatures at different hours. This costs a bit upfront, but can quickly recoup any money spent by not overheating the house all day while the family's at work and school or at night while everyone's sleeping.

✔ If you have a heated waterbed, keep the bed made when you're not in it. The blankets and bedspread help to insulate the bed so the heater doesn't have to work as hard.

## *Improving your appliance efficiency*

Older refrigerators, freezers, and air conditioners are often inefficient and sometimes run constantly, draining needless amounts of electricity and money. Buying a newer appliance is often more economical than using an old one over a long period of time. But if you're planning on moving soon and not taking the appliance with you, replacing it probably isn't worthwhile financially.

If you're in the market for a new major appliance, carefully check the energy ratings. Purchasing a slightly more expensive refrigerator or washing machine that's energy efficient can save you hundreds of dollars in energy bills over the life of the appliance.

Refrigerators and freezers work better if they're full. Fill the empty spaces with clean milk jugs filled with water. Not only will your freezer run more efficiently, but the ice-filled jugs will keep your freezer cold during a power outage. You can also use the water for drinking in an emergency situation.

Here are some other ways to use your appliances efficiently:

✔ Clean the coils of the fridge regularly so the cooling mechanism can run more efficiently.

✔ Whenever you open the refrigerator or freezer, always close it again as quickly as possible. Every time the door's opened, the appliance's cold air is replaced by warm air in the room, so it needs to work harder to cool itself again.

✔ Gas stovetops heat up instantly, so they don't have to run as long as electric. If you're considering replacing your stove and you have access to gas, switch from electric to gas.

✔ Use a water-heater insulation blanket and keep the water heater's temperature set at 120 degrees.

✔ Keep your dryer lint-free. A full lint trap doesn't allow the moist air to escape properly, which slows down the drying cycle, consequently using more energy.

✔ Have your air conditioner inspected and serviced every spring.

✔ If you have a window unit air conditioner, run a fan in the room at the same time. The moving air makes the room feel cooler so that you don't have to set the air conditioner thermostat so low.

## Shedding some light on the subject

After appliances and heating, indoor and outdoor lighting is one of the biggest electricity users in an average home. By cutting down on the number of light bulbs turned on at any one time, you save substantially on your electric bills. Here are some easy tips for lighting-related savings.

✔ If you have outdoor lighting for safety reasons, install motion detectors on the lights. The lights will still come on when you need to see your way or if an intruder needs to be scared away. Limit outside lighting to the minimum required for safety; don't use it just for looks.

✔ Replace frequently used light bulbs with fluorescent bulbs. They're a bit more expensive to buy, but they often last up to ten times longer than incandescent bulbs.

✔ Use sunlight for indoor lighting as much as possible.

# Trash Talk: Controlling Garbage Costs

Garbage happens. Whatcha gonna do about it? Probably the best way to save money on garbage pickup and trips to the landfill is to limit the amount of garbage brought into the home. Remember the three Rs of the anti-trash mantra: reduce, reuse, recycle. You can reduce the frequency of your garbage pickup or at least the size of the container if you reduce the amount of garbage created in your home.

# Reducing what you use and what you throw away

Simple decisions such as using cloth grocery bags rather than disposable paper or plastic bags or choosing items based on whether you can recycle the packaging can make a world of difference in your home garbage situation.

## Avoiding trash by "precycling"

One method of cutting back on garbage production is referred to as "precycling" rather than recycling. Precyclers choose which items to buy based on the amount of garbage the packaging produces. For example, someone who has a precycler mind-set doesn't buy cereal that's packaged in a plastic bag and then inside a cardboard box. They skip that extra layer of potential garbage and go for the cereal that comes only in a plastic bag. The cereal in just the plastic bags is often less expensive, too, so you save money on the cereal and create less garbage.

Back in the long ago days before my family started recycling, the majority of our garbage consisted of paper products: junk mail, cardboard boxes, and newspaper. It's amazing how quickly the paper added up over the course of a week. But once paper and cardboard recycling came into our lives, we cut the amount of actual throw-it-away garbage by more than half. Recycling things like plastic soda bottles, milk jugs, aluminum cans, and glass jars and composting our kitchen and garden scraps reduced our garbage to a fraction of what it was before.

Even a simple thing like purchasing reusable lunchboxes cuts down on the need to throw away paper bags. And reuse plastic containers to store your food instead of using and throwing away single-use plastic wrap and foil. You can also cut down on the amount of garbage you produce by avoiding obviously disposable items such as paper plates, plastic eating utensils, plastic coffee cups, and plastic diapers. Look for labels specifying that a product is rechargeable (batteries, for example) or refillable (such as printer cartridges).

## Recycling to save money and reduce waste

Recycling not only saves money, but has the added benefit of saving the environment. Buying items that are already recycled — and can be recycled again — helps the environment even more.

My family has been fortunate. For much of the past twenty years, we've had curbside recycling pickup. In our old neighborhood in West Seattle, we just tossed everything recyclable into one big can that the city picked up regularly. Now we have to do a bit more work — sort out our paper recyclables from metal, glass, and plastics — but we can use a smaller garbage can and save a bit of money on our utility bill from the city. Even when we lived in a small town with no curbside recycling, we still saved our glass, plastic, metal, cardboard, and paper products in separate bins in the laundry room. We just loaded the full bins into the back of the station wagon and took them to the local recycling station in the parking lot of a grocery store across town. If we hadn't recycled, our garbage bill would've been much higher.

Having a compost pile in the backyard is one of the best ways to recycle assorted vegetable scraps. Just save all your trimmings and discards from salads and veggies, toss 'em on the old compost heap, and use the homemade compost to grow more fresh salads and veggies.

## Reusing household items in creative ways

You can give many everyday trash items a new lease on life by creatively reusing the items in the home or office. Here are few easy examples:

✔ Use the backs of old envelopes for writing out your shopping lists. You can even slip coupons right into the envelope before you leave the house. Handy little trick, isn't it?

✔ Cut cereal boxes to size to use for photo mailers.

✔ Cut off the fronts of old holiday cards and make them into holiday postcards. You save on postage and on the price of new cards.

✔ Instead of grabbing a paper towel next time you spill something or need to dust, keep a supply of wipe cloths made from old T-shirts and other clothes. If someone else can still use an article of clothing, donate it to charity; if it has stains, holes, or bleach marks, it's a prime candidate for a household rag.

✔ If you get plastic grocery bags at the supermarket, don't just throw them away. I personally prefer plastic to paper bags because the plastic bags find so many new uses around my house. I have one of those cute little fabric tubes for storing my plastic bags, but you can just shove 'em all into the empty cardboard tube from a paper towel roll. Plastic grocery bags can be reused in a multitude of simple ways:

    • Pack your lunch in a bag.

- Use as garbage bags for the trash pail under the sink or in the bath and bedrooms.
- Wrap dirty cloth diapers in a plastic bag when you're out and about.
- Put dirty laundry in bags when traveling.
- Store shoes in bags to keep them separate from clothes in suitcases and travel bags.
- Wrap smelly garbage and bloody meat wrappers in plastic bags before putting in the trash.

# Reducing Television and Cable Expenses

Getting rid of cable television can save substantially on your yearly household expenses. If you figure your cable's costing you $25 per month on the low end, you're paying a bare minimum of $300 per year (but I wouldn't be surprised if most people's actual bill is closer to twice that much per year). If you add premium channels to the package, you can spend over $80 per month!

If cable television is absolutely essential to your life, the best way to save money is to stick with the bare-bones basic package. This usually includes the major networks, public broadcasting, assorted educational channels, and a handful of others. It usually doesn't include many of the children's cartoon channels, however. Basic cable seems to run from $10-$15 per month throughout the United States compared to more than $50 per month for expanded cable. You save at least a couple hundred dollars per year. You can take a fraction of that amount and rent all the movies you really want to see.

# Cutting Down on Water Use to Save Money

Some people are a bit more extreme than others about saving water. When I was growing up, a friend's mother had a beautiful sign in calligraphy hanging over the toilet in the main bathroom. It read, "If it's yellow, let it mellow . . . if it's brown, flush it down." I remember coming home all excited and telling my mom what a great idea I thought that sign was . . . but Mom didn't respond the way I'd hoped. She only looked at me meaningfully and wrinkled her nose; that was the end of my days as a toilet-flush reformer.

But conserving water does save money, so here are a few easy, less extreme ideas for cutting back on water use around the house:

✔ Take short showers rather than long showers or baths filled to the brim. Set a timer for three minutes and get in, get soaped, and get back out before it dings at you. Most of us like to take long, soaking baths with the water up to our chins, but if you're willing to take a shallow bath, you actually use less water than an average shower.

✔ Turn off the water while brushing your teeth or shaving.

✔ Rinse fresh vegetables in a sink or pan of standing water rather than under running water from the faucet.

✔ Reduce the amount of water used per flush by placing a tall plastic bottle filled (and sealed!) with sand or rocks in the back of the toilet tank. By displacing some of the water in the tank, you use less water each flush.

✔ Run the washing machine and dishwasher only with full loads. If you do wash your dishes by hand, don't let the rinse water run while you're scrubbing the dishes. Either save all your soapy dishes to be rinsed at once, or use a dishpan of clear water for dipping and rinsing.

✔ Install low-flow showerheads.

✔ Keep a bottle or pitcher of water in the refrigerator to keep it cold. You waste gallons of water running the tap until the water gets cold. Or to chill tap water quickly, add ice to your glass before filling it with tap water. Just don't let the faucet run needlessly.

✔ Fix leaky faucets and running toilets as soon as they occur. These problems can waste gallons of water each day.

✔ Sweep the driveway and walkways instead of spraying them clean with the water hose.

✔ Water your lawns and gardens in the evening or early morning to prevent most evaporation.

✔ Avoid using the garbage disposal. Disposals use a lot of water each time they're turned on, so try to recycle or compost your kitchen waste instead. When you do use the garbage disposal, run cold water only.

✔ Use the water-saving settings on your washing machine, if applicable.

✔ Don't use the toilet as a wastebasket. If you pick up a wad of stray hair or a bit of paper from the floor or carpet, put it in the trash rather than flush it down the commode.

# Chapter 15

# Saving Money on Big-Ticket Items

*H*ousing and transportation: Two of life's biggest budget busters. But you can find simple ways to steer clear of your car taking you to the cleaners or your rent or mortgage payments eating you out of house and home. You also find information in this chapter on saving money on appliances — another one of those big budget-eating categories of life.

## Keeping a Ceiling on Housing Budgets

Housing, food, and car payments are often the most expensive items in anyone's budget. Whether you rent an apartment, live in a mobile home, or are making payments on your own home, you'll find helpful budget-stretching ideas in the following section.

### Saving money on rent

Although I'm currently a homeowner, I've spent most of my adult life as a renter. As I see it, renting has several advantages over owning a home:

✔ Renting allows you the freedom to move if needed.

✔ Renting doesn't saddle you with unexpected repair bills and general upkeep expenses.

✔ Rent in many apartment complexes also includes free use of an on-site gym, pool, and sauna, saving the cost of a membership at the local gym.

✔ Renting doesn't require yearly property taxes.

✔ Rent of an apartment or condominium often includes the cost of some utilities so you don't have additional cable, water, or garbage bills to pay. The included utilities are also set at a flat rate so they don't fluctuate from month to month.

✔ Renting an apartment usually doesn't involve any yard or grounds maintenance costs (unless you're renting a house).

✔ Renting may entitle you to a discount if you don't receive something you've paid for. For example, if your air conditioner doesn't work for a week, or you have to eat out a couple of days while a defective stove is replaced, you may be reimbursed by the property manager for some of the rent you've paid that month.

✔ Renting requires a small upfront investment compared to buying a house, which requires a large down payment usually equal to several years' rent. If you don't have enough money put together for the first and last month's rent and the usual damage deposit, check around. Some apartment complexes offer the first month free for new renters or don't require a deposit if you move in by a certain date. Look for ads in the newspaper, in apartment renters' guides available at newsstands and supermarkets, or on signs outside apartment buildings.

Of course, looking for rentals that are offering deals isn't the only way to save money. You may find that treating your rental as your *own* home (vacuum and clean the carpets, plant flowers, and so on) has some money-saving benefits as well.

For example, we rented a small house for eight years and during that time took care of it as well as our neighbors took care of the homes they owned. Our landlady was so appreciative that she didn't raise our rent more than just a tiny bit in all that time. We ended up paying well below the going market rate for comparable rentals in our area. When our landlady wanted to sell the house, she came to us first to see whether we were interested in buying it. She even offered to carry the mortgage for us herself because she knew by our prompt and regular rent payments over the years that we wouldn't default on a home loan.

One way to save money on rent, and maybe even qualify for free rent, is to become a property manager for an apartment complex. A property manager shows vacant apartments to prospective renters and oversees the general maintenance of the property. Many times they take care of the on-site office work, as well. Look in the classified ads for apartment manager listings.

## Buying into the American dream — Home ownership

Often rental costs are nearly as much — if not more — than the cost of monthly mortgage payments. But even if your monthly mortgage payments will be higher than your current rent, the cost of the mortgage may actually be lower than you think when you take into account the tax deductions you receive when you itemize your tax return. For more information on buying a home, read _Home Buying For Dummies_ by Eric Tyson and Ray Brown (published by Wiley).

### Avoiding "house poverty"

Some people probably think they'll look richer and be happier if they buy the biggest house they can afford. But keep in mind the risk of _house poverty_ — when your house and the related expenses (mortgage payments, taxes, insurance, home and yard maintenance, and so on) swallow up all your expendable income. You may have a nice house but not much of anything else to show for your hard-earned money.

If you make the big decision to buy a house, be sure to buy within your means. You want balance in your life, not just a bigger house. An occasional vacation, money for education, a fun evening out with your spouse or friends, furniture, a retirement account — these things can end up on the wayside of your life if you buy more house than you can reasonably afford.

Be careful when you're house hunting. Realtors and lenders often try to convince you to buy as much house as possible, but they obviously have a vested interest in seeing you spend more of your money. The more money you spend on a house, the more money ends up in their pockets. Beware!

### Coming up with the down payment

Don't assume that just because you don't have much money set aside for a down payment you aren't eligible to buy a home. Ask a real estate agent about home-buying programs available in your area that allow a limited down payment. These programs are more common for first-time home buyers. Several options also exist for low-income buyers, so don't let a lower income scare you away from looking into buying options. You can also ask conventional lenders whether they offer mortgages with low down payments combined with programs like Fannie Mae, Freddie Mac, or other governmental or non-profit agencies.

### Considering homes within your budget

A new, traditionally built home is sometimes out of reach for the frugal person who wants to become a homeowner. But if you're willing to investigate options like older fixer-upper houses or alternative homes (such as mobiles and pre-fabricated homes), you may find home ownership is a very real possibility after all.

Few home buyers are really in the market for fixer-uppers, or houses needing work. Most people want to move right in and enjoy the benefits of their new house without immediately needing to dive in with repairs and elbow grease. But if you want to own your own house, and you're willing to do a little work, a fixer-upper can be just the ticket you've been looking for. The competition for these homes is almost non-existent, giving you time to assess whether the amount of work needed is worth the overall savings.

The ideal fixer-upper requires minimum work, has been on the market for some time, and is being sold at a substantial savings. You can often find fixer-uppers that have been on the market for six months to a year and are being sold for 20 to 30 percent off the market price. Sometimes just a fresh coat of paint, some new windows, or aluminum siding can make a forlorn home dynamite. An older home with avocado green appliances, gold carpets, chipped paint, and out-of-date flooring can be a real eye-sore, but look beyond the surface and you'll find that these cosmetic problems can make it an incredibly easy house to fix for very little money.

Major renovations like a new roof or foundation repairs are expensive and don't usually give a good return on the monetary investment when you resell. If you're thinking of eventually reselling the fixer-upper for a profit, the most profitable repairs are the simple ones — things like adding new wall-to-wall carpeting, painting the house inside and out, replacing kitchen cabinet doors, landscaping, adding new lighting fixtures, and installing up-to-date appliances (for example, a new refrigerator, range, dishwasher, and built-in microwave oven).

Always have a fixer-upper carefully inspected before signing on the dotted line.

# Fixing up a house; financing a dream

I spoke with one woman who put together the money to buy her family's dream home by buying and fixing up two small houses that needed a great deal of love, care, and elbow grease (in other words, *sweat equity*). Four years after buying the two small houses, she sold them for a sizeable profit and had the down payment for her family's dream home on five acres of land — a home they never plan to leave. If you're interested in fixing up and selling an older home, consider selling the house yourself, saving thousands of dollars in commission fees for a real estate agent. If you don't know how to sell your home, take a class. Spending $200 on a "for-sale-by-owner" seminar is a lot cheaper than paying $12,000 (or more!) in commission to an agent.

Another option for low-cost home ownership is to look into manufactured housing. Pre-fabs (modular homes that are built in sections in a factory and then put together on your building site) and mobile homes aren't the big metal boxes of days-gone-by. Many people think they have to live in a crowded mobile home park if they own a mobile home, but many areas allow you to install a mobile home on private property, and pre-fabs usually have the same building codes and requirements as any site-built home. The combined monthly payments for the property and a mobile home or pre-fab are usually significantly less than the payments on traditionally built houses. The resale value and appreciation benefits may not be as great with mobile homes, but if you're just looking for a roof over your head and not a future investment, consider mobile homes. Also, if you've always dreamed of owning acreage, buying a mobile home and putting it down on several acres can be just the answer for affording your "dream-come-true." Check with your local city hall about zoning laws for mobile homes. The resale and appreciation on modular homes is the same as a site-built home.

You can also buy a used mobile home — still in good condition — for a fraction of what you pay for other living arrangements. You definitely want to look into this if money's tight. Used mobile homes can be found in the classified ads or through mobile home dealers that sell new and used mobile homes.

## Refinancing your current home loan

Interest rates tend to fluctuate over time, so you may find yourself in a position where you're paying a much higher interest rate than the current market rate. Look into refinancing your home loan at the lower interest rate, potentially knocking down your monthly mortgage rate considerably. Talk to your bank or mortgage holder for details.

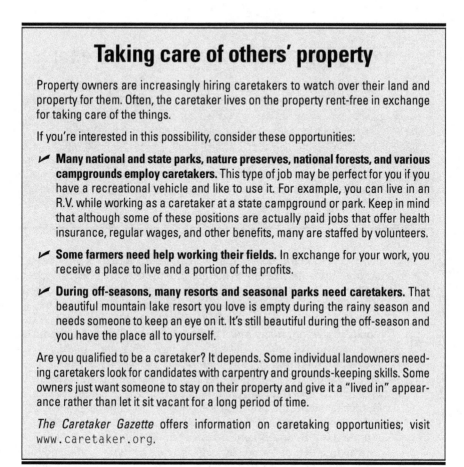

## Taking care of others' property

Property owners are increasingly hiring caretakers to watch over their land and property for them. Often, the caretaker lives on the property rent-free in exchange for taking care of the things.

If you're interested in this possibility, consider these opportunities:

✔ **Many national and state parks, nature preserves, national forests, and various campgrounds employ caretakers.** This type of job may be perfect for you if you have a recreational vehicle and like to use it. For example, you can live in an R.V. while working as a caretaker at a state campground or park. Keep in mind that although some of these positions are actually paid jobs that offer health insurance, regular wages, and other benefits, many are staffed by volunteers.

✔ **Some farmers need help working their fields.** In exchange for your work, you receive a place to live and a portion of the profits.

✔ **During off-seasons, many resorts and seasonal parks need caretakers.** That beautiful mountain lake resort you love is empty during the rainy season and needs someone to keep an eye on it. It's still beautiful during the off-season and you have the place all to yourself.

Are you qualified to be a caretaker? It depends. Some individual landowners needing caretakers look for candidates with carpentry and grounds-keeping skills. Some owners just want someone to stay on their property and give it a "lived in" appearance rather than let it sit vacant for a long period of time.

*The Caretaker Gazette* offers information on caretaking opportunities; visit www.caretaker.org.

# Getting Around: Cutting Transportation Costs

For most of us in the twenty-first century, transportation has progressed a long way from the horse and buggy, which is a good thing . . . most of the time. But when a car payment can be higher than a mortgage and the cost of gasoline can outpace your commuting budgets, you may want to think twice about the sanctity of the family car. Do you have other options? More frugal alternatives? Ways to afford more car for less money? Yep. Read on!

# Finding a deal on a set of wheels

Unless you live in the city on an excellent bus line, you're going to need a vehicle at some point in your life. But paying $400 each month on car payments isn't necessary if you follow some of the simple ideas in this section. For detailed help in buying a car, whether new or used, be sure to read *Buying a Car For Dummies* by Deanna Sclar (published by Wiley).

### Paying upfront and avoiding debt

Many people think monthly car payments are a fact of life, like bad hair days and taxes. But the alternative, owning a car outright with no payments at all, can reduce a family's monthly expenses by several hundred dollars. Take my family, for example: We always drive used cars paid for in full, and even though our maintenance expenses may be a bit higher than if we drove new cars, we've never spent more than an average of $50 per month on maintenance. Fifty dollars is a great deal less than the $300-$400 new car payment many families carry these days. Plus, paying interest on a car loan, whether for a new or used car, only adds more to the total cost of the car.

Most people today choose to take out a loan for a car, but you can save on your car loan by purchasing an older vehicle or one with fewer extras. You can carve as much as $100 a month off your monthly car payment simply by making choices like buying a new car with crank windows instead of power windows. Basically, you're paying yourself $100 a month to roll down the windows. That breaks down to about $3.35 a day — enough to treat your family to a daily movie, or a round of colas, or a new puzzle, or a rented video game.

### Finding a deal on a new-to-you set of wheels

An obvious alternative to buying a new car is to buy a used car. Doing so can save you quite a bit of money.

The moment you drive a brand spanking new vehicle off the car lot, it becomes a used car and begins to depreciate rapidly and drastically. Why not pay thousands of dollars *less* for a used car rather than pay top dollar for a soon-to-be-used car? Either way, you're driving around in a used car the moment you leave the car dealership.

Also, consider carefully the type of car you're buying. You can buy a wide range of car models for the same price, but the insurance rates for those cars can vary significantly. Cars with higher safety ratings insure for less. But if you want the snazzy red sports car, be prepared to pay through the nose to insure it! See the later section in this chapter for additional ways to save on car insurance.

If you're thinking of buying a used car, check for the ratings on used cars that interest you by looking at back issues of *Consumer Reports'* annual auto report. You can also search online for used cars in the price range and locality you need. You can get a general feel for what's available in your price range. For a good place to get started, check out www.autotrader.com.

Get the word out to friends, neighbors, and co-workers when you're in need of another car. Our family has found several reasonably priced used cars in good condition just by telling people what we're looking for. We've even had a couple of cars given to us for free.

If you buy a car from an individual or even a dealer, pay the $30 or so to have it checked out by a mechanic before you sign the papers. A friend of mine learned this lesson the hard way. She bought a great looking Cadillac a couple of years ago for $2,500 and had an $800 repair bill within two weeks. But the car still wasn't fixed, so she decided to cut her losses and trade it in at a dealership. The car needed a new engine; the dealer gave her $1,200 for it. So a month after purchasing her "great deal," she found herself recovering from a financial bloodbath that could have been avoided if she'd simply taken it to a mechanic before she bought it."

Another good idea when you're considering a used car is to view the car's history report online. (You can do this for a $10 - $20 fee at www.carfax.com.) You can tell whether the car has ever been in an accident, how many owners it has had, and whether it has been a rental or fleet car.

Other excellent resources for used cars include:

- ✔ **Rental car companies:** They have to clear out their entire inventory every couple of years, and even though the cars are used, sometimes heavily used, rental cars often get a higher level of continuous maintenance throughout their lives than most cars owned by private individuals. Call and find out when your local rental car businesses are holding sales of their out-of-service fleet of cars.

- ✔ **Auctions:** Be sure to check in various local classified advertisement listings for auctions. Many cars at auctions have either been repossessed, confiscated by the police, or are trade-ins from car dealerships.

- ✔ **Dealer repossession sales:** These sales provide reasonably good cars at less-than-market prices.

For ideas for saving money on basic car care and upkeep, see Chapter 13.

### Saving on car insurance

To save money on car insurance, be sure to shop around. The rates are always higher for young, unmarried drivers compared to people over age 25, but the rates from one insurance carrier to another can vary widely. Call around and give each insurance company you talk to the same details: the amount of coverage you want, the deductible you're willing to pay, your age (or the age of the driver, if you're checking this out for your kids), the type of car, and the average amount of driving you do. Many states require comprehensive insurance on mortgaged vehicles, but switching to liability insurance only once the car's paid off can save you hundred of dollars each year.

The best ways to save money on automobile insurance are to drive safely, get married, and grow older. (Although I wouldn't suggest saying "I do" just to get a lower insurance premium!)

## Using public transportation

If you live out in the country somewhere, chances are good that public transportation isn't much help in your situation. But most people in moderate-sized communities and large cities have access to several transportation options other than their own private vehicle.

### The wheels on the bus go round and round

A monthly bus pass easily pays for itself if you live and work near a local bus route. Buses usually offer low rates, discounts for multiple rides, and convenient locations near business and office centers. I always found commuting on the bus a relaxing way to catch up on my reading and to just sit back and watch the scenery go by without worrying about doing the actual driving myself.

Bus passes for teens also provide some much desired independence for the teens and cut down on the amount of time Mom and Dad spend running a taxi service all over town.

### Catching a ride on the subway or commuter train

Larger cities like Chicago and New York have additional public transportation options like the subway or commuter train. Both of these alternatives offer the same benefits of bus systems. You've probably heard scary stories about subway systems, but most of them are quite safe if you use common sense. Riding a New York subway alone at two o'clock in the morning may not be the wisest course of action, but then most commuters aren't riding the subway home at that time of night anyway.

## Biking or walking to keep your budget intact

Many people are willing to pay high prices for a workout at the health club, but few people consider foregoing the health club and simply biking or walking to work or school five days a week. You also save on parking fees if you usually park your car at a pay lot near your office.

If you have things you need to carry into work with you each day, get an inexpensive saddlebag for bicycles that can probably hold anything you need to transport back and forth. You can find auctions for new and used bicycle saddlebags at `www.ebay.com`. Search for "bicycle saddlebags" or "panniers." If you're walking to work or school, invest in a comfortable backpack. You can also keep a change of shoes in the pack so you don't have wear your dress shoes for the two-mile walk to work.

If your work attire isn't conducive to biking or walking, bring a change of clothes with you and make use of the company washroom to touch-up your hair and make-up before work.

## Finding bargains on airfare and rental cars

Although extremely frugal people probably cringe at the expense of traveling by plane, air travel is often a fact of life. If you own your own business and have frequent travel obligations or you need to travel across the country to visit an ill relative, finding bargain transportation options is important to help keep your budget in line.

To get the best deals on airfare:

- ✔ **Plan ahead.** Reserve your flight as soon as you set your travel plans.

- ✔ **Check online search engines such as** `www.expedia.com` **or** `www.travelocity.com` **for cheap flights.** Be sure to compare the search prices to what the airlines are offering directly.

- ✔ **Purchase electronic tickets (e-tickets) rather than pay for paper tickets to be mailed to your home.** Also, if you lose a paper ticket, you're out of luck and have to buy a new ticket. But with e-tickets, your reservation is still solid and the airline can print you a new ticket.

✔ **Consider bidding for tickets online.** You can save a lot of money on major airlines. Check out www.priceline.com.

When you're searching for price quotes, be sure to vary the details of your trip: time, day, airline, and airport. Sometimes altering your destination slightly by landing in a neighboring city, flying at night rather than the morning, or returning on Sunday can reduce airfares considerably. If your travel plans are flexible, watch for price wars between airlines.

Consider using a travel agent if your trip is going to include airfare and accommodations. Travel agents are experts at ferreting out the best package deals.

The rates for renting a car while you're out of town are varied and depend on things like the size and make of car (ask about which model is cheapest), how long you need the car, how far you are driving, and whether or not you need to purchase additional insurance. Be sure to find out whether it's cheaper to pick your car up at the airport, or at some other location at your destination. You may save money by taking an airport shuttle to your hotel and picking up a rental car there. You don't know unless you ask. Also, when you call to reserve your rental car, ask if they have any special promotional rates. Sometimes car rental agencies have lower rates on weekends, or a special rate if you rent the car for a full week rather than just for a few days.

Check to see how much the car rental agency charges you per gallon if you bring the car back without filling up the gas tank first. You usually save more than a few cents if you top off the tank at a local gas station before you return the car to the rental agency.

If you're a member of a frequent-flier program, you may get some special car rental discounts. You also may be eligible for discounts if you're a senior citizen or a member of AARP or AAA. Be sure to ask. If you're buying a package deal that includes airfare and accommodations, ask if a car rental can be included in the package (and be sure to find out how much it will add to your package). Some travel packages include unlimited car rental for free or for a greatly reduced price.

You can often find discounted car rental prices online at www.orbitz.com.

## Opting to travel by train or bus

Before you commit to long distance air travel, compare the cost of airfare to the cost of a bus or train ticket. Sometimes (but not always) you can find great deals on bus and train fare if you have extra time to spend reaching your destination.

If you don't have far to travel, taking the bus can be a really good idea. But be sure to comparison shop. Don't assume the bus is always cheaper. The same goes for train travel. A friend of mine decided to take a train from the Seattle area to southern California, thinking that a train trip would be less expensive than flying even though it would take much longer to reach her destination. She was surprised to discover flying was considerably less expensive.

# Purchasing Appliances

Everyone needs something to cook on, a way to get clothes clean, and a heating system to keep the cold away during the winter. Here are some ideas for saving money on this very expensive — yet very important — part of life.

Take your time making a decision about any major appliances you need to purchase. Even if your stove's broken down completely, or the washing machine is beyond repair, don't make snap decisions. You can cook for a few days in the slow cooker or microwave, and you can always go to the all-night laundromat down the street if you're facing a dirty clothes emergency. Taking your time to shop around and perhaps look for good quality secondhand appliances can save lots of money if you're patient and don't make a hasty decision.

## Keeping energy efficiency in mind

If you're in the market for an appliance (whether you buy it new or used), consider buying one that's more economical to use. For example, in many parts of the United States, the cost of electricity has far outpaced the cost of natural gas. Consider switching to a gas clothes dryer rather than another electric dryer when you need a new one.

Also some local utilities give rebates to customers who purchase energy-efficient models of major appliances. Be sure to check whether any programs exist in your area before you buy. The rebate may mean the difference between buying just a standard washer or being able to afford a top-of-the-line energy-efficient model.

For detailed information on shopping for new energy-efficient appliances, check out the Pacific Gas and Electric Company's advice on the Web at www.pge.com/003_save_energy/003a_res/pdf/appliance.pdf.

Used appliances are often not very energy efficient. Sometimes the increased cost per month on your utility bill from an older appliance can be more than the monthly payments on a new, more efficient model. Check around to see if you can find the details about the energy efficiency of an older appliance you're considering buying. Often you can find a label on the appliance itself or information on the manufacturer's Web site. Figure out the energy efficiency of an appliance at `www.eren.doe.gov/consumerinfo/refbriefs/ec7.html`.

## *Shopping for scratch-and-dent and secondhand*

You can find slightly used appliances for a fraction of the cost of new appliances by shopping the following locations:

- ✔ **Outlet, clearance, or warehouse stores:** Slightly damaged appliances (external scratches or small dents) are sometimes sold for a substantial discount compared to new, undamaged or unscratched items. Call around to large stores and ask what they do with their scratch-and-dent merchandise.

- ✔ **Furniture rental stores:** You can find good deals on rental returns from furniture rental stores. The appliances are used, but usually not for a long time.

- ✔ **Used appliance stores:** You can find reconditioned appliances that often come with warranties.

- ✔ **Auctions:** You can get really rock-bottom prices on good appliances at auctions. But remember, go early because the good items go quickly.

- ✔ **Family or neighbors:** Ask around. Let the word out that you're in need of a washer/dryer or freezer. Someone you talk to may have neighbors or family members who are updating their kitchen or moving out of state.

## *Thinking twice about the rent-to-own option*

Ever see those rent-to-own ads on TV for complete furniture suites or big screen television sets? Renting-to-own usually appeals to people who have a limited budget but are in need of some basics, like a living room couch or a washer and dryer. If you're renting-to-own an appliance, the store usually includes all repair work as part of the rental agreement.

The credit checks for rent-to-own businesses are usually minimal or non-existent. If you stop making payments for some reason, the dealer simply takes back the appliance or piece of furniture. When we were young and newly married, my husband and I were trying to establish credit, so we went down to the rent-to-own store and rented a new, inexpensive stereo system. We enjoyed our new sound system, could easily afford the monthly payments, and at the end of the rental term, we owned the stereo and had the beginnings of a good credit record.

By the time you've rented your rent-to-own appliance to the point of outright ownership, you've probably paid two to five times the retail price of your appliance. If you're short on upfront cash or need to build a credit rating, renting-to-own might be a good idea. But please note the word *might*.

# Chapter 16

# Calling Secondhand Rose: Finding Quality in Previously Owned Merchandise

*In This Chapter*

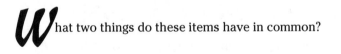 Adjusting attitudes about secondhand shopping

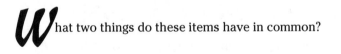 Discovering hidden treasure in unlikely places

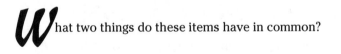 Giving high-quality, bargain-priced gifts

*W*hat two things do these items have in common?

- ✔ Three wooden bookshelves overflowing with classic books and educational supplies
- ✔ A framed, matted, and autographed bald eagle photo by a famous wildlife photographer
- ✔ A school backpack
- ✔ A mahogany formal dining table with six matching chairs
- ✔ An office-quality paper cutter
- ✔ A huge, comfortable couch
- ✔ A slow cooker
- ✔ The shirt on my back

Give up? Well, for starters, 1) I can see everything on that list from where I'm sitting in my family room at the computer desk, and 2) not one of these items was purchased new from the store — they're all secondhand!

Yep, everything on the list — from the couch where my dearly-beloveds sit in blissful family togetherness ("Mom! He's got his feet on my side of the cushion again!") to my well-loved comfy shirt — came from secondhand sources. Whether we're talking Grandma's attic, an upscale consignment shop, the Salvation Army Thrift Store, or a neighbor's clean-out-the-closets yard sale, you can find almost anything at these resources.

Secondhand shopping can give a wonderful outlet for latent creative talents. Look beyond the surface and what do you see? That old, rugged, saggy leather boot can be filled with potting soil and made into a one-of-a-kind outdoor planter. Does that wooden chair just need a fresh coat of paint to look wonderful in the den?

In this chapter, I share common sources for secondhand purchases, and give hints on creative, easy ways to find quality merchandise in your local garage sale or thrift store. Sometimes you just need to view something slightly different in order to see the creative possibilities around you.

Let's go shopping!

# Thinking Thrifty Thoughts

They call me Secondhand Rose. Well, actually they don't call me anything of the sort, but maybe they should. Secondhand shopping has been one of the single greatest helps to our family's tight budget over the years. Although I'm the first to admit I like to buy new items, I'm often in a tight place financially, requiring more than a little creative maneuvering to stay afloat. But I've heard various excuses from people who don't like purchasing items secondhand. Most of their excuses can be divided into the following categories:

- ✔ It's dirty.
- ✔ It's used.
- ✔ It's out-of-date.
- ✔ It's unattractive.
- ✔ It's unkind (yes, you read that right).

Here are some ideas to think about before you write off the idea of secondhand shopping completely.

## *It's dirty: Clean it up!*

If you're worried about something being dirty, remember, you won't be using it or wearing it "as is" right off the rack. By all means, wash everything you buy at a thrift store or garage sale before using or wearing. This statement bears repeating: Wash everything!

Other than an occasional sweaty preteen boy dirty shoe problem, if you wash your secondhand purchases thoroughly with a quality laundry detergent or cleaning product, then voilá, they're clean.

## *It's used . . . but gently*

Guess what happens after you wear your brand-new $40 blouse just once? It's now a used shirt. Do you rush right out and buy a replacement blouse because you can't wear something that's been worn before? No, probably not, unless you're bucking for a television spot on *Lifestyles of the Rich and Wasteful.* You don't replace each item of clothing simply because you've worn it before. You just deal subconsciously with the fact that everything in your closet is used.

If environmental awareness is high on your list of personal priorities, buying used clothing and other household items is the ultimate form of reducing/reusing/recycling. Not only does it save you money, secondhand shopping also cuts down on the number of new items needing to be manufactured. Less waste and pollution mean fewer resources being used. Wow, what a deal! Even the environment comes out ahead!

## *It's out-of-date: But "retro" is in!*

Yes, many items in thrift stores and garage sales are out-of-date. But who says you have to buy the ones that are out-of-date? By looking carefully, you can find a large selection of fashionable, sometimes even brand-new, clothing and decorative items. If you shop at consignment stores, they usually sort through the items carefully and have already rejected the floral housedresses and avocado green appliances.

Think of secondhand shopping as an expedition after gold. You only find the really valuable items if you're willing to dig a little — and then dig a little more — and then keep on digging until you've sifted the gold nuggets out from the polyester pant suits.

Besides, haven't you heard the word *retro* bandied about in fashionable circles lately? Out-of-date is now often considered up-to-date and chic. Why, oh why, did I clean those old bell-bottoms and tie-dyed T-shirts out my closet? Who would've thought they'd come back in style with a vengeance?

## It's unattractive: Keep digging for the gold

By all means, if the item is unattractive, don't buy it! You may have to sort through a large number of unattractive items on the racks and in the bins until you find your gold hidden in them thar hills. Don't bring home plain rocks with zero value to you. Go for the gold! Only buy what you really love.

## It's unkind: Don't buy what the kids don't like

Oh, no! It's the dreaded Secondhand Rose Syndrome!

One man I spoke with said he'd rather not have children at all than have kids of his wear something that didn't come new from a prestigious department store. If you know the secrets to successful second-hand shopping, you can have your kids dressed in clothes from your favorite department stores, or wearing whatever brand names meet your particular style of "dress-your-kid-for-success" criteria. Read Chapter 7 for further information on dressing children on a budget.

To give some attention to my acquaintance's complaint, you want your children to wear clothes that aren't completely unfashionable or out-of-date. Once again, while shopping at secondhand sources, keep in mind that you don't need to buy anything for yourself or your child that's unattractive or out-of-style.

# Discovering Treasure: Old and New

You can find good stuff, and the clothes aren't all polyester suits, feather boas your Great Grandma wore, and shirts with pointy collars. You can actually find treasure in that hope chest after all. Believe it or not, you may even find some nifty dishware from the days when astronaut Neil Armstrong first walked on the moon.

The most common sources for secondhand items are garage sales, estate sales, auctions, thrift stores, and consignment stores. The following sections detail the benefits of these different types of resources.

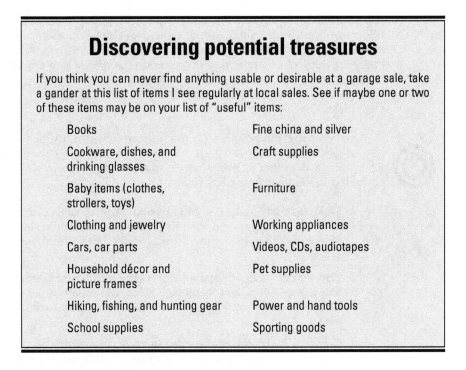

## Discovering potential treasures

If you think you can never find anything usable or desirable at a garage sale, take a gander at this list of items I see regularly at local sales. See if maybe one or two of these items may be on your list of "useful" items:

| | |
|---|---|
| Books | Fine china and silver |
| Cookware, dishes, and drinking glasses | Craft supplies |
| Baby items (clothes, strollers, toys) | Furniture |
| Clothing and jewelry | Working appliances |
| Cars, car parts | Videos, CDs, audiotapes |
| Household décor and picture frames | Pet supplies |
| Hiking, fishing, and hunting gear | Power and hand tools |
| School supplies | Sporting goods |

## *Garage sales*

Whether you call them garage sales, yard sales, tag sales, rummage sales, or church jumble sales, this secondhand option represents an excellent means of recycling someone else's castoffs, finding a new treasure, and hanging onto some of your hard-earned money. Remember, someone else's trash is another person's treasure.

Occasionally stopping at a single garage sale every six months probably won't produce the exact items on your shopping list. I've discovered that the garage sale game is all about quantity — the more sales you visit, the more likely you'll find something worthwhile. I usually try to allow at least one Saturday every other month to make the rounds of the local garage sale circuit. During peak garage sale months, the late spring through early fall, I may go as often as every other weekend. Hard-core garage sale shoppers usually wait in their car for the first garage sale of the weekend every Saturday morning. But be careful — if you love to shop, garage sales can be addicting! Unfortunately, Bargain Hunters Anonymous hasn't started a chapter in my area yet.

### *Mapping out your shopping plan*

Don't make a big mistake when hitting the garage sale circuit. Don't leave your driveway without a game plan, and then wander around town aimlessly, hoping to see a sign pointing the way to a local sale. Hit-or-miss garage sale shopping isn't the most efficient use of your time and effort, and if you've ever tried shopping this way, you've had your share of frustrations. Ask around to discover which day of the week is the best for garage sales in your area. In one town, Wednesday may be the hot garage sale day, while it's Thursday someplace else.

Map out your route in advance. My mother carefully instilled her garage sale techniques in me from the time I was old enough to read a map. She was a bit of a Garage Sale Guru and highly organized about her battle plan. According to Mom:

1. **Wake up early and eat a good breakfast.** Most sales start before 9:00 a.m., so you want to get your battle plan in place in plenty of time before the opening of the most promising sales.

2. **Check your local newspaper's classified ads under Garage Sales, Yard Sales, and Rummage Sales.** (Newspapers list these sales differently from one part of the country to the next.)

3. **Circle or highlight all the sales in your community or general vicinity that sound even vaguely interesting.** If a sale is spread out over several days, plan on shopping that one the first day. (If you'll be back in the neighborhood, ask if they'll be adding merchandise in subsequent days.)

4. **Decide which sales sound the most promising — you want to hit those first while the selection is best.** The more space the notice takes up in the paper, the more money those folks spent to post the ad. You can bet they have a large quantity of treasures for sale, because they anticipate being able to recoup their advertising investment.

5. **Cut out the ads for the sales you want to visit.** A handy trick I discovered from Mom is to take a piece of transparent tape and stick it down firmly over the ad (so the ad shows through the tape). After the ad has adhered completely to the tape, carefully lift the tape back off the newspaper. The ad miraculously lifts right off the page. Try it!

6. **Tape the ads onto a blank piece of paper, arranging them in the order you want to shop.** You can also organize the sales by general locations or neighborhoods.

7. **Get out your handy-dandy city map and plan your driving route.**

8. **Make sure you have plenty of gas in the car.**

9. **Go shopping!**

When planning your route, take into account the types of neighborhoods where sales are located. If you're looking for baby clothes or children's toys, you don't need to visit the local retirement community, and you probably won't find antiques in the neighborhoods with tricycles and wading pools in every yard. But then again, you never know. Maybe the young family with the jungle gym just inherited a houseful of antique furniture from Great-Aunt Belle. Or the retired couple may have kept toys, books, and children's clothing on hand for visiting grandkids. Another criterion for choosing a promising garage sale is to remember that nicer neighborhoods usually have nicer items for sale.

When you arrive at a sale, take a fast walk through the entire sale to get an initial overview of what's for sale. If you start at the curb and work your way in, another shopper may nab that beautiful $10 bunk bed in the back of the garage while you're busy surveying 25-cent fashion dolls in the driveway!

### *Preparing your garage sale expedition kit*

When heading out the door on a hiking expedition to the high mountain backcountry, you probably wouldn't leave home without at least the bare essentials of survival. Perhaps a compass, a map, and a canteen. You also need to prepare yourself when heading out the door for uncharted garage sale territory. You need supplies so you don't get lost, run out of energy, or use up needless time following dead-end paths. The following list of items can easily fit into a small bag or purse to keep in your car when you journey out on a Garage Sale Safari. Watch out for stampeding white elephants!

- ✔ **A map.** Not all garage sales have effective signs marking the way. Your best bet is to find the address and then locate the sale on your map.

- ✔ **The local newspaper or a list of garage sales.** Look over the local offerings before you leave home and bring the list with you in the car.

- ✔ **Cold, hard cash.** Stop by the cash machine or bank before you start your journey through your neighbors' garages. Most yard sales don't accept credit cards or personal checks, although some estate sales do. Be sure to stock up on $1 bills and change, especially quarters.

- ✔ **Shopping list.** Everyone has a list of items they're meaning to buy, whether it's items for the home, seasonal decorations, gifts, toys, videos, tools, linens, books, or clothing needs. By carrying this list with you while you're out perusing this week's yard sales, you may find some items for a fraction of the cost you would've paid new.

✔ **Measurements.** Keep a list of measurements you may need, such as the size of your tabletop, the width of your windows, the length of wall spaces throughout your house, and so on.

✔ **Sizes.** Make a list of clothing sizes for all family members or people on your gift list. Also make a paper outline of your children's current shoe sizes. Over time, the size markings on shoes fade, so having a template of their foot is the next best thing to your child being there to try on shoes.

✔ **Tape measure.** Don't trust yourself to accurately eyeball whether that beautiful hutch will fit in your dining room or not. Measure it!

✔ **A handy length of strong rope.** Occasionally I buy items that don't quite fit in the car or trunk. If you have a rope, you can tie your purchases down, rather than hoping the person you're buying from has an extra rope to spare.

✔ **A snack and water bottle.** Everyone needs a little nutrition break at some point. Carrying your own snacks cuts down on the temptation to spend extra money at the corner convenience store or fast-food restaurant.

✔ **A money belt or fanny pack.** You have a much easier time jumping in and out of your car quickly if you're wearing a fanny pack rather than carrying a purse. A fanny pack also keeps your hands free for shopping, browsing, and carrying items around while you make your decisions.

✔ **Pen and paper.** You may need to take down names and phone numbers so you can call back later. "Do you still have that toddler bed you said you'd sell at half price if it hadn't sold by the end of the day?"

## Estate sales and auctions

Check for any estate sale listings while you're browsing through your local classified ads. You can often find antique furniture and glassware, general housewares, jewelry, and classic books at estate sales. Usually an estate sale occurs after someone dies and is run by professionals. They price the items and then hold the actual sale for the heirs, receiving a percentage of the profits for their work. Many estate sales accept checks and credit cards, too. Come early for the best selection — the early bird really does get the worm. Estate sales usually have people lined up outside the door before the sale even officially opens.

Auctions can be a fun way to spend a weekend. Look in your newspaper's classified ads or the business section of the phone book under auctions to discover where auctions are being held in your local area. Auction houses usually offer a special preview time when prospective shoppers can see the items that are up for auction. The preview is usually either the day before the auction, or earlier the same day. A friend of mine who loves to frequent auctions told me that the best time to make purchases is to stay late. Most people leave long before the auction is over, so the late bird gets the worm. Many times, the auctioneer will start boxing items together to help speed things along at the end of the sale. Auctions are run differently from place to place, so come early, ask questions, look around, and generally get a feel for how the auction's being conducted.

An auction can be a fun and emotional experience as the bidding gets higher and higher. To avoid getting caught up in the experience and unintentionally overspending, know the value of the items you're bidding on. You don't want to get home and find you could've bought the same items for less money (and brand new!) at a discount store down the street.

## Thrift stores

Thrift stores are usually more expensive than garage sales. For example, at garage sales, you can find nice women's blouses for $1 (or less), while thrift stores charge in the range of $3-$10 for the same item. Compared to the same blouse being sold in a department store for $40, thrift store prices are still rock bottom.

Shopping at thrift stores provides a successful way of recycling clothing and other functional household goods. Furthermore, many charities operate thrift stores so your patronage could be helping the Salvation Army or Goodwill, a battered women's shelter, cancer research, or any number of other worthwhile causes. Some of these stores provide entry-level employment and training for people getting back on their feet.

Many thrift stores offer frequent discounts, so it pays to stop by regularly. One of my favorite stores places different colored tags on all its merchandise, and each day a different color is discounted (for example: red tags = 75 percent off, blue = 50 percent off, green = 25 percent off). Always check near the store's entrance for signs or posters announcing current discounts or upcoming sale events. Military personnel and seniors often qualify for additional discounts.

At most thrift stores all sales are final, so try on clothing before leaving the store.

## Consignment stores

Consignment stores are the most expensive of the secondhand alternatives, but they're also my favorite. The majority of consignment stores are well organized, provide a higher level of customer service than you find at thrift stores, and most of the junk has already been culled so your chances of finding a few gold nuggets are much better.

Consignment stores split their profits with the people who bring in items. Either the store pays cash or store credit upfront for the items (often about half the intended selling price), or the store pays the consignor a percentage of the final selling price for the items, usually about 60/40, in favor of the store.

With consignment shops, you get the best of both worlds. You save money by shopping at the consignment store, and you can also make a few extra pennies by consigning your own castoffs or your children's out-grown items. The rate of return is usually much higher per item than selling at your own garage sale. Keep in mind that consignment stores only want high-quality, well-cared-for items currently in season. Don't try to consign your ski boots in mid-summer.

When my youngest child was a baby — and growing out of clothes faster than seemed humanly possible — I took her outgrown clothes to the local children's consignment store and received store credit. I took the proceeds and turned right around and shopped for clothes in her current size. It saved us a bundle on clothing expenses.

Consignment stores often specialize in a particular niche market. You can find consignment stores that cater to women, children, sporting goods, music, and even books. Usually the used bookstores only give store credit rather than cash, but you can still recycle books you're finished with, especially paperbacks. Read Chapter 10 for information on frugal book buying.

Look for these businesses in the phone book under Consignment Stores and Secondhand Stores.

# Checking for Quality and Safety While Secondhand Shopping

Shopping for secondhand items can be fun, rewarding, and incredibly inexpensive. But if you come home to find the zipper doesn't work in the "like-new" jeans you bought for your son, or the collectible pottery mug has a hairline crack making it unusable, your inexpensive shopping expedition quickly turns into a frustrating trip back to the store to find out if items are returnable. By checking for hidden flaws and avoiding some problem items altogether, your adventures in the world of bargain hunting can yield more big game than big duds.

## Consulting secondhand checklists

Although you can find beautiful, like-new items at secondhand outlets, look over your finds for any hidden flaws. You may want to consider making a copy of the following check lists to take with you on your next secondhand shopping spree.

### Clothing

Double-check each item of clothing before heading to the checkout counter. Remember, most secondhand items can't be returned. Refer to the following list as you decide on any clothing purchases:

- ✔ Check tags for brand name, size (especially when the outfit has multiple pieces), and fabric content.

- ✔ Read any special laundry instructions. You aren't saving money if you buy a $2 blouse that needs dry cleaning after each wearing.

- ✔ Look carefully at seams (under arms, across shoulders, legs, crotch, and back end).

- ✔ Make sure pockets aren't ripping out or coming undone. Check for holes inside the pockets.

- ✔ Check the buttons. Are they all there? Do they match? Have they been replaced?

- ✔ Make sure zippers work properly and aren't broken or previously replaced.

- ✔ Carefully check the entire garment for stains, rips, holes, snags, runs, bleach marks, loose hems, or defects.

- ✔ Try the clothing on. Don't trust the sizes on the labels. The previous owner may have laundered the sweater inappropriately and changed its size, or the item may have been altered after someone lost weight.

If you're a seamstress, or know a good one, you can alter some clothing slightly (for example, shorten a skirt or pant length).

### Appliances, radios, and televisions (oh, my)

Garage sales and thrifts stores are usually teeming with used small appliances. Don't assume that if someone's getting rid of it, it doesn't work. Sometimes the previous owner just tired of the style, or wanted to update to a new model. This list gives you ideas of what to look for to see if that cute little toaster oven is really a lemon in disguise:

- ✔ Test all electrical appliances to make sure they work properly. Don't hesitate to ask to use an electrical outlet.

- ✔ Check for frayed cords or plugs.

- ✔ Try bulbs in lighting fixtures.

- ✔ Open battery compartments and look for corrosion from old batteries.

### Books

Books and other reading material, such as reference works and magazines, are common at garage sales and thrift stores. If you're anything like me, going to your local library book sale is like a little slice of heaven here on earth. I never have a problem finding enough books. My problem is finding enough bookshelves to store all my bargains! But not all books are worth bringing home. Here are some tips for looking over that pile of bedtime reading:

- ✔ Smell for musty odors (those odors are difficult to remove).

- ✔ Scan through the book for ripped, marked up, or stuck-together pages.

- ✔ Look at the spine to make sure it's not broken or damaged.

- ✔ Check for water damage or stains.

### Jewelry

If you love costume jewelry, you can find a never-ending source of it at garage sales and thrift stores. Why spend $20 on a necklace when you can find a similar one for 25 cents? Here are a couple of tips to make sure your necklace doesn't unravel the first time you wear it:

- ✔ Check clasps to make sure they close and aren't falling apart.

- ✔ Make sure beads are strung securely on a strong wire or string.

### Glassware/china

I can't even begin to tell you the number of times I've seen pieces of my mother's china at garage sales. Before purchasing it, though, I always check quickly for the following flaws:

- ✔ Look for chips, cracks, scratches, and stains.

- ✔ Feel along the lip of the glass or plate with your hand for chips or nicks (many imperfections on the edge can be felt but not easily seen).

### Videos, DVDs, CDs, and tapes

Purchasing used videos and DVDs, compact discs, and audiotapes is always a bit chancy. You never really know until you get home what condition the merchandise is in, but by looking each item over carefully, you increase your chances of finding a good quality tape or CD. And when you find a movie you've wanted to see for only 50 cents, you can take the chance.

- ✔ Check the contents of the box to make sure it matches the cover.

- ✔ If you're at a garage sale, ask the owner if they have a player where you can test a tape, CD, or video.

- ✔ Look for scratches or damage.

## Avoiding potential problem purchases

A few items commonly found at garage sales and thrift stores actually have the potential to be dangerous. Here's a list of items to watch out for:

- ✔ Older infant car seats (if a car seat has previously been through an accident, the seat is no longer safe to use with a child — also, regulations and recommendations for car seat manufacturers change regularly).

- ✔ Baby walkers (the ones that roll around on the floor) are no longer considered safe at any time. Avoid these items completely.

- ✔ Older strollers, cribs, play pens (damage can be hidden or regulations may have changed in recent years — older cribs may contain harmful paints or have slats spaced too widely apart).

- ✔ Painted toys (if they're old, they may contain lead paint).

- ✔ Drawstring hoods on children's clothing can entangle the child and cause choking or strangulation.

- ✔ Electrical items (may have electrical shorts inside).

- ✔ Hair dryers without electrocution protection.

- ✔ Lawn darts (unsafe at any speed).

- ✔ Bean bag chairs (small children can choke on the beans if they leak out of the chairs).

## A-tisket, a-tasket, making a gift basket

You can find perfectly good cookie tins (which sell for $3-$10 new) for about a quarter to fifty cents a piece. You can use the tins for storing home-baked treats to give as gifts (fudge, cookies, candies, and so on). A dozen homemade cookies and a 39-cent tin make a fun, frugal gift appreciated by everyone. Check tins for signs of damage or rust. If you plan to add food to the tins, wash and dry thoroughly, and then line with waxed paper cut to size.

I'm amazed at the number of quality wicker baskets for sale at thrift stores. These baskets are expensive items if bought new in craft stores, but are usually less than a dollar when purchased used. They are perfect for homemade gift baskets. If the baskets are a little worn, a thorough scrubbing followed by a coat of spray-on paint can work wonders.

A little wadded up gift wrap in the bottom of the basket, two china tea cups and saucers (also found secondhand), a box of assorted gourmet teas (buy new, please), a lace doily or two, a bit of cellophane (bought by the roll on sale at the craft store) over the entire basket, a bow, and you've got yourself a tea-party-to-go gift basket. Or use a coffee theme, bubble bath with bathtub toys, or whatever strikes the interest of your friends and family members.

# *Bargain Hunting for Gift-Giving Occasions*

Most people aren't completely comfortable giving used gifts for birthdays and holidays, but a large number of gift ideas are still available through secondhand sources — and many of these items aren't really previously used purchases at all. They're brand new. Many items may have been purchased and long forgotten ("Baby will grow into this someday"), or were received as gifts and weren't appropriate for the recipient ("Why did Aunt Martha think I needed another carved wooden nut dish?"). Sometimes I find useful household items still in their original packaging and never opened. Perhaps the new bride didn't want to bother returning four extra toasters, so she dropped them off at the Goodwill on the corner. Any one of these items can be the perfect gift just waiting to help you fill your gift list.

Another common item on the thrift store/garage sale circuit is gift-wrapping supplies. You can find wrapping paper, bows and ribbon, gift boxes and bags, and even greeting cards in perfect condition at secondhand shops.

# Part V
# Part of Tens

# In this part . . .

Sometimes it feels like a frugal gift will tell your friends and loved ones that you're cheap, but money spent on gifts doesn't have to be equal to how much love you feel toward the recipient. If birthdays, anniversaries, and holidays such as Valentine's Day keep you scrambling, looking for something to give that's more creative than a box of chocolates and a card from the supermarket, you'll find plenty of frugal — and even romantic — suggestions here. The chapters in this part contain lists of frugal gift ideas and inexpensive — yet meaningful — ways to tell your sweetheart, "I love you!"

# Chapter 17

# Ten Frugal Ways to Tell Your Sweetheart, "I Love You!"

*W*hether it's Valentine's Day or the anniversary of your first date, here are ten simple ideas for expressing your love . . . without taking out a bank loan!

## *Baking Heart-shaped Food Items*

Preparing a heart-shaped anything is a romantic gesture. Make heart-shaped pancakes for breakfast, heart-shaped crispy rice treats for a snack, or a heart-shaped pizza for dinner. You can also use a heart-shaped cookie cutter to cut the crust off sandwiches. How romantic — heart-shaped PBJs for that special someone!

You can easily bake a heart-shaped cake without any special heart-shaped pans. Just make a cake recipe for a double-layered cake. Bake one layer in an 8-inch round cake pan and the other layer in an 8-inch square cake pan. After the cake is cool, cut the round layer into half-circles. On a large serving platter or cookie sheet, place the two half-circles along two adjoining edges of the square layer. Surprise, surprise — a heart-shaped cake! Covered in frosting, your loved one won't even realize the secret of your cake's shape. I mean when the cake's covered in frosting, not your sweetie, although that may be fun, too.

# Making a "100 Reasons Why I Love You" List

Write out a list of 100 reasons why you love your dear one. Does he always put the toilet seat down? Does she remember your birthday? Does he wash the dishes regularly? Does she maintain the yard's appearance? Anything and everything can become an item on this list. Have some of the reasons be funny, some just plain silly, and some sentimental and romantic. Just make them all true! If you can't bring yourself to be creative enough to do 100 reasons, I bet you can at least come up with 20 reasons, right? Ten? Oh, c'mon!

# Reading Love Poems Together at a Local Bookstore

Browse a local bookstore that has a coffee shop, grab a latte and a stack of books of love poetry, and read quietly to each across a small, intimate table. Don't forget to play footsie under the table, too!

# Sharing Romantic Greeting Cards

Sometimes money's so tight, even the expense of a nice card for Valentine's Day may be out of the question. Making cards for each other is simple and inexpensive. Use a card-making program on your computer or draw your own cards on scraps of paper. If drawing your own designs is beyond your artistic abilities, glue on magazine clippings, pressed flowers, dried leaves, photos, ticket stubs, or any other meaningful or romantic items.

Plan a fun date for just the two of you and visit the local card shop at the mall. Or go to your favorite quirky gift shop with the unusual cards. Browse through the romantic greeting card racks and read aloud the cards that you would want to give each other. Laugh at the funny ones, gaze lovingly at each other over the sentimental ones, and blush visibly over the embarrassing joke cards.

# Bringing Chocolate

Bring chocolates to your honey. And not just a plain ol' candy heart from the bargain bin at the grocery store. Go out of your way to visit that special little gift shop downtown with the handmade specialty candy selection. Even a single, elegantly wrapped, hand-dipped almond-flavored bonbon makes a heart-felt gift and shows that you're paying attention when your loved one sighs over the chocolate counter at the expensive department store. And besides, nobody ever shot someone bearing chocolate.

# Leaving Love Notes in Unexpected Places

Write "I love you!" in the fog on the bathroom mirror while your sweetie's in the shower. Pack a love note in his or her lunch or briefcase. Set one on the car seat while your honey is at work. A note is a tangible way to remind your loved one of your devotion, but if you're looking to make a bigger, noisier splash in the "loving expressions" department, try the following tip.

# Sending a Singing Love-O-Gram

You may want to hire a real singing telegram company to serenade your dear one, but we're supposed to be talking frugal tips, here. How about hiring a group of neighborhood children to sing a love song to your sweetie? Have the kids ring the bell, hand Sweetie-Pie a note stating who the song is from, and then let them belt out the song. On-key or off, the song is a touching expression of your love.

# Making a Scroll-of-Love

To make your scroll, use either a receipt roll from an office supply store or a paper roll from an adding machine. Start at the loose end of the roll and then write down romantic quotes, loving thoughts, or any number of favorite feelings you want to share with your loved one. Take your time. You can make your writings an ongoing project while you watch television. Or keep it next to your computer so you can jot down ideas while you're browsing online. You want to keep this project a secret, so make sure you work on it when your honey isn't around. When you're finished, wrap each end of the scroll around a dowel cut to size, and then, when you give it as a gift, plan on reading through it together with your dearly beloved. Don't forget to bring a box of tissue if your honey's a sop for the emotional stuff.

# Getting Sentimental at a Wedding

Next time you're invited to a wedding, hold hands with your honey through the entire ceremony. Every time something sweet, profoundly moving, or romantic is said during the ceremony, squeeze your loved one's hand meaningfully. Try to catch your sweetie's eye and smile shyly at appropriately mushy times, too.

# Saying "I Love You!"

The most frugal way of all to say "I love you!" is just to say the words. Some people think their love goes without saying, but you need to express your love in as many tangible ways as possible — through looks, small attentions, personal nuances, but especially through the actual words. Say it. Say it every day for the rest of your life. Trust me, you won't regret it.

# Chapter 18

# Ten Frugal Gift-Giving Ideas

*T*he majority of most people's holiday expenses go for gifts. Giving to others is definitely a wonderful and important part of the holiday season, but is going to the store and paying top dollar for household clutter really the answer?

In this chapter, I give you some gift ideas to help you think creatively about the holidays. Sometimes giving gifts is really a matter of creativity versus cash. This list isn't exhaustive by any stretch of the imagination, but let your mind ponder these ideas for a while. You may be surprised how much fun you have finding creative gift-giving alternatives.

## *Making a Personalized Calendar*

Creating your own personalized calendar can be as simple as buying a store-bought calendar and writing important family days to remember throughout the year, such as birthdays, anniversaries, and so on. Or buy a blank calendar at the rubber stamp store and decorate the entire calendar yourself. These calendars usually come with a top section that you can decorate with photos or mementos, just like a scrapbook page. Add the important family dates to the calendar, and then when the year's over, the recipient can cut off the calendar section and keep the scrapbook pages together as a memory book. You can also design a personalized calendar on your computer's desktop publishing program. Rather than photos or artwork at the top of each calendar page, how about a simple layout design with favorite family recipes, quotations, and so forth?

# Putting Together Favorite Family Recipes

Many families pass down favorite recipes almost like treasured family heirlooms. Request that family members send you a couple of their favorite recipes, and maybe even a sentence or two about the recipe, its history or origin, any traditions surrounding the recipe, or even funny family stories. Then, if you have access to a computer, put together your own cookbook. (Even if you have the booklets professionally copied and bound, it's still a relatively inexpensive gift.) If you don't have access to a computer, handwritten recipes put onto index cards are an inexpensive gift as well. Put the recipes together in a nice recipe box found during your garage sale travels or on sale at the kitchen supply store. Or buy an inexpensive plain card file box at the office supply store, and decorate it with paint or stickers. Recipes make for especially nice gifts for young adults going out on their own or for a newly married couple.

# Giving a "Learn to Cook" Gift Set to a Child

Whether you're giving a gift to your own child or to a niece or neighbor, teaching children to cook is a great inexpensive gift idea that has lasting significance and helps children through the rest of their lives. For your learn-to-cook gift set, sew a child's apron and include a cookbook and some cooking utensils. Even folks with very little sewing experience can cut out a child-sized apron pattern. Sew the edges with bias tape, and then add some ribbon for ties around the neck and waist. I find children's cookbooks all the time at thrift stores and garage sales, and most of them look like they're brand new. Occasionally I've seen offers for inexpensive — and sometimes free — children's cookbooks on the back of boxed mixes and flour bags. You can also pick up some brand new inexpensive kitchen supplies (like stirring spoons, spatulas, and measuring cups) at the dollar store. This gift can also include a handmade certificate for time spent with you in the kitchen baking chocolate chip cookies, or prepare one of the recipes in the cookbook you're including with the gift.

# Giving a Coffee Mug or Tea Cup Along with a Tasty Treat

In a pretty, tasteful, or humorous coffee mug, include a selection of small bags of coffee mix or favorite coffee beans, spiced cider mix, a selection of gourmet teas, a pretty silver-plated spoon found at a thrift store, or other favorite tea time or coffee break treats. Wrap in cellophane and tie with a pretty ribbon. You can even make this gift into a tea-for-two basket by including two teacups and saucers, a variety of gourmet teabags, a box of scone or muffin mix, and a small jar of jam or lemon curd. You can often find inexpensive, "like-new" baskets at thrift stores and garage sales.

# Putting Together a Box of "Loving Memories"

Save small souvenirs (theater tickets, seashells, matchbooks with restaurant logos, and so on) from previous dates or activities you shared with your loved one. Put them into a special gift box on an anniversary or a "just because" day. If you can find an inexpensive framed display box, you can use it to arrange your special mementos. For the friend or relative far from home — perhaps in the military or away at college for the first time — this can make an especially meaningful gift.

# Acquiring Cotton Scraps for Your Favorite Seamstress

Quilting and sewing are popular pastimes. Small pieces of colorful fabric can be used in a variety of creative ways, so if you have a sewing fanatic in your circle of friends, keep your eyes open while you're at garage sales for cotton shirts, sheets, and pillowcases in nice patterns or plain colors. Pick scraps in colors that blend well together. Cut out large squares of useable material from the backs and fronts of the shirts, fold the material into neat squares, and then tie a ribbon around the stack of colorful scraps.

# Making a Soup Can Planter

Use cuttings from your own plants or buy small, inexpensive houseplants from the store. Clean out a soup can and keep the label intact. Try not to get the label wet. After the can is dry, punch a few drainage holes in the bottom with a hammer and nail (don't hammer the can to your kitchen counters!). Cover the label with clear adhesive paper to protect it from water damage, fill with potting soil, and then add a cutting or small plant. You may even want to include a small thrift store plate to catch water under the drainage holes. These gifts make nice teacher appreciation presents. Hey, even Andy Warhol thought soup cans were valid art objects!

# Giving a "Dress-Up" Bin to a Family with Small Children

After you've scoured through your own supplies of castoff clothing and jewelry, head out to the garage sale circuit, or visit your local thrift store on one of their clearance sale days. Stock up on inexpensive dress-up clothes and accessories: prom dresses, hats, shawls, scarves, cowboy paraphernalia, costumes, surgical attire, costume jewelry, men's suit jackets, clip-on ties, and fancy shoes. Old lace tablecloths and curtains make perfect "wedding veils." Most dress-up clothes are bigger than the kids, so keep a look out for cute belts for cinching up gowns and over-sized shirts. Look for a suitable storage bin for the clothes. Plastic bins with lids work well, but even just a big cardboard box covered with wrapping paper can work for this much-appreciated gift.

# Delivering a Gift of Homemade Goodies

If you love to bake and have the time, giving homemade goodies is always a welcome treat, especially during the holidays. Some ideas include: homemade breads, dessert loaves, cookies, cakes, muffins, sweet rolls, and candies. (Pick up *Baking For Dummies* by Emily Nolan and published by Wiley for more yummy ideas.) Other folks appreciate anything your own family enjoys eating as a special treat. Delivering the gifts personally provides a fun time visiting with treasured friends and family, too.

# Hand-decorating Glass Ornaments

Buy a set of inexpensive clear glass ball ornaments at your local craft store. Remove the hanging wires and, using various colors of craft paint, pour a few drops of the paint into the balls. Swirl the balls around gently to make lines and designs with the various colors. When the inside of the balls are covered fully with paint, place the balls upside down on paper towels. Allow the ornaments to dry completely before reattaching the hanging wires. Hand-decorated glass ornaments make great gifts for grandparents, teachers, neighbors, and children's friends. If you see clear glass ornaments on sale after Christmas, you can stock up for next year's gift-giving at great discount.

# Index

### • D •

# • *H* •

# • N •

# FOR DUMMIES®

## A world of resources to help you grow

---

## TRAVEL

**0-7645-5453-0**  **0-7645-5438-7**  **0-7645-5444-1**

**Also available:**

America's National Parks For Dummies
(0-7645-6204-5)

Caribbean For Dummies
(0-7645-5445-X)

Cruise Vacations For Dummies 2003
(0-7645-5459-X)

Europe For Dummies
(0-7645-5456-5)

Ireland For Dummies
(0-7645-6199-5)

France For Dummies
(0-7645-6292-4)

Las Vegas For Dummies
(0-7645-5448-4)

London For Dummies
(0-7645-5416-6)

Mexico's Beach Resorts For Dummies
(0-7645-6262-2)

Paris For Dummies
(0-7645-5494-8)

RV Vacations For Dummies
(0-7645-5443-3)

---

## EDUCATION & TEST PREPARATION

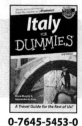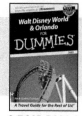

**0-7645-5194-9**  **0-7645-5325-9**  **0-7645-5249-X**

**Also available:**

The ACT For Dummies
(0-7645-5210-4)

Chemistry For Dummies
(0-7645-5430-1)

English Grammar For Dummies
(0-7645-5322-4)

French For Dummies
(0-7645-5193-0)

GMAT For Dummies
(0-7645-5251-1)

Inglés Para Dummies
(0-7645-5427-1)

Italian For Dummies
(0-7645-5196-5)

Research Papers For Dummies
(0-7645-5426-3)

SAT I For Dummies
(0-7645-5472-7)

U.S. History For Dummies
(0-7645-5249-X)

World History For Dummies
(0-7645-5242-2)

---

## HEALTH, SELF-HELP & SPIRITUALITY

**0-7645-5154-X**  **0-7645-5302-X**  **0-7645-5418-2**

**Also available:**

The Bible For Dummies
(0-7645-5296-1)

Controlling Cholesterol For Dummies
(0-7645-5440-9)

Dating For Dummies
(0-7645-5072-1)

Dieting For Dummies
(0-7645-5126-4)

High Blood Pressure For Dummies
(0-7645-5424-7)

Judaism For Dummies
(0-7645-5299-6)

Menopause For Dummies
(0-7645-5458-1)

Nutrition For Dummies
(0-7645-5180-9)

Potty Training For Dummies
(0-7645-5417-4)

Pregnancy For Dummies
(0-7645-5074-8)

Rekindling Romance For Dummies
(0-7645-5303-8)

Religion For Dummies
(0-7645-5264-3)

---

**Available wherever books are sold. Go to www.dummies.com or call 1-877-762-2974 to order direct**

## FOR DUMMIES®

### A world of resources to help you grow

---

## HOME & BUSINESS COMPUTER BASICS

**0-7645-0838-5**

**0-7645-1663-9**

**0-7645-1548-9**

**Also available:**

Excel 2002 All-in-One Desk Reference For Dummies
(0-7645-1794-5)

Office XP 9-in-1 Desk Reference For Dummies
(0-7645-0819-9)

PCs All-in-One Desk Reference For Dummies
(0-7645-0791-5)

Troubleshooting Your PC For Dummies
(0-7645-1669-8)

Upgrading & Fixing PCs For Dummies
(0-7645-1665-5)

Windows XP For Dummies
(0-7645-0893-8)

Windows XP For Dummies Quick Reference
(0-7645-0897-0)

Word 2002 For Dummies
(0-7645-0839-3)

---

## INTERNET & DIGITAL MEDIA

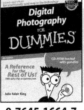

**0-7645-0894-6**

**0-7645-1642-6**

**0-7645-1664-7**

**Also available:**

CD and DVD Recording For Dummies
(0-7645-1627-2)

Digital Photography All-in-One Desk Reference For Dummies
(0-7645-1800-3)

eBay For Dummies
(0-7645-1642-6)

Genealogy Online For Dummies
(0-7645-0807-5)

Internet All-in-One Desk Reference For Dummies
(0-7645-1659-0)

Internet For Dummies Quick Reference
(0-7645-1645-0)

Internet Privacy For Dummies
(0-7645-0846-6)

Paint Shop Pro For Dummies
(0-7645-2440-2)

Photo Retouching & Restoration For Dummies
(0-7645-1662-0)

Photoshop Elements For Dummies
(0-7645-1675-2)

Scanners For Dummies
(0-7645-0783-4)

### Get smart! Visit www.dummies.com

- **Find listings of even more Dummies titles**

- **Browse online articles, excerpts, and how-to's**

- **Sign up for daily or weekly e-mail tips**

- **Check out Dummies fitness videos and other products**

- **Order from our online bookstore**

---

**Available wherever books are sold. Go to www.dummies.com or call 1-877-762-2974 to order direct**

# FOR DUMMIES®

## Helping you expand your horizons and realize your potential

---

## GRAPHICS & WEB SITE DEVELOPMENT

Photoshop 7 For Dummies
**0-7645-1651-5**

Creating Web Pages For Dummies
**0-7645-1643-4**

Macromedia Flash MX For Dummies
**0-7645-0895-4**

**Also available:**

Adobe Acrobat 5 PDF For Dummies
(0-7645-1652-3)

ASP.NET For Dummies
(0-7645-0866-0)

ColdFusion MX for Dummies
(0-7645-1672-8)

Dreamweaver MX For Dummies
(0-7645-1630-2)

FrontPage 2002 For Dummies
(0-7645-0821-0)

HTML 4 For Dummies
(0-7645-0723-0)

Illustrator 10 For Dummies
(0-7645-3636-2)

PowerPoint 2002 For Dummies
(0-7645-0817-2)

Web Design For Dummies
(0-7645-0823-7)

---

## PROGRAMMING & DATABASES

C++ For Dummies
**0-7645-0746-X**

Visual Studio .NET All-in-One Desk Reference For Dummies
**0-7645-1626-4**

XML For Dummies
**0-7645-1657-4**

**Also available:**

Access 2002 For Dummies
(0-7645-0818-0)

Beginning Programming For Dummies
(0-7645-0835-0)

Crystal Reports 9 For Dummies
(0-7645-1641-8)

Java & XML For Dummies
(0-7645-1658-2)

Java 2 For Dummies
(0-7645-0765-6)

JavaScript For Dummies
(0-7645-0633-1)

Oracle9i For Dummies
(0-7645-0880-6)

Perl For Dummies
(0-7645-0776-1)

PHP and MySQL For Dummies
(0-7645-1650-7)

SQL For Dummies
(0-7645-0737-0)

Visual Basic .NET For Dummies
(0-7645-0867-9)

---

## LINUX, NETWORKING & CERTIFICATION

Red Hat Linux 7.3 For Dummies
**0-7645-1545-4**

TCP/IP For Dummies
**0-7645-1760-0**

Networking For Dummies
**0-7645-0772-9**

**Also available:**

A+ Certification For Dummies
(0-7645-0812-1)

CCNP All-in-One Certification For Dummies
(0-7645-1648-5)

Cisco Networking For Dummies
(0-7645-1668-X)

CISSP For Dummies
(0-7645-1670-1)

CIW Foundations For Dummies
(0-7645-1635-3)

Firewalls For Dummies
(0-7645-0884-9)

Home Networking For Dummies
(0-7645-0857-1)

Red Hat Linux All-in-One Desk Reference For Dummies
(0-7645-2442-9)

UNIX For Dummies
(0-7645-0419-3)

---

**Available wherever books are sold.**
**Go to www.dummies.com or call 1-877-762-2974 to order direct**

WILEY

CPSIA information can be obtained
at www.ICGtesting.com
Printed in the USA
LVHW052151290519
619527LV00010B/412/P